To Irva, a good
Sunday school worker and
teacher.

Loftis J Sheffield

3/26/78

The Power
of Teaching
with
New Techniques

The Power of Teaching with New Techniques

by Charles R. Hobbs

Published by Deseret Book Company
Salt Lake City, Utah
1973

Library of Congress No. 72-92037
ISBN Number 0-87747-267-X
© 1972
Deseret Book Company
First Edition 1964
Second Printing 1965
Second Edition
Revised and Enlarged 1972
Revised Edition Reprint 1973

Don't Just Read This Book . . .

...*Study It*

1

Look at the chapter headings in the Contents to get an idea of what is coming.

2

Read through the first nineteen chapters carefully. Keep in mind that many important ideas are presented in pictures, charts, and graphs.

3

Stop reading now and then and think of ways you can adapt the ideas to your teaching. Write your ideas on a card to be placed in your file, or write them in the margin of the book. Underline key sentences in the book for later review. Do exactly as instructed in chapters 15-18 on chalkboard illustrating.

4

Skim over Part 4, Classified Methods of Teaching, to get an idea of many teaching methods available to you.

5

Study the Teaching Methods Chart on pages 269-71.

6

Use the Teaching Methods Chart with accompanying references each time you prepare a gospel lesson.

Contents

Part 2 Techniques for Teaching Subject Matter to Students

Part 3 Special Techniques Using Instructional Materials

Acknowledgments

This book is dedicated to four people who are a constant source of inspiration in my life. They are my eternal companion, Nola, and our three children, Christine, Mark, and Janice.

Helpful assistance has been given in preparation of this edition by Rex A. Skidmore, Boyd D. Beagley, Darrel J. Monson, and Della Mae Rasmussen.

The production of this work has resulted from the timely encouragement and help of James Mortimer. I would also like to thank Gary Gillespie for his competent performance as editor. Keith E. Montague and Travis A. Winn provided the layout and art, which in quality speaks for itself. They were kind enough to straighten out my crooked lines in the chapters on chalkboard illustrating. My secretaries, Mary Ann Nielson and Laura Smout, offered much help in typing and preparing the manuscript.

I would also like to express appreciation to those who helped with the first edition of this book, which was entitled *Teaching with New Techniques*. They are Ernest Eberhard, Jr., Marba C. Josephson, John M. Richards, Alvah H. Parry, Dick and Mary Scopes, Garry W. Graf, Alma P. Burton, Dale T. Tingey, Odessa Hunter, F. Weldon Thacker, my parents Milo and Bertha Hobbs, Renee Vandenberghe, Mary G. Dalley, Irwin Goodman, Eileen Dunyon, Don F. Colvin, Hal G. Ferguson, Kay V. Fellows, Leland E. Anderson, Alma A. Gardiner, Jack C. Raymond, Donald B. Jessee, and the late Merrill D. Clayson and Raymond T. Bailey.

Teachers of the Southern Utah Seminary District, when I was coordinator several years ago, also provided much help in preparation of the first edition.

Introduction

When a truth is effectively shared by a teacher with his students, it lives on, woven into the very fabric of their lives. Having been enriched, they in turn share with others, and all within reach become edified. The influence of that one qualified teacher touches many and, with the many, grows and continues into the eternities. A teacher who produces a worthy effect transmits a power that bears upon the destiny of life itself.

Some time ago I visited a teacher who desired to have such a notable influence upon his students. But far from his ideal, Bill was presently having difficulty holding the attention of his class members. After class he walked to the back of the room where I was sitting. With outstretched arms he pleaded, "Help me reach my students." I wanted to help Bill. But how? After discussing the problem and offering Bill a few suggestions, we parted company.

I returned home deeply concerned about Bill's desire to change the lives of his students and about the limited help I was then able to offer. During the following two hours of lonely travel, those pleading words "Help me!" echoed and re-echoed through the stillness of the night. They reverberated not only Bill's petition, but also cries from another teacher I was supervising who lived fifty miles to the west. I could hear the pleading voice of a parent to the south asking for practical methods for teaching his children in family home evenings. These multiplied into yearning appeals from teachers and parents throughout the Church.

During these thoughtful hours I visualized many arms outstretched as were Bill's that late afternoon—teachers' and parents' arms groping, each pleading, "Help me motivate my students and children. Help me help them practice the principles of the gospel. Help me with specific teaching procedures that will increase my power of influence."

That was one of the several occasions that led me into a systematic study of teaching processes and the eventual publication of this book. One of the greatest needs in the Church is to help teachers and parents to be more effective in changing the lives of individuals in living gospel ideals.

I would like to refer you to a teacher of influence in introducing the organizing ideas of this book. On his tombstone is written: Mark Hopkins 1802-1887.

The influence of Mark Hopkins has unquestionably extended into the lives of many thousands of people. There is a common expression in educational circles that keeps our awareness of his power alive. The expression goes something like this: "The ideal teaching situation consists of Mark Hopkins sitting on one end of a log and on the other end, a pupil."[1]

What I read into these words is the ideal of a great teacher (in certain ways the Bill of the future) in a face-to-face relationship with a student. Together the two are meaningfully sharing ideas presented by the teacher with the intent of bringing about change in the student. Much can be said for such an ideal. But we must first consider what exists in this situation.

The Mark Hopkins arrangement consists of a *teacher,* a *student,* an *idea,* and a *log.* These properties exist in all teaching.

It is usually the teacher who sets the stage in presenting the ideas. And the student ordinarily is the receiver of them. The ideas we will call subject matter, or that which is being taught.[2] The log represents materials, or physical resources, used to help present ideas. Materials would of course include such items as books and instructional equipment as well as a chair, a desk, or other furniture on which to perform. Materials consist of all physical properties useful in teaching and indeed can be taken to represent the overall nonhuman physical environment for instruction.

Each of these four components—teacher, student, subject matter, and materials—is related to the others. It is the way in which their related parts are organized that largely determines the outcome of certain desired change in the student. As in systems theory, which has made success possible in notable undertakings such as placing man on the moon, effective teaching calls for planning the interrelationships of vital factors that have bearing on hoped-for results. Our basic model then would appear as given in figure 1.

Wherever the four teaching components interrelate in process, teaching exists in some form. Therefore, all teaching situations have these four parts. Instructional power, or the ability to effect change in the student, is directly related to the ways in which the teaching components are arranged with purpose. How these components are arranged in process is what we call teaching procedures, techniques, or methods. Latter-day Saint teaching then is a process, an organized system of procedures, techniques, or methods used with the idea of helping the student understand and practice the subject matter of the revealed doctrines of Jesus Christ. The model in figure 1 provides a basis for

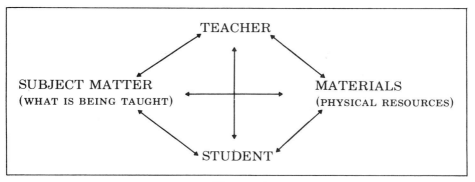

Figure 1
Basic Components of Teaching

talking about Bill's problem and the problems of many other teachers. This model will be used in the chapters that follow in helping you increase your power to influence others.

In these chapters we will be discussing teaching in the gospel instructional setting. This setting includes priesthood and auxiliary classes; home evening sessions; professional religion classes such as those taught in seminary, institute, Church colleges, and adult education courses. Many of these teaching techniques should be useful to missionaries in teaching investigators. In short, this book is intended for anyone who is interested in increasing his power for influencing children, youth, or adults through organized instruction in gospel ideals.

A parent, missionary, instructor, or anyone who is in the role of influencing others is ordinarily called a *teacher* in this book. Children in the home, investigators, or anyone being taught of all age levels are usually called *students*. *Classroom* is also used in a broad sense to include the physical environment where students are being taught; thus a classroom might be found almost anywhere—in a home, around a campfire, on a street, in a school, in a chapel of worship, or in a formal classroom.

The earlier edition of this book, under the title *Teaching with New Techniques,* has been used by educational systems outside of the Latter-day Saint Church. I anticipate that the many changes made in the present edition will be of even more help to teachers both in and out of the Church.

To speak here of teaching with new techniques is not to imply that the ideas in this book are all new or even mostly new. Many of the teaching strategies will likely be new to you, however. Also, each teaching situation you face is a new experience, even with the methods long known to you. In this sense, whenever you teach, you are *teaching with new techniques.* As you strive to enliven the student's world by giving him a variety of new worthwhile learning experiences, you will find that there can be *power in teaching with new techniques.*

Although it is tempting to wax philosophical when writing a book on teaching, I have made a conscientious effort to give primary attention to specific *how-to* ideas, believing these to be a more genuine public need. John W. Gardner at least partly justifies my effort in writing and your effort in studying this book with his remark, "A concern for how to do it is the root impulse in all great craftsmanship, and accounts for all of the style in human performance. Without it we would never know the peaks of human achievement."[3]

But as we give concern to the *how-to* in method, we must also alert ourselves to the hazards of losing sight of valued goals, the natural flow of expression, and other important conditions in teaching.

One of my former professors at Columbia University, Leland Jacobs, gave warning of certain hazards when he told me, "Charles, if you're mechanics are showing, you are not teaching." The implication in Dr. Jacobs' statement is that to be mechanical in teaching is to limit effect.

There is power in useful new teaching techniques, but the methods must be used naturally and spontaneously and must not become the "end" as well as the "means."

I agree with William James' position that an emphasis on teaching processes need in no way weaken an intellectual or subject matter emphasis in teaching,[4] nor need it limit spiritual effect. Proper attention to method and teaching style will actually strengthen spirituality and transmission of the subject matter to students. The distinctive feature of the teacher development program of the Latter-day Saint Church is the emphasis it places on teaching processes, on how to teach the principles of the gospel with effect.

This book is organized in four parts, using as framework the Basic Components of Teaching model that we have discussed on page xviii. Part 1 is a discussion about you, the *teacher,* with a few ideas on how you might increase your personal power to influence students. Part 2 will help you with specific techniques for teaching *subject matter* to *students.* Attention is then turned in Part 3 to some practical, but uncommon, techniques in the use of instructional *materials.* The first three parts of this book have been written with two purposes: (1) To help you be aware of ideas that would seem fundamental to effective gospel teaching, and (2) to introduce you to a few practical techniques not commonly understood or practiced. Fifty-six methods of teaching are then presented in Part 4 to orient you to a variety of techniques. These fifty-six teaching procedures, along with the accompanying chart (pages 269-71), are intended for your use in planning lessons. Each method in this section is briefly defined and explained with examples given to assist you in its implementation in your own teaching. There are of course many teaching methods, including uses of materials, that we do not consider in this book. There are actually as many teaching methods as teaching moments. Hopefully you will use your own creative imagination and go beyond the techniques suggested in this book.

Now let's get on with the business of increasing your power as a *teacher* to influence your *students* with the *subject matter* of the gospel and the *log*.

xxii

Introduction
NOTES AND REFERENCES

[1]This remark originated from a speech delivered to the Williams College alumni on December 28, 1871, by General (later President) James A. Garfield. Garfield was a student of Mark Hopkins, the latter having served with distinction as professor of philosophy at Williams College for over fifty years and as college president thirty-six of these years. Garfield has also been quoted by some as saying, "The ideal college is Mark Hopkins on one end of a log and a student on the other." Possibly a more accurate account by Garfield, however, is the statement, "I am not willing that this discussion should close without mention of the value of a true teacher. Give me a log hut, with only a simple bench, Mark Hopkins at one end and I on the other, and you may have all the buildings, apparatus and libraries without him." See Houston Peterson, *Great Teachers* (New York: Vintage Books, 1946), p. 75; *Encyclopedia Britannica* (Chicago: William Benton, 1960), 11:738; Dumas Malone, ed., *Dictionary of American Biography* (New York: Charles Scribner, 1964), 5:216.

[2]This definition of subject matter was taken from John Herbert, *A System for Analyzing Lessons* (New York: Teachers College Press, 1967), p. 17.

[3]John W. Gardner, *Self Renewal* (New York: Harper and Row, 1965), p. 47.

[4]For a brief discussion on James' position, see William James, *Talks to Teachers* (New York: W. W. Norton and Company, 1958), pp. 16-17.

THE TEACHER AND THE STUDENT

Power
Through
Spiritual Excellence

One of the most vital questions to you as a Latter-day Saint teacher is *How can I increase my power to influence students to practice the revealed doctrines of Jesus Christ?*

Power is used here simply as the ability to produce effect. This is not to suggest dominion, coercion, manipulation, or compulsion over people. I would rather stipulate power to be worthy influence on others. Power generates largely from within the individual as he sifts the realities of life to which he is exposed, casting aside the undesirable and embracing that which is of worth. Instructional power has something to do with how the individual as a teacher relates with his students, subject matter, and materials and, drawing upon his accumulated understanding, organizes and controls this teaching environment.

There is merit, virtue, indeed preeminence, in power. Power, therefore, has a close kinship with excellence. For a teacher to excel above mediocrity in influencing students in righteous conduct is to produce a desired effect. One may have authority to teach, but in the last analysis it is his level of excellence in bringing about worthy results in changing others that gives him a claim on power.

Power of God in Man

Achieving power of excellence in teaching is of course made possible through various undertakings. But it would be well for us to commence with those considerations that offer the most significant effect.

As we consider the realm of human endeavor, surely the most pervasive and penetrating power is the Spirit of God in man. This truth has been chronicled by the prophets since ancient times. In the Old Testament it is recorded, "Thine, O Lord, is the greatness, and the power, and the glory, . . . and thou art exalted as head above all. . . . In thine hand is power and might; and in thine hand it is to make great, and to give strength unto all."[1]

Apostle Paul promised, "But ye shall receive power, after that the Holy Ghost is come upon you."[2]

And from Moroni we learn that "by the power of the Holy Ghost ye may know the truth of all things."[3]

God is all powerful. It is from this divine source that we as gospel teachers can derive the greatest strength. President Joseph Fielding Smith taught that "the Spirit of God speaking to the spirit of man has power to impart truth with greater effect and understanding than the truth can be imparted by personal contact even with heavenly beings."[4]

Granted that a teacher can be of much influence by drawing upon the wisdom of the world. But the wisdom of the world sees "through the glass darkly." It falls short of the excellence of God's wisdom. In order to teach Christ's doctrine effectively, one must function within the spirit of that doctrine.

Paul, who had considerable understanding of the wisdom of the world, nevertheless put first the wisdom of God. He said that "my speech and my preaching was not with enticing words of man's wisdom, but in demonstration of the Spirit and of power."[5] Paul went on to say:

> Now we have received, not the spirit of the world, but the spirit which is of God; that we might know the things that are freely given to us of God.
> Which things also we speak, not in the words which man's wisdom teacheth, *but which the Holy Ghost teacheth;* comparing spiritual things with spiritual.
> But the natural man receiveth not the things of the Spirit of God: for they are foolishness unto him: neither can he know them, because they are spiritually discerned (italics added).[6]

Gospel instruction is necessarily a team-teaching effort. We must take into our classrooms, at home or church or wherever they might be, that divine companion teacher, the *Holy Ghost.*

We then have one more factor, the Holy Ghost, to add to the Basic Components of Teaching (see figure 2).

How can we as teachers lay claim to spiritual power? We received a special right to the Holy Spirit through baptism and the laying on of hands for the gift of the Holy Ghost by the proper priesthood authority. But the divine ordinances of baptism and confirmation are not enough. "He that keepeth God's commandments receives truth and light."[7] For "the Lord worketh not in darkness."[8] Our lives must then also be in harmony with God's value system.

The Lord taught, "And if your eye be single to my glory, your

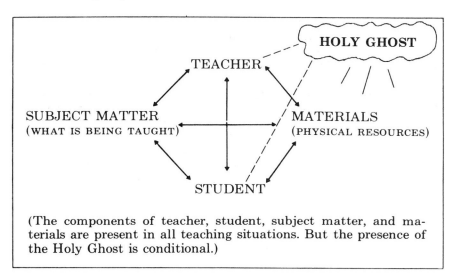

(The components of teacher, student, subject matter, and materials are present in all teaching situations. But the presence of the Holy Ghost is conditional.)

Figure 2
Basic Components of Teaching

whole bodies shall be filled with light, and there shall be no darkness in you."[9]

One of the most powerful scriptures for teachers of divine truth comes to us from him who gave more light than any teacher who has graced this earth, Jesus Christ. To paraphrase, "Let your light so shine before *your students,* that they may see your good works, and glorify your Father which is in heaven."[10]

There is a spiritual aura of light that emanates from an individual who lives with an eye single to the glory of God. We all have a spiritual aura of light—some more than others. At one time when I was teaching seminary, three students transferred into my class. I had never seen them before. I knew nothing of their past lives. As they walked into the classroom, I detected a spirit of darkness. It was as if there were a black light transmitted from them. Their faces were dirty, but I thought, "A hundred baths would not make them clean." I learned later that the boys had been released from reform school "to get another chance." Their histories, including police records, confirmed what I had discerned. Unfortunately these boys were returned to the reform school two weeks later.

In that same class I remember vividly a young lady who radiated light to others. Her brilliant smile and the sparkle in her eyes contributed to the illuminating effect she had on those around her. She was a good girl, a prototype of spiritual excellence.

I have known some *teachers* who carried the lantern of black light in their countenances and others who radiated peace and who transmitted an exalted feeling of enlightenment to students. Most teachers, as well as their students, are somewhere between these two extreme examples. All too many, unfortunately, are on a level of mediocrity.

Several years ago in Phoenix, Arizona, after I had delivered a lecture on the power of God's light in man, a good sister came up to me and said, "Brother Hobbs, I can testify from firsthand experience that the light of which you spoke is a reality. Two weeks ago I was sitting in a sacrament meeting when I felt the presence of a great spirit in the room. Immediately I glanced to the back of the chapel to see President David O. McKay standing in the open doorway. Others in the chapel later testified of having had the same edifying experience."

One need not have the authority of a prophet to possess a spiritual aura. This power is a consequence of righteous living.

What the Lord asks from each of us as teachers is to keep His commandments so that we can be blessed by the power of the Holy Spirit to *put light in students' faces.*

The divine light comes to us by our being humble, patient, honest, kind, respectful, unselfish, and free from idolatry, anger, hate, and distrust. It comes from exercising faith in the Lord Jesus Christ and in believing in ourselves and in those around us. It comes from continuous church activity, payment of tithes, and living the Word of Wisdom.

This spiritual power is made possible, as the sons of Mosiah testified, from much prayer and fasting.[11] It grows from giving noble service to others and, in this process of self-sacrifice, freeing oneself if necessary from the bondage of sexual passion, obsession for material wealth, and greed for the honors of men. And most significant of all, the way to obtain the power of God's light is through practicing that overarching commandment within which all of God's laws are circumscribed—*love.* Jesus Christ taught that on love hang "all the law and the prophets."[12] To paraphrase John, "He that loveth his *students* abideth in the light, and there is none occasion of stumbling in him."[13]

Power Through Love

At one time a professor at Johns Hopkins University assigned a group of graduate students to: "Go to the slums. Take 200 boys between the ages of twelve and sixteen. Investigate their background and environment. Then predict the chance for their future success."

After consulting social statistics, talking to the boys, and compiling as much data as they could, the researchers concluded that 90 percent of the boys would spend some time in a penitentiary.

Twenty-five years later another group of graduate students was given the job of testing the prediction. Returning to the slum area 180 of the original 200 boys were located. It was found that only four of the group had served time.

Why was it that these boys, who lived in a breeding place of crime, developed into manhood with such an excellent record? The researchers were consistently told by each of the questioned, "Well, there was a teacher . . ."

Pressing the matter further, it was found that 75 percent of the cases reported the same woman. The graduate students searched out and found this teacher in a rest home for retired educators.

After introductions came the interrogations: "How did you exert this remarkable influence over the slum children? Could you give us any reason why these boys should have remembered you?"

"No," she meekly replied. "No, I really couldn't." And then thinking back over the years, she musingly responded, more to herself than to her questioners, "I loved those boys!"[14] This noble teacher put light in students' faces. This is power in teaching. A worthy effect was produced. Should not teachers of the gospel also qualify in the practice of communicating love as did this public school teacher?

The first and great commandment to all teachers of the gospel is, "Thou shalt love the Lord thy God with all thy heart, and with all thy soul, and with all thy mind." And paraphrasing the second great commandment, which is like unto it, "Thou shalt love thy *students* as thyself."[15] On these two charges hang all the commandments of God and a key to effecting change in students' lives.

When my oldest daughter was five, we were living in Cedar City, Utah. My office was only one-half block from home. One afternoon little Christi called me on the telephone at the end of the day and said, "Daddy, may I come to the office and pick you up?" I responded, "Sure, Christi, come on."

I stepped to the large front glass doors of the school building and waited. Shortly I saw the little tot skipping along the sidewalk with her flowered dress bouncing above her two tiny knobby knees. Her long golden hair reflected the orange rays of a setting sun. The clear complexion of her face glowed with happiness. I became overwhelmed with the joy of love for this little angel—my very own daughter. I slipped back into my office, which was near the front door, and thoughtfully waited.

Christi struggled at the door but finally pulled it open wide enough to squeeze herself inside. When she entered the office, I was sitting low in a chair weeping. Very concerned, she said, "What's the matter, Daddy?" And I responded with broken voice, "Chris, it's just that I love you so much."

Without hesitation she crawled upon my knee, and with the sensitivity of a mother of twelve children, she placed her little arm as far around my shoulder as it could reach and patted me on the back. Then came one of the most precious of all conversations. Not another word was spoken. But as I looked into her eyes and as she looked into mine, we were saying, "Christi, I love you" and "Daddy, I love you."

In this deep, meaningful relationship there was a fusion that took place, a *spiritual interpersonal fusion.* After a few moments of unspoken conversation, Christi slid to the floor, and together we walked home hand in hand. From that eventful day on, Christi has been a different person and so has her "daddy." We have since been very close. On that spring day in Cedar City, we both learned something about the power of God's light of love.

I believe that we as teachers must strive to love our students, whatever their age or disposition, as we would love one that is our very own. It is a fatherly or motherly dimension of love of which I speak.[16] This challenge often becomes particularly difficult when the student is not a carrier of the light, when he is obstreperous, steeped in sin, and insecure about accepting love from us. It is easy to love the sweet and innocent child who has the light. Loving one who does not possess the Spirit of the Lord and who "esteems you as his enemy" is equally important and much harder. Our real challenge is to love those whom some would consider to be unlovable.

To feel love is not enough in acquisition of spiritual excellence in teaching. We as teachers must develop the Christlike powers within us to *communicate* that love. This we do in part by focusing on the *here* and *now* with others. We have no power in the *there* and *then,* because *there* is away from us and *then* has either already happened or has not yet occurred. As Tolstoi wrote, *now* "is the most important time because it is the only time when we have any power."[17] We communicate love through delicate sensitivity to the feelings of others, by getting out of ourselves and into their worlds, by feeling what they feel. We must teach in the *here* and *now* with affection and not simply attempt to transmit the ideas of subject matter with the thought that "later on" we will get around to trying ways of better communicating love to those we teach.

Let's now move into the specifics of a few of the many ideas that should be helpful to you in developing your powers of communicating love to students. Try these techniques. They have been helpful to many other people.

1. Make the idea of loving your students continuously accessible to you. One teacher posted small signs on the sun visor of his car and on the bathroom mirror that read, "Love Your Students."

2. Evaluate your actions with students the past week. Did you communicate to them feelings of care, respect, kindness, and trust?

3. Pray earnestly for your students' welfare.

4. Visit students when they are ill. Take time to counsel students when they need help.

5. If a student has a serious problem, fast with him.

6. Invite students to your home for dinner and talk about their interests.

7. Visit a student and his parents at home with the singular purpose of expressing appreciation for him. If you are the parent, express your affection openly to the child.

8. Attend activities where your students perform, such as a football game, recital, or meeting. Let them know that you are interested in their success beyond class requirements.

9. When greeting students, shake their hands warmly. Talk to them of their main interests.

10. Send each student a birthday card or a Christmas card or present.

11. Think of your students as your sons and daughters or as other close relatives.

12. Think yourself into being an example for students. The way you act around a student becomes the message to him every bit as much as the gospel subject matter you teach. The greatest effect is produced by sincerely expressing care, respect, kindness, and trust to that individual who sits "on the other end of the log."

13. If you are a parent or regular formal teacher of small children, get down on the floor with the students. On all age levels, including children's, attempt to see the student's world through his eyes. Try to understand his likes and dislikes. See if you can feel as he feels.

I am compelled to expand this last matter by mention of Charles Lutwidge Dodgson.[18] He is better known to most of us by the pen name Lewis Carroll. By profession, he was a clergyman and mathematician at Oxford. But he claims particular respect for his rare standard of excellence in communicating love to children.

Lewis spent a happy childhood inventing games, mathematical puzzles, and puppet plays for seven younger sisters. His happiest moments even in adulthood were when a group of children gathered closely around him, listening intently to his imaginative tales. Children in the neighborhood would regularly invade his room at storytime.

One of the welcomed intruders was a little girl, Alice Liddell, who one afternoon asked for a special story. Mr. Carroll complied, and thus was the beginning of the many exciting adventures of *Alice in Wonderland*. "Straight down the rabbit hole went the most lovely, the most confused, and the most appealing little girl that English literature has produced," wrote Warren Weaver some time later. Alice's new wonderland later became a wonderland for millions of little girls and boys throughout the world.

Lewis Carroll's wit and charm won the friendship of such great Victorians as Rossetti, Tennyson, and Ruskin. Yet he preferred the company of children. One day Mr. Carroll was invited to a children's party. Entering the house, he dropped on all fours and headed for the drawing room growling like a bear. But to his surprise, the children's party was next door. The "bear" found himself confronting an astonished women's party and immediately fled, this time using only his two hind legs for a speedy exit.

Mr. Carroll wrote thousands of playful letters to his young friends. One letter ended, "Give my love to any children you happen to meet." And that's precisely what "Mr. Alice in Wonderland" did all his life.

Mr. Carroll knew how to get on the floor with children and feel the pulsations of their little hearts. Whether teaching children, youth, or adults, bring yourself into their worlds to the point of feeling the pulsations of their hearts.

In developing skill in the *how-to* of loving students, ask yourself:

1. Do I avoid rejecting or embarrassing students?
2. Do I give each student a reputation to live up to and praise him sincerely for his slightest accomplishments?
3. Do I look only for the good in each student? Do I accept him for what he is? Am I positive?
4. Do I build a personable relationship with each student? Do I take a special interest in what he likes?
5. Do I avoid showing partiality?
6. Do I do little things to show my interest?
7. Do I respect the student's right to question and raise issues?

Do not judge a student's action until you have made an effort to get all of the facts. He always has a reason for what he does. Try to understand this reason.

When teaching a student, give him rapt attention. Talk about that which will help him and that in which he is interested.

After he is no more your direct responsibility, follow his activities and assist him throughout life.

These specific ideas should help you in part with the practice of love. Love expressed in righteous perspective generates spiritual excellence.

Summary

In all probability the most vital question to you as a Latter-day Saint teacher is, "How can I increase my power to influence students to practice the revealed doctrines of Jesus Christ?" The most significant power in human activity is the power of God in man, and it is toward achieving power through spiritual excellence that every Latter-day Saint teacher should attend. Rather than man's wisdom, God's wisdom should first be sought. This wisdom comes through the power of the Holy Ghost. You should strive to make the Holy Ghost your constant companion. Through righteous living, the Holy Spirit will descend upon you, the teacher, and illuminate not only your heart and mind but also your countenance.

Your challenge as a teacher *is to put light in students' faces.* The excellence of this highly valued spiritual aura is generated from keeping God's commandments, every whit. In particular, the development of spiritual light in a teacher has much bearing upon the extent to which that teacher genuinely communicates love to students. The teacher's wellspring of spiritual power is love of God and love of students.

Chapter 1
NOTES AND REFERENCES

[1]1 Chronicles 29:11-12.

[2]Acts 1:8.

[3]Moroni 10:5.

[4]Joseph Fielding Smith, *Doctrines of Salvation* (Salt Lake City: Bookcraft, 1954), 1:47-48.

[5]1 Corinthians 2:4.

[6]1 Corinthians 2:12-14.

[7]D&C 93:29.

[8]2 Nephi 26:23.

[9]D&C 88:67.

[10]Matthew 5:16.

[11]Alma 17:3.

[12]Matthew 22:40.

[13]1 John 2:10.

[14]Milton Britten, "Education for Life," *Reader's Digest,* June 1953, p. 131.

[15]Matthew 22:37.

[16]For an interesting discussion on the fatherly dimension of love, see Ernest M. Ligon, *The Psychology of Christian Personality* (New York: The Macmillan Company, 1957), pp. 63-91.

[17]Leo Tolstoi, "The Three Questions," *The Works of Leo Tolstoi* (New York: Black's Readers Service Company, 1928), p. 25.

[18]*Great Lives, Great Deeds* (New York: The Reader's Digest Association, 1964), pp. 570-75.

The YOU in Teaching

In this chapter I would like to consider three additional qualities that are essential in your growth toward acquiring power in changing the lives of students. We will discuss here dedication through commitment to a worthy purpose, knowledge of the subject matter, and humility.

Dedication Through Commitment to a Worthy Purpose

One of the great personalities who has rightfully earned a place among the immortals of the classics is King Richard. So dynamic and forceful a personality was this man that he became known as the "lion-hearted."

With an army of loyal followers, King Richard the Lion-hearted entered the Holy Land to dispose of the Turks. This uneventful expedition failed, and King Richard was captured. While confined in the foreign prison, Richard's kingdom in England fell into the hands of traitors. During these trying days, it appeared that all was lost. But not so—with odds against him, an escape was effected and King Richard returned to his homeland.

Disguised in plain armor, the Lion-hearted gathered some of his loyal followers around him. The plan, according to Sir Walter Scott's novel *Ivanhoe,* was to attack the Castle of Torquilstone, a stronghold of the enemy—thus England would come back into the hands of its rightful heir.

Ivanhoe, a loyal subject of Richard, lay wounded in the Castle of Torquilstone. Because of loss of blood, Ivanhoe was unable to raise himself from his couch to view the onslaught of clanging armor. He asked Rebecca to stand by the window and give an account of what was going on. With a desire to know who the leader was, the loyal knight asked Rebecca to describe the insignia on the armor of the leader.

She said, "He fights in plain black unmarked armor."

Ivanhoe responded, "Describe then the acts of this leader, that I might identify him."

And so Rebecca related how this great man, clad in massive armor, swung his ponderous ax with thunderous blows. She said, "Stone and beams are hurled down from the castle walls upon him, but he regards them no more than if they were thistledown or feathers. . . . He fights as if there were twenty men's strength in his single arm. . . . It is fearful, yet magnificent, to behold how the arm and heart of one man can triumph over hundreds."

Ivanhoe thought that his beloved king was a prisoner in an Austrian dungeon. Yet with such a description he could think of but one man, his king. The wounded knight then expressed a noble tribute to his great teacher-leader. "I swear by the honor of my house, I would endure ten years' captivity to fight a single day by that great man's side in such a quarrel of this."[1]

What gave King Richard the strength of twenty men in one arm? Why did Richard's heart triumph against the enemy? Was it years of skillful practice with a battle-ax? Was it the type of ax he swung? Was it the power of the steed he rode? Or was it the psychological effect of his armor? Surely all of these factors had some bearing on his success. Yet there is a deeper-seated aspect that made all of the above possible: King Richard the Lion-hearted was dedicated to restoring justice to his people. This knight was committed to a worthy purpose.

There is no more noble cause than effective teaching of the gospel of Jesus Christ. What we have to offer our students is the plan of eternal life. Should not then even greater dedication be given by us to our students than the Lion-hearted offered to his subjects? Many teachers in the Church have earned the name *faint-hearted,* considering their faint preparation for lessons, their faint enthusiasm, their faint efforts toward personal contact with students outside of class, their faint courage in trying new methods of teaching, their faint and infrequent bearing of testimonies in word and deed. Their power of light is all too often so very dim.

The *lion-hearted* teacher will not hesitate to prepare several hours for a lesson presentation. He will be willing to utilize evenings in personal contact with his students. A constant search for new methods of teaching the gospel is important to him. This valiant teacher-leader guides his small army of students into the battle of life bearing the banner of self-sacrifice. Yes, the soldiers of the Lord's army combat the adversary best when there is a totally committed teacher out front.

By being committed to a worthy purpose, you will be more aware of what needs to be acted upon, because having a purpose helps you to know where you are headed. And your commitment will bless you with abilities to accomplish the same.

Thomas H. Huxley taught that the first lesson in education that ought to be learned is to do the thing that has to be done when it ought to be done whether you like it or not. This is probably the last lesson that an individual learns thoroughly.[2] He who is without commitment to worthy purpose is without that certain something that "has to be done." He is like a ship without a sail that never feels the strength of the wind that carries it to new horizons of accomplishment.

To speak of worthy purpose in the Church brings immediately to mind the long-range aspiration of attaining exaltation. But the question at hand is how to increase your powers to *influence students* in achieving this most worthy condition. Taking this latter question seriously will help advance your success, and theirs, in attaining exaltation.

In a general sense, I would define success as the self-direction in acquiring whatever one desires of life that contributes to the peace, happiness, and personal achievement of himself and others. Success is advanced by application of the following four principles:

1. *Set a goal, defining clearly what it is you want.* Keep in mind that the suggested goal you adopt as your very own is to attain a level of excellence, in your own right, to influence students to live gospel ideals.

2. *While working toward this goal, nourish the desire into a passion for its fulfillment.* Do not allow fear or incompatible desires to block your way. Someone once said, "In almost any subject your passion for the subject will save you. If you care enough for a result, you will most certainly attain it. If you wish to be rich, you will be rich. If you wish to be learned, you will be learned. If you wish to be good, you will be good. Only then, you must really wish these things, and wish them with exclusiveness, and not wish one hundred other incompatible things as strongly." If you really wish to become a teacher with power, you will become a teacher with power.

3. *Organize and follow industriously a specific plan to achieve your goal.* Our goal in teaching is long range. It is almost more than a goal—it is an aspiration. Therefore, long-range planning with realistic short-range goals is necessary. You must first decide what kind of a teacher you want to become and then what techniques and skills you must develop that will lead you to your ultimate desire. Do not attempt to become a carbon copy

of a great teacher. Rather, plan to enlarge upon your own personality, adapting ideas to yourself from what you see in great
teaching. Neither I nor anyone else can give you a standardized
prescription to accomplish this task. I have never seen any two
outstanding teachers teach alike. You must make your own plan
and develop the distinctive *you* in teaching. Others can give you
some specific helps in getting started, however. That is the purpose of this book.

Select any section of any chapter and go to work on it. Don't
try to do everything at once. You may wish to start by developing skill in the use of your eyes or voice while teaching (see pp. 28,
33); you may wish to practice some of the techniques in communicating love to students (see pp. 6, 40, 48); or you may wish to
begin now in developing chalkboard skills (see pp. 171-262). Many
teachers have found that using the chart on pages 269-71 of the
book during lesson preparation adds effectiveness to their teaching. There are a number of useful ideas in this book to help you
achieve your goal, but in the main you must focus on one specific
goal at a time. Remember, your time of power was not yesterday
and is not tomorrow—it is *now*.

On a sheet of paper, write down your long-range aspiration
with an expanded list of short-range goals. Spell out in specific
terms the teaching skills and techniques you hope to acquire.
Identify the knowledge you will need. You would do well to
devote a page or two to a description of the type of teacher you
hope to become.

4. *Recognize that our Master Teacher was talking to you
when He said, "If thou canst believe, all things are possible
to him that believeth."*[3]

Lack of self-assurance has probably ruined more potentially
great gospel teachers than any other single factor, other than
sin. The teacher who believes in himself is one who has faith in
his own abilities as a teacher. He is self-reliant and harbors within
his mind the trust or certainty that he will succeed. He is not
bound by the oppressive hand of fear. He is not afraid of his
students, an unfamiliar teaching method, his subject matter,
instructional materials, or himself. Deep within his soul is the
assurance that nothing is impossible to him because he *believes*
in himself, in his students, and in his message. It is this rare
commodity of unquestioning faith that moves mountains.

Here are some of the many specific *how-to* approaches that you
can go to work on in strengthening your commitment to the worthy
purpose of building personal confidence:

Be thoroughly prepared with every lesson presentation. Only
the prepared teacher can claim the right to being confident. Only
hours of detailed preparation qualify you as the classroom authority.

Never express a fear or offer an excuse to students when unprepared or in doubt. If you do a poor job of teaching, you don't have to tell them about it. They will find out soon enough.

Don't be afraid of making mistakes. Everybody does.

Act as if you are now a master teacher.

Again, keep the commandments. The Lord said, "Let virtue garnish thy thoughts unceasingly; then shall thy confidence wax strong in the presence of God."[4]

While teaching, let profound truths flow from you as the authority. If one who you feel is more qualified on the subject is seated in the class, do not ask him to answer the tough questions with the attitude that he is the ultimate interpreter. Likewise, in this same spirit, do not ask him to verify answers you might give. This would make *him* the class authority and cause you to lose status with the students. If the visitor chooses to respond on his own volition, respect his comments and give him recognition for what he says.

It will help your confidence to dress in good taste. As a teacher receives student feedback of acceptance of his appearance, it fortifies his self-confidence. Do you keep your hair, shoes, and suit or dress immaculate? Do you keep up with the styles as long as they conform to gospel standards? Do you brush your teeth and bathe frequently?

However you set up your plan of action, have faith in your goal and in your potential. Take up your armor and prepare to face the challenge of growth that awaits you. By committing yourself to the purpose of more effective teaching, you will experience a joy of dedication in the service of building other people that is almost unexcelled in human activity.

Knowledge of Subject Matter

One cannot succeed in teaching without knowledge of his subject matter. Knowledge directed to worthy purpose generates power. If there is anything that instills student confidence within a teacher, it is for the teacher to know what he is talking about.

Louis Agassiz is considered by many to be the ablest teacher of natural science America has ever known. It has been said that "every notable teacher of natural history in the United States for the second half of the 19th century was at some time a pupil of Agassiz or of one of his students."[5] His method of instruction at Harvard resulted in a complete revolution in the study of natural history in America. Agassiz was also one of the best informed men in the world on certain subjects in biology that he was teaching.

From his early years, Agassiz studied intensively. As a boy he was a student at the gymnasium in Bienne, Switzerland, and later at the Academy at Lausanne and the universities of Zurich, Heidelberg, and Munich. He received a doctor of philosophy degree from Erlangen and doctor of medicine from Munich. Agassiz' knowledge of the subject matter he researched and taught expanded year after year due to an unwavering commitment to a worthy purpose.

We have already made mention of Mark Hopkins and his student on the other end of a log. Hopkins had considerable power by sheer virtue of his personality, but he also knew his subject matter of philosophy well. Even at age eighty-five his intellectual powers with his subject matter were brilliant.[6]

When I was a student at Teachers College, one of the most respected instructors was Professor Phillip H. Phenix, chairman of the Department of Philosophy and Social Sciences. I remember sitting in Professor Phenix' course entitled "Ways of Knowing" and being inspired by his vast knowledge. He lectured on each of about thirteen academic disciplines and discussed with us how knowledge of such subjects as mathematics, philosophy, biology, psychology, and sociology is structured. In each field of knowledge he had a depth of understanding that appeared to exceed the understandings of some teachers in their singular fields. I believe that Dr. Phenix' considerable influence with students and faculty had a good deal to do with his breadth and depth of knowledge and how he used it.

You of course are not an Agassiz, a Hopkins, nor a Phenix. But these influential teachers suggest an important lesson: The extent of the breadth and depth of knowledge you have in the subject matter you teach has much to do with your power of influence on students. This knowledge is attained to considerable extent through discipline in personal study.

As a teacher of the revealed doctrines of Jesus Christ, you must know well these doctrines. You do not need a diploma from a university to qualify. But you do need to make a thorough and continuous study of the scriptures and of other materials that relate to them. Particularly literature written by Church authorities should be part of your library and frequently used. But this is not all. Christ's doctrines are found in all truth. His doctrines are meshed within the fabric of life itself. By acquiring knowledge in many fields and carefully integrating "outside" knowledge into the framework of gospel ideals, you can greatly increase your effect on students. You will be better equipped to prepare them to meet outside influences. Also, your extended knowledge of "the world" can be used when teaching students to justify Church doctrine, as well as to bring the interest of new knowledge into the lesson. A caution in studying and teaching about the "theories of men" is that this be done within the framework of revealed truth.[7] You must know the subject matter you teach, and you would do well to expand your knowledge in many fields.

Humility

An accompanying hazard with acquiring knowledge is becoming trapped in the self-sufficiency of pride. Any time a teacher comes to feel that he has arrived, that he has ample ideas and skills to get by, that he knows more than others on a given subject, he has set the stage for power reduction. For by such presumption, he has closed the doors to further inquiry, to new ideas, to more useful skills, and possibly in a degree to the guidance of the Holy Spirit. The power of growth through self-renewal is found only in humble men.

The Giver of light said, "Be thou humble; and the Lord thy God shall lead thee by the hand, and give thee answer to thy prayers."[8] I can visualize our Master Teacher tenderly lifting a little child to a position where all could see him when He uttered these words:

Except ye be converted, and become as little children, ye shall not enter into the kingdom of heaven.

Whosoever therefore shall humble himself as this little child, the same is greatest in the kingdom of heaven.[9]

There is power in humility.

May I illustrate how we as teachers sometimes climb the mountain of knowledge and forget to return to the vale of humility and become as little children. Here is a story of a man who remembered. He was a giant of a man and in his Alpine village everyone called him Magnus, meaning "big." Although his muscles were tough from climbing the mountains, his heart was tender for his little boy, Angelo.

One spring morning Magnus took little Angelo by the hand and said, "Son, you are old enough to climb the mountain; come with me." Off they went, Magnus the giant and little Angelo running at his heels.

The neighbors smiled as they saw the two of them head for the mountain. At the edge of town, old Solomon cried out from his shop, "Be careful, Magnus. Don't you lose that little angel in the mountains." With a swing of his arms, Magnus answered by lifting the boy above his head, and off he strode like a proud elephant with his small driver astride his mighty shoulders.

After climbing for a long time, with Angelo sometimes running and sometimes riding, Magnus saw the high cliff, and through the underbrush he spotted a little glen by a stream. He said to Angelo, "Let's rest here by this pool and eat our lunch." He lifted his little boy to the ground, and Angelo ran to the stream and dipped his face into the fresh clear water. They ate their cheese and bread, and as Magnus stretched out for a rest, he sank into the soft grass and murmured, "Angelo, stay close by. We'll soon be going home."

Angelo did not hear, or pretended not to, because he wanted to put his face in the water again—it felt so cool and tasted so good.

As he leaned over, a gentle breeze carried the fragrance of mountain violets to his nostrils. As he turned to see where they grew, he spied them in little clusters by the stream. His legs flew as up the hillside he climbed to pick the purple flowers.

As he leaned over one cluster, he saw water was bubbling up from under a large rock. To see more clearly, he pushed aside some bushes near the rock, and there to his amazement was a hole. "Is this where the mountain hides its water?" he asked himself. "I shall find out!" And in through the hole he crawled.

It was dark inside—only a faint glow from a few rays of the sun lit the dim cavern. As he crept forward, his foot dislodged a rock and he heard it rumble down below. The sound echoed on and on, never seeming to end. Little Angelo called out, "Halloo," and he heard his voice again and again, and it sounded big and deep like that of his father. Never had he heard anything like this, so he sat down and began to talk to the mountain.

Meanwhile down by the pool, Magnus awakened with a start. He jumped to his feet and called, "Angelo! Angelo! Where are you?" But there was no answer.

Frantically he climbed to the top of the cliff, but he could see nothing of his little Angelo. Inside his heaving shoulders he felt the sharp pain of fear—it drove him back down the rocks to the pool, where in despair he fell to his knees and sobbed out his prayer to God. "Help me find my little Angelo," he cried.

As he opened his eyes, he looked into the water at his own troubled face. There he saw a strange sight, something long forgotten. Looking back from the mirrored pool was not the face of Magnus the giant, but the face of Magnus the boy. He knelt closer to see if it were some strange formation of rocks that made him see this long-forgotten image. As he leaned over the bank, he caught the fragrance of mountain violets. On his knees he followed their scent and remembered a childhood adventure in the mountains.

Faster he scrambled up the side of the stream until he came to the rock, and there it was—the bubbling spring. And beside the rock, hidden behind the bushes, was the hole where once he had entered the mountain and heard it speak. He stood up and pulled away the bushes, but he could not crawl in, for the opening was so small and he was so big. He shook with terror as he imagined his Angelo in the cavern alone and lost. Back to his knees he fell, and with a prayer on his lips, he wiggled and squirmed his way through the small tunnel.

Once inside, he lay panting on the damp earth, and then faintly above the pounding of his own heart he heard a distant sound echoing over and over, "Halloo! Halloo! Halloo!"

"Angelo! Angelo! Angelo!" he answered.

In the dim light he could not see his little boy, but he could hear little feet running toward him. In a moment he reached out into the darkness and clasped his son to his heart. Then Angelo spoke, "Daddy! Daddy! How did you find me?"

And Magnus, with tears running down his cheeks sobbed, "I found you by becoming a child again."

And in that village they still talk about Magnus the giant who remembered to become as a little child so that he could enter the mighty mountain and find his lost son.[10]

We have seen that it is requisite for the successful teacher to climb the majestic mountain of knowledge. Success makes equal demands, however, that the truly effective teacher then return himself to the vale of humility. Magnus was a giant, but not until he lowered himself from the towering heights of a proud heart and became once again as his little child was he able to save Angelo. Do you return often to the vale of humility? When was the last time you tried?

Most of us like to consider ourselves as humble people; yet no mortal is *all humble* or *all proud*. We can be humble in one character index and proud in another. Further, it seems that often when we think of ourselves as humble, we are proud. To be humble to the point that the Lord can work within us requires continuous effort and concentration and a realization that we are seldom as humble as we ought to be. Ask yourself, "Am I truly as humble as I ought to be?"

You might make a personal evaluation by asking yourself such questions about humility as the following:

Do I praise my students and not belittle them?

Do I have an unhostile sense of humor?

Am I willing to sacrifice my own ego to save face for my students?

Am I thoughtful before speaking so as not to do a student injury?

Am I patient with my students' frailties, and am I slow to be moved to anger or displeasure?

Do I respect everyone?

Do I seek to lift my students to a high plateau of success?

Do I avoid bragging to students about my personal recognitions or abilities I possess?

Do I take a sincere interest in students as they seek to express their feelings?

Do I express appreciation to my students?

Am I modest in dress?

Do I have self-respect, and yet am I thoughtful of my weaknesses as a teacher and person?

Do I abide gladly the decisions and policies of those in authority over me?

Am I willing to learn from anyone who may have something good to offer?

Do I guard against the opinion that I know enough?

Do I seek wise counsel and constructive criticism?

Do I aspire toward personal development and ability to contribute, rather than toward office and honor of men?

Do I acknowledge the almighty power of a loving Father?

Summary

We have seen that the power of a teacher in changing the lives of students is generated in part through the teacher's commitment to a worthy purpose. Through such commitment you will have direction and will thereby be aware of what needs to be acted upon and how better to accomplish it.

Success in developing your powers as an influential teacher is promoted by applying four basic principles:

1. Commit yourself to the aspiration of attaining a level of excellence to influence students in living gospel ideals.

2. While working toward this goal, nourish the desire into a fervor. You must become fully committed to its attainment in order to succeed.

3. Organize and follow industriously a specific plan to achieve your goal.

4. Recognize that if you believe you will become a teacher of influence, it can be done—for nothing is impossible to "him that believeth."

Included within your plan should be a description of the type of teaching personality you hope to become. You should identify the teaching methods with which you will become proficient. Your plan should include a designation of the breadth and depth of knowledge you will acquire. You must recognize and act upon the fact that one thing all influential teachers have in common is knowledge of the subject matter they teach.

As you grow in knowledge of the subject matter of the gospel, of related fields, and of life in general, you will face the hazard of becoming trapped in the self-sufficiency of pride. A constant vigilance toward being humble is therefore essential.

To be dedicated through commitment to worthy purpose, to seek knowledge, and to strive toward humility will certainly make a greater *you* in teaching.

Chapter 2
NOTES AND REFERENCES

[1]Sir Walter Scott, *Ivanhoe.*

[2]In A. Hamer Reiser, *A Reader for the Teacher* (Salt Lake City: Deseret Book Company, 1960), p. 357.

[3]Mark 9:23.

[4]D&C 121:45.

[5]*Encyclopedia Britannica* (Chicago: William Benton, 1960), 1:340.

[6]Houston Peterson, *Great Teachers* (New York: Vintage Books, 1946), pp. 77-104.

[7]The Lord also said, "Seek ye first the kingdom of God" (Matthew 6:33); "Seek ye out of the best books words of wisdom" (D&C 88:118); "To be learned is good if [you] hearken unto the counsels of God" (2 Nephi 9:29).

[8]D&C 112:10.

[9]Matthew 18:3-4.

[10]Adapted from Lorin F. Wheelwright, *Convention Instructor* (Salt Lake City: Deseret Sunday School Union, 1963), pp. 25-26.

Does Your Personality Appeal to Students?

There are probably as many appealing types of teacher personalities as there are appealing teachers. As was suggested earlier, there is no standard prescription for what one might mistakenly consider to be the "best personality" for teaching. You must enlarge upon your own personality and develop your own individualistic style. Again, the question at hand is, "How can I increase my power to influence students to live the revealed doctrines of Jesus Christ?" How you develop your personality has a good deal to do with accomplishing this desired effect. If you do not appeal to your students, you are operating at a considerable disadvantage in influencing their lives. A lack of appeal would make it difficult for students to accept you or your message.

There are certain basic principles beyond those we have already discussed that have utility for the many personality types in promoting appeal to students. And no matter how effective or ineffective your personality might be, you can improve.

By being enthusiastic and flexible and by developing skill in what you say and how you say it, your powers will be increased.

Enthusiasm

A gallon of vaporized gas with a fire kindled beneath has the power to send an average car sailing over a four-story building. A teacher with enthusiasm can inspire a class of students to almost unlimited heights of motivation.

Emerson said that "nothing important was ever accomplished without enthusiasm." Enthusiasm has two sets of relatives—the synonyms and the *aunt*onyms. The synonyms are the *in*laws whose company is to be sought, for they help to make enthusiasm the desirable influence that it is in teaching. The *aunt*onyms are the undesirables, the *out*laws, with whom you cannot afford to associate if you keep your good name as a teacher. May I first introduce to you the family of synonyms? They are:

intensity
ecstasy
eagerness
devotion
excitement
fervency
spirituality
ardent zeal

Now for that particular set of undesirables. They too can exercise influence on your teaching if you will let them. They are good to know—at a distance. They are:

aloofness
indifference
unconcern
apathy
flippancy
coldness
disinterest
boredom

With which set of enthusiasm's relatives do you most frequently associate? Perhaps you spend some time with both sides of the family. But in practice only the synonyms offer you effective power.

Because of too much mixing of enthusiasm's relatives, many teachers fit somewhere in between—on the plane of mediocrity. And as long as they stay there, the credit for students' becoming "doers of the word" rightfully belongs to the more influential teachers who "had the gas."

We all like to eat, and some foods are better for us than others. A proper teaching diet calls for a main course of "enthusiastic stew" in every lesson you cook up. The recipe is to *put everything you've got into it.* King Frederick rose before dawn so that he would have a longer day to enjoy being king. Let's have the stew and take a lesson about enthusiasm from the man who enjoyed being king.

In short, be so enthusiastic with life and your teaching that you would inspire the cigar-store Indian.

Enthusiasm grows out of—

An inner conviction of the eternal value of the gospel plan.

A deep appreciation for the wonderful blessings of being alive.

A feeling that life is a great adventure.

A keen power of observation.

An obsession to do simple things better than they have ever been done before.

Being filled with the conviction from the top of your head to the bottom of your feet that your subject matter is truth and that it is of the most exceptional importance.

Before each class, try winding yourself up. Tell yourself how exciting it is to be alive, to teach such wonderful students, to teach the gospel. Enter the class *sitting on top of the world* and stay there. During the lesson keep things moving. Allow not even a five-second lag. Plan more than can be presented during the lesson period. Give the students the feeling that every second together is a golden moment to be used productively. Then, in your own unique style, use spontaneous humor and smile with a sparkle.

Lively spontaneous humor is closely allied to enthusiasm. Both require a keen, alert mind. Both excite the students' thinking. Spontaneous humor holds a rightful place in our pedagogy because it has no equal as a release mechanism for strained classroom relationships (and no class is immune or free from such relationships). Students of all ages want to laugh. They want a teacher who will laugh with them.

Here are a few ideas that should help you develop your humor:

Generally a joke in class has more assured utility when it relates to the lesson objective. If the joke happens to fall flat, the teacher still has the objective on which he can hang his story. A concept brought out in a lesson that does not relate to the lesson objective can easily misdirect the students' thinking from what is intended to be taught. Ideas expounded in jokes are no exception to this rule. Abraham Lincoln was a prolific storyteller, but he always used jokes to put over a lesson.

Screen all jokes for "shadiness" and vulgarity. This includes jokes by students. It is better to sacrifice the joke than oneself as a poor example and teacher of wrongdoing.

Much of Christ's strength as the Master Teacher was His spontaneity. Often His lessons grew out of an immediate happening. When possible, let your humor also follow this effective style of teaching.

A humorous experience often grows out of the unexpected. Therefore, watch for opportunities to create the unexpected. I heard one individual jest, "I just flew here all the way from New York. And, boy, are my arms tired!"

Listen carefully to those who have developed spontaneous humor. Observe how they play with words. Then practice playing with words yourself. The quip about flying was a play on words as well as a way of saying the unexpected. When I heard this joke, it was well timed and relevant to the situation at hand. It got a good laugh.

It is all right for the teacher to use himself as a scapegoat when jesting, as long as the students do not use him as such.

The teacher should be a good sport and laugh with the students.

The teacher should be sensitive to student feedback. One teacher told a joke, and he was the only one that laughed. So he told another one that was also coldly received. Had he been sensitive to what the class members wanted to hear, he probably would not have started on the first joke, not to mention the second attempt that also failed.

The teacher should not allow spontaneous student wise-cracking when he is trying to put over a lesson. Some students have not yet learned how to be funny without doing damage to a friend or to the spirit of a lesson.

Ordinarily do not tell a joke on someone unless it really happened to him. There is such a thing as humorous sincerity.

A word of caution: Jesting with students usually loosens the classroom atmosphere, and discipline problems might result. Keep your humor within the bounds of control.

In addition to using humor, there are also ways of communicating enthusiasm with your eyes and mouth. Every student of cartooning learns early that the eyes and mouth are in fact the most expressive parts of the body. This is a lesson also in the art of living that each of us as teachers of the gospel should learn early.

Jesus Christ said, "The light of the body is the eye."[1] Our eyes are the "windows of our mobile tabernacles." They have much potential for communicating ideas and feelings to others. They can be a useful tool to the effective teacher.

Here are a few ideas to begin practicing immediately:

1. Go to the mirror and take a good look at yourself. Look at your eyes. Do they sparkle? If so, go on to the next suggestion. Do they appear dull? Try making them smile. Do you see some wrinkles in the outer corners of your eyes? This is good if you are not just squinting. Wrinkles are a complement, even to a woman, if they are in the right places. Practice sparkling your eyes. When you get the feel of it before the mirror, you are ready to practice at any time—while walking down the street, while driving to the grocery store, while eating your dinner, while talking with a friend.

Concentrate on making the light of your body sparkle, and you will soon form a worthy habit.

2. The eyes are one of the most effective disciplining aids

at a teacher's disposal. If you can pinpoint a discipline problem in its budding stage, hardly a word need be said. Just move over to the center of the problem in the room and look the offender straight in the eye. This calls for more practice. So back to the mirror. Look at yourself and try squinting this time. Try to look determined. Look angry. Look furious. Isn't it amazing what can be done with the eyes during a lesson? Keep in mind that only a slight glance may be necessary for a slight student distraction. Where confusion prevails, a cold stare may be in order. Don't let a problem get beyond this point. Like anything else of value, skillful disciplining with the eyes comes through conscientious practice.

3. While presenting a lesson, make it a practice to look into the eyes of individuals in the room. Let your eyes remain on each person long enough to let him know you are looking at him as a special person. This gives each student the feeling that the lesson is specifically for him. If the listener is in close proximity, look at the bridge of his nose. This is more restful to you, and your eyes won't be shifting and dancing to the distraction of the listener.

4. If you are asking a favor of a student and are not sure your request will be granted, ordinarily do not let your eyes meet his. If this happens, he will immediately be placed on the defensive and your petition may not be granted. Another time that it may be useful to turn your eyes away from a student is when he is taking part but begins to appear insecure in your presence. Not looking directly at the student helps him assume the offensive position.

5. When bearing testimony or expressing conviction of a principle of truth, do not look up at the ceiling or down at the floor, but look squarely into the eyes of each student. This is a time when the light of the teacher is to penetrate his students, and it should take place frequently. Never underestimate the power of direct eye contact in expressing a sincere emotional conviction.

6. If you sit while presenting a lesson, keep in mind that this usually brings you on the same eye level with your students, placing them on an equal plateau of authority. Standing raises your eyes over the students and gives you greater command.

7. Oral reading by the teacher should not be excessive, because teacher-student eye contact is often lost as the teacher reads from the printed page. It is almost unforgivable for a teacher to read a lesson to his students. Effective teaching is "eye-to-eye," as has been taught in the Church teacher development program.[2]

8. We learned in chapter 1 that every person radiates light

according to his righteousness. The Lord declared, "If your eye be single to my glory, your whole bodies shall be filled with light, and there shall be no darkness in you."[3] Practice keeping the commandments, and your whole person will radiate light. Again, your challenge is to *put light in students' faces.*

While practicing sparkling your eyes before the mirror, you probably found that the corners of your mouth simultaneously turned up. That's the way it should be, because the eyes and mouth are a team in creating facial expressions. Have you noticed, however, that the majority of facial expressions most of the time are deadpan? Most people's eyes and mouths work in harmony all right—the eyes are dull and the mouth is sober. Homer S. Jones, professional photographer and winner of the coveted National Master's Award for Service in Photography, told me, "I generally do not ask an adult to laugh or grin while he is posing for a picture because I want him clothed in his natural expression." He then added, "A smiling portrait photograph is much more popular than a sober photo *when the smile is natural.* But it is difficult to capture a natural smile on adults." No wonder the smiling face stands out in a group as a light upon a hill!

There's something pleasantly different and contagious about the teacher who smiles and sparkles. A smile says, "I'm glad to see you. I feel at ease in your presence. You make me happy. I love you." Isn't this particularly true when it is a heartwarming smile that comes from within?

These suggestions may help the "dull eyes and sagging mouth" disease:

1. A smile grows out of one's positive happy attitudes. Therefore, replace criticism with appreciation. Overlook others' faults and consider mainly the good in associates.

2. Observe those around you who smile and those who don't. Whom would you prefer to be like? This activity has tremendous converting power in favor of the smile.

3. When in the gloomiest mood, try humming, whistling, or singing a happy song. A good one to have on hand is "Smiles" by Daniel Taylor:

If you chance to meet a frown,
Do not let it stay,
Quickly turn it upside down,
And smile that frown away.

No one likes a frowning face,
Change it for a smile,
Make the world a better place
By smiling all the while.

4. Set up a project of smiling at everyone you meet every waking hour for one week.

5. Talk with your class about smiling. Get students to laugh with you. Show how smiles are contagious by having each student look at his neighbor and smile.

Do you remember the old-time song "Let a Smile Be Your Umbrella on a Rainy, Rainy Day"? No matter how discouraging or depressing the day is, smile—*because a smile* is *your salvation on any rainy day*. Smile, and your class smiles with you.

There are many ways of practicing enthusiasm. Spontaneous humor and smiling with a sparkle are two useful approaches among the many. In the final analysis, enthusiasm is "God within" and carries with it an exalted feeling. This feeling is essential to your success.

Flexibility

Wings of the best-built planes, branches of the healthiest trees, and teachers of the greatest influence usually have the capacity to bend with the pressures that confront them. On the other hand, an airplane that is of rigid construction, a tree that is dry and brittle, and a teacher who lacks resilience may not be equal to the tests that lie ahead.

Flexibility is the capability of responding appropriately to changing or new conditions. Every teaching moment introduces a new situation. Therefore, a teacher with a non-adaptive, rigid personality may be in for trouble.

Most gospel teachers are adults and have patterns of performance so deeply entrenched within them that it would seem their ways of thinking and acting are set in cement. As William James put it, we are a "bundle of habits." Of all attributes we ought to seek to change within us, foremost should be the ability to change. I believe that even a rigid individual with much desire and effort can develop a more elastic personality.

A flexible personality has the power to "lose himself" in his students. He has a delicate sensitivity to others and is capable of reading feedback accurately as he acts and then receives responses from students. With each new input of information, he makes appropriate adjustment for subsequent action.

To illustrate ineffective use of this technique, one teacher demanded that students sit in alphabetical order in the classroom. One day when a student was absent, another student left his assigned chair to sit in the empty one. The teacher demanded that he return to his assigned chair. The student said, "Try and make me!" The student, being larger in size than the teacher, grabbed hold of the neck and pants of the advancing teacher and literally threw the teacher out of the classroom.

Had the teacher been sensitive to his students' feelings, he would not have assigned seats alphabetically in the first place, and the whole problem would have been averted.

The adaptive teacher will preassess the needs, feelings, temperaments, understandings, fears, and interests of his students. Once the teacher has determined where the student is at, he will adjust his personality, techniques, subject matter, and materials accordingly. Much thought should go into preassessment while preparing lessons.

As a lesson is prepared, alternate approaches should be considered to enhance spontaneity. The forthcoming moments of teaching are the moments of power when the prepared approaches are then used to influence students. Being prepared with various ways of approaching a situation enhances spontaneity in the teaching moments.

One must of course be flexible to be spontaneous. A spontaneous act by the teacher arises from what would appear as a momentary impulse controlled and directed by the teacher. You must quickly read each situation with your students and act upon it in good judgment. Previous experience and proper preparation, as well as alertness, are necessary conditions, just as they are in sight-reading music.

A good sight reader of music is one who has had many experiences with various patterns of notes and harmonies. He hasn't seen the melody before, but he has practiced many times the various combinations of notes in the melody. For the most part, an individual who is sight-reading plays what he already knows, but acts quickly and spontaneously to smoothly adapt the patterns into the unified whole of the melody. Likewise the power of spontaneity in teaching is made possible through experience, proper preparation, and the capability of being an adaptive quick-change artist.

We might go one step further in this analogy by comparing masterful musical performance with masterful teaching. In his *Success in Music,* Henry Finck describes the moving spontaneous renditions of Paderewski. His description could well be interpreted into performances of great teaching:

> No matter what Paderewski plays, he usually seems to be improvising, to follow the inspiration of the moment, to create the music while he performs it. His playing is the negation of the mechanical in music. When ordinary pianists play a Liszt rhapsody there is nothing in their performance that a musical stenographer could not note down just as it is played. But what Paderewski plays could not be put down on paper. . . . It is precisely these unwritten and unwritable things that constitute the soul of music and the instinctive command of which distinguishes a genius from a mere player.[4]

The flexible teacher is constantly "improvising" by following the "inspiration of the moment." And what he does cannot adequately be recorded on paper. There is much more than rote performance in the art of masterful teaching.

Jesus Christ, who gave His first allegiance to God, was one time asked by a conniving student, "Is it lawful to give tribute unto Caesar, or not?" Jesus preassessed the evil designs of His students and responded, "Why tempt ye me, ye hypocrites?" Then taking a Roman coin, He asked, "Whose is this image and superscription?" They responded that it was Caesar's. Christ said, "Render therefore unto Caesar the things which are Caesar's; and unto God the things that are God's."[5]

Here is a classic example of spontaneous teaching. Christ acted upon what appears in the scripture to be a momentary impulse to a question raised. Drawing upon His knowledge of students, subject matter, and the coin as instructional material, the Savior taught a penetrating message of loyalty. His hearers "marvelled." Christ was a master at responding to new situations. His was a flexible personality. He acted on the moment with judgment. His experience, preparation, and alertness made possible His wise spontaneous performance. Surely how Christ taught could never adequately be put down on paper, as impressive as the above written scriptural account of His teaching is.

Now let's consider how pliable you are with students. Would you interact with a quiet insecure student the same way you would interact with an outgoing openly expressive one? Are your students left with a feeling that they must do most all of the adjusting to fit *your* personality? It may be appropriate to greet the wrestler who attempts to demonstrate his masculinity to others with, "How's the toughest kid in town today?" The quiet insecure student might best be approached with a warm smile and a quiet word of encouragement. Talk sports with the football enthusiast, needlepoint with the seamstress, power of car engines with the racing enthusiast, and the best ski slopes with the skier. Laugh with the humorist and cry with the broken-hearted. You will do these things if you have that essential elastic quality that makes your personality relevant to the varied personalities and moods of students. This is what we mean by relating to students. We have to get into their worlds by making our personalities relevant to theirs.

Flexibility also suggests the power of inventiveness and imagination as you deal with students, subject matter, instructional materials, and methods. An adaptive teaching personality will draw heavily upon his own creative capacity in planning for instruction. He will not hesitate to experiment with his new ideas in lessons. The flexible teacher has the power not only to respond to change but to cause change.

Developing Skill in What You Say and How You Say It

There are about 600,000 words in our English language as listed in the Merriam Webster unabridged dictionary.[6] Yet 50 percent of the average person's vocabulary consists of not more than seventy words. The other 50 percent are words pertinent to the subject under discussion. Although a large vocabulary is conducive to academic excellence, many people with limited vocabularies are persuasive and successful lecturers. It is proper choice of words, grammar, syntax, fluency, and voice modulation that are particularly important to the teacher as he speaks.[7] And these are vitally important because no other method of communication is used so frequently in the classroom as is speaking. We have to talk to teach.[8]

Here are some ideas on how to effective in what you say:

Professional journalists recognize that important parts of a publication are the opening and closing. They therefore often use a "snapper" at the start and finish of their presentations. The "snapper" jolts the reader into an unexpected emotional experience. You might try being fluent and stimulating with the first and last verbal expressions of a lesson. It will help you to think through every word you are going to open and close with before presenting the lesson. Do not memorize these words. This could weaken your spontaneity. Plan to use action words.

We all enjoy the uplift of polished and refined words. For example, use *obtain*, not *get; pursue*, not *go after; soiled*, not *dirty; excess*, not *too much*. Keep your vocabulary simple and avoid a big word where a simple term will do the job. Don't use an unfamiliar word merely to make an impression. When using a word that might be unfamiliar to the students, define it. For example, Brother Jones is teaching a group of sixteen-year-old students about the condescension of God as found in 1 Nephi 11:16. *Condescension* is a king-sized word for most teenagers. So Brother Jones clarifies, "Here, students, we learn that Christ *condescended* to take upon Himself a body like ours. He thus had the humility to experience the type of life we experience. Because He loved you and me, He willingly became one of us and taught, through example, that we can rise above ourselves."

Combine action words with the simple polished vocabulary. Such words captivate the listeners and help assure an engaging experience for students. How is it done? Simply be specific and vivid. Rather than saying, "A dog ran toward me." Say, "A monstrous German police dog came at me in great leaps and bounds." Don't say, "He prayed and got a testimony of the Book of Mormon." But rather, "Upon completing the Book of Mormon, he fell to his knees, overwhelmed by the power of the great book. With head bowed low and tears streaming down his cheeks, Jim pleaded to the Lord for a witness that the Book of Mormon is true. It was not until then that a feeling of peace and assurance filled his soul and he could say with certainty, 'This book of scripture is of God.' "

In describing his first vision, the Prophet Joseph didn't just say, "I had a vision." The young prophet declared, "I saw two Personages, whose brightness and glory defy all description, standing above me in the air. One of them spake unto me, calling me by name and said, pointing to the other—*This is My Beloved Son. Hear Him!*"[9]

Are *your* expressions presented vividly through use of action words and through specific descriptions?

To use poor grammar often detracts from the message of the lesson, and it certainly doesn't provide a desirable example for students to emulate. Grammatical errors common among teachers are presented below.

Grammatical Error	Incorrect	Correct
1. Plural subject with singular verb.	We *was* there. Jack and Char *was* coming. There *goes* two horses.	We *were* there. Jack and Char *were* coming. There *go* two horses.
2. Misuse of adverb for adjective form.	I feel *badly*. She felt *poorly* this morning.	I feel *bad*. She felt *poor* this morning.
3. Improper case of pronouns.	They rode with Kerry and *I*. Kerry and *me* are going to ride. Kerry is going to ride with Bill and *I*.	They rode with Kerry and *me*. Kerry and *I* are going to ride. Kerry is going to ride with Bill and *me*.
4. Use of double negatives.	He *hadn't hardly* got there. There *wasn't no* one inside. They *aren't no* cowards. *Ir*regardless	He *hardly* got there. There *was no* one inside. They *aren't* cowards. Regardless
5. Split infinitives.	He decided *to not do* the work. George said that I was *to never talk* to him again.	He decided *not to do* the work. George said that I was *never to talk* to him again.
6. Extra and useless prepositions.	Where did he go *to*? Where is the book *at*?	Where did he go? Where is the book?
7. Incorrect pronunciations.	goin or gonna runnen ridin git jist wuz	going running riding get just was

Grammatical Error	Incorrect	Correct
	probly	probably
	comfortbly	comfortably
	patriarichal	patriarchal
	Melchezedek	Melchizedek
	athalete	athlete

Students are often irritated with overuse of such speech manner-isms as *a; ah; unda; oh, a; well, ah; ya see; yah; etc., etc., etc.; and so forth and so forth.*

Let's consider for a moment some hints on using your voice ef-fectively. How effectively you use your voice is an important quality in teaching. The unmodulated monotonous voice is torturous to students and death to learning. Skillful voice inflection is a significant key to engaging attention of a listening audience. Many are deceived in what they think they hear as they speak. The voice sounds different to the speaker than it does to the listener. I have worked with many trainees with a video tape recorder. Almost without exception every student, when seeing and hearing himself perform for the first time on television, responded that he appeared unenthusiastic or that his voice was not as inspiring as he had previously thought.

Dr. Turner, formerly director of speech training for some sixty thousand telephone operators in New York City, once said, "Most girls carry a little pocket mirror to check up on how they look; it would be an excellent thing if we all could have some such simple device to check on how we sound."[10] You may not have a video tape recorder or a pocket voice evaluator, but here are two substitutes:

1. Conceal a tape recorder somewhere near your general standing position in the classroom. Start the machine recording before the students arrive. During the lesson, forget that it is recording and be your natural self. After the students have de-parted, play back the lesson and study your voice quality and voice inflection.

2. Have a friend visit your class with the singular purpose of making an evaluation of your voice.

Along with what your friend tells you, the following ideas might be helpful:

Use syncopated speech. Let the accents fall in unexpected places. Cut into silence suddenly. One teacher, upon seeing that half of his class was in slumber, shrieked, *"You can all go to hell!"* Then after a pause came the gentle, *". . . or you can go to heaven."*

Practice accentuating key words. Try reading the following sen-tences out loud, emphasizing the italicized words:

He *is* right.
Jesus Christ is *resurrected* from the *dead.*
He is *risen.*
Each of *you* has a *great mission* to perform on this earth.
Can *no one* answer *this* question?
Here is an *assignment* that you will *all* enjoy.

One who has a monotone voice can improve his voice inflection by playing various notes within his range on the piano while speaking in these same tones.

Remember to stand erect and speak audibly. Open your mouth wide. Pronounce every syllable distinctly. A speech instructor once said, "I never saw a meadow lark with its beak tucked under its wing." Raise your voice at times and be emphatic. Let the sound come from your toes to your head.

Don't speak so rapidly with slurred words that you sound like the two students who met each other during the school lunch hour. Their speedy conversation went something like this:

"Jeet yet?"
"No, jew?"
"No, squeet!"

In the classroom the soft pleasant, but flexible, voice is not without power. Speak so softly some of the time that the students have to slide out on the edge of their seats to hear your important message. Never talk above classroom noises. At the slightest noise, stop talking long enough to restore order. I have observed instances where the louder a teacher talks, the greater the noise and confusion that prevail.

Summarizing Thought

Every teaching personality is different. There can be only one *you* in teaching. Your challenge is to enlarge upon your own personality. Three fundamental qualities were discussed in this chapter that should be useful as you develop your individualistic style toward increasing power to influence students. Specific "how-to" ideas in developing enthusiasm, flexibility, and what you say and how you say it were presented.

Tackle even the little techniques with the spirit of mighty accomplishment and carry with you the spirit of great-mindedness. The power is potentially within you.

Chapter 3
NOTES AND REFERENCES

[1]Matthew 6:22.

[2]*Teacher Development Program Inservice Administrator-Instructor Materials* (Salt Lake City, Utah: The Church of Jesus Christ of Latter-day Saints, 1971), p. 41.

[3]D&C 88:67.

[4]Henry Finck, *Success in Music,* in Ruth Sawyer, *The Way of the Storyteller,* p. 31.

[5]Matthew 22:17-21.

[6]Clarence A. Schoenfeld, *Effective Feature Writing* (New York: Harper & Brothers, 1960), p. 269.

[7]Adapted from "Effective Persuasion" from Employers Overload Company, p. 5.

[8]While the teacher verbalizing is necessary, it is important that the teacher provide for much student involvement. There is substantial evidence that students learn more effectively when they are doing.

[9]Joseph Smith 2:17.

[10]A. Hamer Reiser, *A Reader for the Teacher* (Viking Press, 1942), p. 353; Howard R. Driggs, "The Voice in Gospel Teaching."

Maintaining Control in the Classroom

The atmosphere of the classroom was cold and uninviting. Walls were bare except for a dog-eared corkboard that had been slashed with a knife. Chipped and scarred desks offered visual evidence of student abuse. The one door was locked so that the thirty students could not leave the classroom.

The teacher was now barking out his imposed rules of conduct with calculated determination, apparently hoping to protect the students from each other and himself from the students. On the back of the teacher's right hand were three ugly wounds, deep scratches that extended from knuckles into the sleeve of his shirt.

The day before, a fight had broken out in class. It seems that two fourteen-year-old girls with old enmities did not agree on a point in the lesson. When the teacher attempted to break up the fight, he became the object of attack. Clawlike fingernails became a weapon against the teacher.

Now, a day later, with ultimatums explained, the teacher attempted to involve class members in a discussion. The discussion failed. The teacher was left to answer his own questions. Not one student would respond. Ironically the main discussion question was, "What is a ghetto?"

I was a firsthand witness to the above happening. The class I visited was in a junior high school located in the heart of Harlem, the largest ghetto in the United States. Much more could be said of this and other brief visits to schools in the ghetto for research purposes. In the extreme problem classroom situations in deprived areas I observed that the object, to be sure, was not learning but self-protection.

The above example is of course an extreme case. It is not typical of the Latter-day Saint problem classroom, but it does show how intense a classroom problem might become. To be sure, there are many classroom discipline problems in the Church where better control is needed.

If you are having any degree of difficulty in controlling students, you are certainly not alone. Many thousands of teachers, both in and out of the Church, are having difficulty. I mention this not to justify uncontrolled classroom situations, but to point out that many classroom situations at all student age levels are not easy to control. There is much need for help in maintaining control in classrooms.

In my observation, at least two distinctive conditions fundamental to maintaining control in the classroom are more or less being violated where discipline problems prevail: (1) the condition of communicating love, and (2) the condition of involving students in responsible performances.

In this chapter we will discuss control in relation to love and responsibility. This will be followed with a presentation of some practical approaches for maintaining control in the classroom.

Control

Acquiring control over oneself in learning to act appropriately in the many situations that might be encountered is an ideal basic to living. Truth represents the standard by which appropriate action can be determined. It is commitment to truth that makes control possible.

When we talk about maintaining control in the classroom, we are then talking about a principle that is basic to life itself. Experience in the classroom can provide both the student and teacher with opportunities to practice control over themselves in learning to act appropriately in various situations. Or the classroom, as in the extreme example above, can become a battleground for transmitting disruption and chaos.

Life in and out of the classroom is both an individual and social concern. It is individual in the sense that one strives to attain self-control. It is social in the sense that one strives to attain control over himself in relation to others.

It of course should be acknowledged that the teacher or student with self-control is in a much better position to succeed socially than the individual with less of this prized human commodity. Seneca said it well: "Most powerful is he who has himself in his own power." The place for a teacher to start in controlling a group of students is with himself.

Control by Communicating Love

Maintaining control in the classroom is not simply a matter of the teacher presenting a stimulating lesson, although this almost always helps. Classroom control goes much deeper to the very roots of human experience. *Wouldst thou control thy students? Then love them with all thy heart, mind, and strength.*

In most instances a teacher who truly communicates love to his students is loved by his students, for love breaks down the walls of separateness that might otherwise exist between teacher and students. On the other hand, discipline problems, in the main, generate out of existing barriers between either teacher and student or student and student. Where love is manifest, there will be a spiritual fusion among those who are meaningfully involved. Enlarging on chapter 1, we can say that *love is an "interpersonal fusion" between two or more individuals within the framework of God's laws.* The practice of love in its highest form knows no barrier between people, no separateness, no aloofness—only fusion, a pulling together in feeling, in thought, in divine precept.[1]

A teacher must understand that love is more than having endearing thoughts and feelings toward someone. It is *sharing* such thoughts and feelings with that someone; it is giving of oneself to another. The loving teacher makes of himself an instrument for the growth of individuals outside himself.

As feelings and thoughts are shared and fused in righteous perspective between teacher and students, love becomes evident as an active power. In the social setting of the classroom, love is reciprocated action. The active power of love is a vehicle in achieving control in the classroom. The teacher is firm with students in his commitment to truth and order, but he is not coercive. Love persuades but does not manipulate.

Every student on the face of the earth has a need to love and be loved and thus to feel of worth to himself and others. The task of the teacher is to strive to meet these needs, thereby strengthening each student's identity with himself and others.[2] It is at this point that the teacher's preassessment[3] of each student's needs, feelings, interests, and understandings becomes clearly significant. The more he knows and is sensitive to these factors in his students, the more able he will be to blend his subject matter, materials, methods, and personality with their worlds. By preassessing students, the teacher equips himself with essential knowledge that helps to make an interpersonal fusion with students possible.

Control by Giving Students Responsibility

Equipped with knowledge about his students, how does the teacher make of himself an instrument for their growth? One of the foremost ways is by giving the students *responsibility* and the payoff of appreciation and sincere praise when the responsibility is carried out.[4]

The responsibility should not be more or less than the student is capable of handling, and the student should be given the right to be himself and carry out the responsibility in his own creative or uncreative way. He should be given the right to make mistakes without severe rebuke as he conscientiously attempts to contribute. At times misbehaving students must be chastized, but the correction should be followed with increased care and concern from the teacher. Love calls down from the heavens kindness and patience interwoven with firmness in seeing that student responsibilities are fulfilled.

When giving responsibility, the teacher's task is to widen channels whereby the students can openly communicate their thoughts and feelings to the teacher and to each other. The teacher should be sincere and not act as though he is something he is not. If the teacher is artificial, the students will have difficulty in identifying who he really is.

Practical Approaches for Maintaining Control in the Classroom

Having discussed principles concerning control and how control can be maintained through involved responsible action and through communicating love to students, we will now consider a few practical approaches in applying these principles of *control, responsibility,* and *love.*

Some Practical Tips on Control

1. *If there is a problem in class, catch it early and take immediate action.* Don't let uncontrolled problems drag out. Be quick to observe what needs to be done. Try to anticipate problems before they occur. Then take immediate and necessary action. It is easier to prevent than correct.

Use your eyes to discipline. If there is a slight disturbance, suddenly stop talking and look the offender straight in the eye.

As you anticipate a problem, move near the potential offender.

It is effective to hold a steer in a pasture with a slight pulsating shock from the fence. Give little shocks when a problem is barely detectable to prevent students' crossing the fence of disturbance.

2. *Make the students physically comfortable.* Watch for and improve extreme temperatures, foul air, poor lighting, dirty floors, marked desks and walls, and extraneous noises. Do you have a place for everything? Is your classroom neat? Is your classroom clean?

3. *Avoid becoming involved with trivialities.* Overlook insignificant actions of students that may tend to annoy you but do not add to lack of classroom control. Be aware of what is going on among the students, but don't concern yourself with the trivialities.

Learn to live with the fads of the age group you are teaching.

Do not interrupt a study period unless you have something important to present.

In a class with more than five to eight students, do not pass out papers individually to each student. Rather place a few papers at the beginning of each row. Then instruct class members to take a paper and pass the pile along the row. Collect papers by reversing the process. When scrap paper is to be discarded, you might have one student take the wastebasket around the room, rather than allow each one to leave his chair for the wastebasket. Follow the motto, "Delegate classroom management activities to students whenever possible."

4. *Use social pressure.* Social acceptance is a big thing with all age levels. If a student feels that his behavior is unacceptable to his peers, unless he has deep-seated problems, he will tend to do that which will bring group acceptance. Therefore, get the class to show disapproval of his inappropriate behavior. If the climate is right, you might say, for example, "Students, are you willing to accept the disruption in the back of the room? What do you propose in solving this disturbance?"

I know of a professor who was teaching a large group of coeds in a college class. Many of the girls were knitting while halfway listening to the lecture. The professor one day quickly solved the knitting problem by announcing, "All of you girls who are pregnant may continue to knit. Would the rest of you kindly put your knitting away?" That took care of the knitting problem. Use social pressure on offending students.

5. *When possible, avoid ultimatums.* An ultimatum is a binding rule that if not adhered to will bring speedy decisive punishment. Do not set long lists of ultimatums. *A teacher is committed to follow up on every rule he makes or else lose face.* Therefore, never make a rule you cannot carry out. Let the rules be few and meaningful. Never punish the whole class for the misdeeds of one person. Nor should you threaten a written assignment as punishment. Giving black marks for punishment is repulsive. I know of an effective teacher of adolescents who gives two rules the first day with students. The rules are: (1) never speak out during a lesson without raising your hand and/or being recognized by the teacher, and (2) do not use books, papers, or objects in class that do not relate to the course work. This teacher is successful with these rules because he sees to it that they are carried out.

Make it understood that you are not imposing your own rules but those that are accepted as contributing to the welfare of the group and to each individual in the group. Let students help formulate the rules. Make the rules clear. In classes with younger students, have them recite the rules back to you as a check to see whether they understand. See footnote 5, page 52, for a discussion by Les Johnson on rule setting by teachers and parents.

Rather than tell an offender exactly what you are going to do to him if he doesn't behave, one technique is to use the "principle of the unknown." Let him know the punishment will be swift and severe, but do not indicate what the punishment will be. For example, one teacher, while presenting a lesson to young students, walked back to an offender and whispered in his ear (so as not to embarrass), "What time will your father be home tonight?" The boy froze in his seat, and nothing more was said. He had no idea what would happen to him if he continued making trouble, but both he and the teacher knew the father.

One time a teacher put his arm around an offender and said, "Son, we're going to miss you around here."

6. *Be prompt.* Promptness in starting a lesson prevents student idleness and thus is a safeguard in preventing discipline problems. How often have you been late for class during the past month? Do you make it a habit to arrive in the classroom early to prepare lesson materials and talk with students who come early to class?

7. *Allow no time lags once the lesson has started.* Keep a jump ahead of the students. Give them the feeling that there is only a short time to do an important job. Keep things moving. Prepare more than you will have time to present in each lesson. Try not to allow even a five-second time lag during the lesson.

8. *Teach individuals, not groups.* If you direct your lesson to the level of the uninformed student, the more informed student will not be challenged. If you teach to the level of only the better informed one, the less informed may be confused and possibly become a troublemaker. Therefore, plan the lesson with questions and ideas on the understanding levels of the well informed, the average, and the less informed student so they will all be challenged. For example, a question to the better informed student might be, "Define the word *decalogue.*" The same question to the average student might be stated, *"Deca* means 'ten.' What is the *decalogue?"* To the less informed student you might ask, "Moses received the *decalogue* on Mount Sinai. What is another name for this record?"

When making an assignment, give students alternate choices to meet their abilities and interests.

Handle problems on an individual basis.

Some Practical Tips on Responsibility

1. *Be prepared.* Responsibility rests with the teacher as well as with the students. In fact, from the standpoint of our discussion, responsibility rests particularly with the teacher. Among the most significant of the teacher's responsibilities is being prepared. Preparation calls for more than simply knowing the subject matter that is to be taught. Preparation calls additionally for a working knowledge of instructional materials and the know-how with a variety of stimulating methods. And of course a prepared teacher knows his students.

It would be well for the teacher during his preparation period to premeditate the many possible actions and reactions of each student in relation to the subject matter, materials, and methods that might be used. The teacher should be prepared with plans and alternate plans to meet each of the possible questions and problems that might arise. Imagine yourself in the class for which you are preparing. Here are examples of questions you might raise as you imagine yourself teaching the lesson before you:

Child or adolescent class: What will I do if a student—
Throws a paper wad?
Passes a note?
Plays with a toy?
Chews gum?
Pops out with a smart-aleck remark?
Taps his foot?
Groans when I introduce a new activity?
Asks for a popsicle party while I am relating a spiritual story?
Says to me, "I won't do it!" when I ask a favor?
Combs a girl friend's hair during a lesson?

Adult class: What will I do if a class member—
Tries to dominate a discussion?
Talks to a neighbor?
Disagrees openly with me?
Refuses to answer a question?
Shows disinterest in the lesson?
Takes issue with a basic truth in the subject matter of the lesson?
Acts indifferently to me?

As sure as you are a teacher, you will be confronted with such questions as those enumerated above.

2. *Plan your lesson to be student involved.* The few class rules that are made should often be self-initiated, meaningful, and understood clearly by each student.

Students who feel they are making their own rules will be more likely to support them. The possibility of a problem student confronting a teacher and breaking the rules is minimized when the students have participated in making the rules.

Help students understand that the welfare of classmates should often come before personal desires.

In formal classroom settings, it may be a good idea to allow students to choose their own seats at the beginning of the course. This shows that you have confidence in them. Make it understood that if there is any disturbance, you hold the right to shuffle the entire group, if necessary, and that they are not to move away from their self-appointed seat during the lesson and from lesson to lesson. The day before they choose their seats, give them the responsibility of seating themselves away from those with whom they might be chummy and talkative. In some cases there is wisdom in the teacher's assigning seats the first day of class.

Let students feel that some decisions are theirs. Be sure that you are not setting only your own standards. Keep the few class rules within student reach.

If the need arises, have a pet-peeve session where the group is given opportunity to speak openly and frankly on how the class climate can be improved.

Have students handle class routine procedures such as shutting the door, opening a window, running the filmstrip projector, and calling the roll. In fact, do not do that which can be delegated to a student. Keep students busy.

If you are doing most of the talking in class, you may be doing too much. Use a variety of student-centered teaching methods.

Student-involved teaching methods can be used as a way of opening the channels of communication. Consider, for example, problem-solving discussion, buzz sessions, and the tutorial method (see "Student Centered Methods," chapter 21). When these methods are used effectively, the students are given the responsibility of thinking and performing together under controlled conditions.

3. *Use student leaders as an extension to yourself.* Another approach in opening the channels of communication by assigned responsibility is through organized student leadership. Some teachers have the misconception that a teacher is a teacher because his knowledge is greater, his performance is better, and his judgment is superior to that of his students. This is not always true, particularly in gospel instruction where the subject matter of revealed truth is common property among the students. In adult gospel classes many class members have been or are presently gospel teachers. Even in classes with younger pupils there are students who frequently have some knowledge and skills that extend beyond that of the teacher. Responsibility concerns involvement in a classroom. A wise teacher will draw upon his students' knowledge, skills, and judgments for leadership to achieve change of behavior in class members.

By using a student president or chairman and other class officers to carry out leadership functions, the teacher increases his power to influence. He uses capable students as an extension to his own personality. The student leaders join with the teacher in a type of alliance as instruments for the growth of fellow students.

Let's assume that a class has a president, vice-president, and secretary. If other student officers are in your class, the roles of the three officers in the following example can be adapted. Also special adaptation of leadership roles will necessarily be made with small children's classes. If your class has no officers, you will need to create new leadership positions. In family activities, carefully defined positions and roles can be helpful to the growth of the children. The duties must be specifically defined to the officers, and the officers must be fully committed to their clearly understood responsibilities.

Here are the three example positions of president, vice-president, and secretary.

The *class president* is given full responsibility for the spiritual leadership development of each classmate. Student discipline, tardiness, absences, and classroom solidarity should be numbered among his duties. He is to delegate lesson planning and evaluation to his vice-president. Through special assignments and committees, the president is to provide opportunities to every student in the class in the development of creative talents.

The president conducts a weekly class council meeting wherein the needs and problems of class members are considered in relation to the lessons presented by the teacher. The class council is made up of the president, vice-president, and secretary, with the teacher as adviser. The president prepares a written agendum for each class council meeting. He carries a small notebook. Upon observing problems arising in the class or in other everyday activities, he jots them down in the notebook. Before the class council meeting is held, he organizes his notes, placing each item to be brought forth in the most effective order for presentation. This agendum must be approved by the teacher before the meeting. The average class council meeting should be held no longer than twenty minutes with all present functioning at a high level of efficiency.

The *class vice-president* serves as counselor to the president. In the absence of the president, the vice-president assumes the president's role. The major responsibility of the vice-president, however, is the promotion of an effective class curriculum. Working jointly with the teacher, the vice-president raises questions in the class council meeting as to how the teacher might effectively meet the needs of class members in relation to the subject matter that is to be presented in subsequent lessons. Other class members might be invited to class council meetings to participate in the lesson planning discussions as the teacher and council determine the need. This procedure can be a powerful means in the improvement of lessons and in preventing or reducing discipline problems in the class. At least two factors lend to success in such an effort: (1) the teacher is open to constructive criticism, and (2) a meaningful rapport exists between class officers and teacher to enable the students to be free in expressing useful ideas.

The *class secretary* keeps all attendance records. She calls the roll silently in class. She also takes minutes in the class council meeting, which are read by her at the beginning of each meeting. The minutes are kept confidential. She, along with other members of the class who have been appointed by her, might also assist the teacher in preparing handouts for future lessons.

4. *Be firm.* Make it understood with your students from the outset that it is their class, yet you are in command and hold the right and responsibility to remove any obstacle that might stand in the way of the students' learning.

Being firm does not mean complete domination or unyielding rigidity to class rules, but simply adhering to the standards that have been set. The first impression is the lasting one. It is much easier to relax firm controls than to gain proper conduct after starting out too lax.

Give yourself the full responsibility of carrying out and delegating responsibilities in maintaining group control. Do not depend on someone in authority to solve your problems. Seek assistance only when you really need it.

Don't compromise a standard to win popularity.

When a problem needs to be ironed out, don't hesitate.

Never try to speak over a noisy situation. Unless a learning activity suggests otherwise, only one person should talk at one time during a lesson.

5. *Admit your errors.* If you have taught a misconception, admit it emphatically. If you have wronged a student, ask forgiveness. Be willing to concede when you see the students have a point.

If you are not certain of the correct answer to a question, say, "I don't know the answer, but I will be happy to look it up for you." Then be sure to find the answer and give it to the class.

Some Practical Tips on Love

1. *Build a personal relationship with each student.* Learn the name of each student and use his name. To him, it is the most priceless word in the English language.

The accepted norm is to call adolescents and children by their first given names. Out of respect, young students should call the teacher by his or her last name, which should be preceded by *Brother* or *Sister*. In adult gospel classes the general practice is for teacher and class members to address each other as Brother _____ or Sister _____. In intimate relationships among teacher and adult class members, first names may be used to promote personal meaningful involvement.

Talk with class members about their problems, hopes, and aspirations. In order to succeed in the best possible way, you must establish a warm meaningful relationship with each student.

Help your students save face. Rather than rebuking a student before his peers, call him in after class. One approach when you get alone with him is to talk about his interests. Give him a happy experience with you. During the discussion casually mention the problem at hand.

As you seek to learn about the background of each student, watch for little things he does. Listen to conversations of class members. Give activities and assignments that provide students with opportunities to talk or write about themselves.

Do you always show genuine interest in each student? Are you friendly to everyone at all times? A good practice is to greet students as they enter the classroom. Be friendly. The student who knows that you really care will care in return and lend you his support.

2. *Be consistent.* While answering the questions presented in the first practical tip on responsibility (p. 45), keep the answers well in mind. Then be consistent in how you use them. If you don't follow a consistent philosophy, the students will be frustrated and confused. Not knowing where they stand, they will disrespect you for wavering.

Are you just and fair? Students are different. They cannot all be treated alike. Yet the same basic rules and philosophy should be adapted to all.

If you accept a certain behavior one day, this same behavior should be accepted every day.

3. *Give each student a reputation to live up to.* When starting out with a new group of students, you might let them know that you are unaware of any bad habits they may have. To you, they have possibilities. Then request that they do nothing to destroy this destiny you see for them. Drop your eyelids to half-mast for the rest of the course and overlook many of their errors.

Do you make them feel that they are important? Do you honor their decisions? Do you focus on their strong points? Do you give them a chance to excel? A teacher has no right to tear down the self-esteem of an individual. Are you willing to protect each student's sense of personal worth even at your own expense?

Do not embarrass a student before his classmates. If a student gives a stupid answer, you don't need to announce publicly that it is stupid. Silence is one approach. If the class snickers at his response, side in with him. Somehow help him save face.

Do you really contribute to a student's sense of personal worth? One teacher bluntly reprimanded a student before the class by saying, "Jack thinks he's a wit, but he's only half right!" Another teacher, upon observing Alfred's restlessness, ignored the slight distraction of the student. To help put over the day's lesson, the teacher told of Alfred's persistence and self-control while training on the football field. Jack became even more antagonistic. Alfred took a liking to his teacher and began controlling himself in class. Try to give each student a little success every day.

4. *Be enthusiastic and laugh with your students.* Radiate enthusiasm. When a tense situation arises in class, say something funny.

It is often effective to approach an unruly student jokingly. In one class I visited, two boys were causing a slight disturbance during a study period. The teacher casually walked over to them and without a word handed a slip of paper to the main offender. The note read, "You two have the same promise America does—that is, if you serve me and keep my commandments, you shall stay together and prosper in the class. But *if you don't,* behold, you shall utterly be separated (Teacher 4:22)."

Do you avoid all forms of *SOURcasm?* Do you *smile?*

Do you let your students know how much you enjoy teaching?

Do you laugh *with* your students and *at* yourself?

5. *Look for the positive.* Seek the positive side of student behavior. At least recognize the good as much as that which is to be changed in a student. It's easier to reinforce a student's good conduct than to change an incorrect habit. Then, by reinforcing the good in him, he will be more apt to do something about his inappropriate actions.

Emphasize *do's,* not *don'ts.*

No matter how unruly a student may be, he is loved by God. He is a god in embryo, not a devil.

6. *Don't nag, threat, or argue.* Nagging and threatening secure no more than surface conformity. Instead use praise and encouragement.

Get students saying yes, yes, yes immediately.

Save raising your voice at students for the rare occasions. You'll be most effective this way. There was a teacher who seldom raised his voice. His discipline was good. During one lesson, however, the class became unruly. The teacher was patient for a short time. Finally with every ounce of energy available, he yelled, *"Silence!"* His wish was granted by thirty surprised and humbled students.

7. *If you must criticize, let it be criticism of a student's behavior, not criticism of him as a person.* Reassure him that you accept and love him, but not his actions. Convince him that you are suggesting changed actions because you know he is able to behave more acceptably. Assure him that he belongs. Make his mistakes seem easy to correct. Make him feel good about doing the thing you suggest. All of this will help him build a sense of personal worth.

Follow the Lord's law of discipline: "Reproving betimes with sharpness, when moved upon by the Holy Ghost; and then showing forth afterwards an increase of love toward him whom thou hast reproved, lest he esteem thee to be his enemy." (D&C 121:43.) Rebuke when moved upon by the *Holy Ghost,* not by *anger.* If you must criticize a student's behavior, it is better to do it privately and not in class.

8. *Step into your student's shoes.* Empathize with a student who is in trouble. Try to think out his problem as he would think it out. *Re-*

member there is a reason for everything he does. Try to understand that reason. Do everything you can to learn the facts before taking action on a problem with a student.

9. *Take no personal offense.* If a student strikes out at you, try not to take it as a personal affront. If you do and the student does not accept you, he may feel justified in his thinking—and there will be more trouble. Often to the student you are the authority against which he feels he must fight. Therefore, reject his actions but do not reject him as a person.

Have you tried ignoring one's questionable behavior? This is often an effective disciplining technique.

10. *Maintain group solidarity.* Don't allow splits or schisms among students. Get them to love one another and to extend friendships to individuals outside of their own cliques. Do not allow a student to embarrass a classmate.

In Conclusion

Posted on the bulletin board in a school at North Carolina was a list of penalties for infractions of school rules. The year was 1848. Here are some of the rules:

Quarreling at school ---------------------- *4 lashes*
Playing cards at school -------------------*10 lashes*
Swearing at school ----------------------- *8 lashes*
Misbehaving with girls --------------------*10 lashes*
Drinking liquor at school ------------------ *8 lashes*
Wearing long fingernails ------------------ *2 lashes*
Blotting your copy book ------------------- *2 lashes*
Breaking your slate --------------------- *6 lashes*
Wrestling at school --------------------- *4 lashes*
Not bowing to the teacher when leaving ------- *3 lashes*
Not saying "Yes, Sir" or "No, Sir" ----------- *2 lashes*
Not washing before using school books -------- *4 lashes*
Playing about the millstream --------------- *6 lashes*

Such coercion may yet be practiced in some school systems, but as we have seen, success in classroom management and consequently the attainment of instructional power are logically effected by communicating love to and among students and by giving students responsibility in a controlled but democratic environment.

Chapter 4
NOTES AND REFERENCES

[1]The concepts of "interpersonal fusion" vs. separateness, love as an active power, and a person's making himself an instrument for others are adapted from Erich Fromm, *The Art of Loving* (New York: Harper and Row, 1963), see chapter 2, "The Theory of Love."

[2]William Glasser, *Schools Without Failure* (New York: Harper and Row, 1969), pp. 12-13; see also, William Glasser, *Reality Therapy* (New York: Harper and Row, 1965), p. 9. Glasser's position is that man has the following basic psychological needs: (1) to love and be loved, and (2) to feel of worth to himself and others.

[3]See chapter 21, "Student-Centered Methods," for a definition and brief discussion of preassessment.

[4]In *Reality Therapy* Glasser insists that the best remedy for inappropriate behavior of an individual is to give him responsibility. This helps to bring the individual in direct confrontation with reality.

[5]Following is a discussion by Les Johnson that gives useful helps to teachers and parents on setting rules:

You're doing children a favor when you establish and enforce rules for them to follow and respect.

On the farm where I spent my youth, I noticed that the first thing that the cattle did when they were let out in the spring was to head for the nearest fence. They leaned on it, marched along it, crawled through it, or jumped over it. There was no apparent reason for their action since the other side of the fence was summer fallow—sandy, dry, undigestible summer fallow.

I believe my father correctly psychoanalyzed the action of the cattle. They were looking for a fence. They wanted to find out as quickly as they could just how far they could go. They wanted to find the limitations of their newfound freedom.

After years of teaching, I have come to the conclusion that people, especially young people, have that same natural urge to find the fence. In adults we call it the urge to explore, and we say it is wonderful. Most psychologists admire this quality in children, and so do I. But . . . there must be a fence to limit the exploration. Cattle will not prosper if they spend their time crawling through a fence or unhappily staring down at dusty summer fallow. They will be as unhappy as the child who can't find the borders of his existence.

How secure it is to look across your yard in the spring and think that from here to there is mine! How happy is the crawling baby to find the comforting four walls of his home! How confident and secure is the youth who can say to himself, "This, this, and this I can do—but that I cannot do!"

How miserably uncomfortable is the child who cannot find his fence! He is the wild young boy who runs away from home. She is the wayward girl who finds her fence too late. He is the juvenile delinquent who gets arrested for stealing cigarettes, cars, and money from milk bottles. He is the "bad boy" who cripples himself (and maybe others) for life going ninety miles an hour down a residential street, who tears trees and flowers from public parks, who breaks into a house and rips up furniture with a knife. He is the delinquent whose only real crime is in not being able to find his fence. In his mind is that horrible turmoil of a picture reaching out to find its frame.

In my classroom I have students whose parents have all but disowned them. They have given up trying to understand them. Yet after a week or two these young people are no trouble at all.

What marvelous pedagogical discovery did I make to accomplish this miracle? I applied a lesson I learned from my father. He simply electrified the fence.

Within a few days the cattle knew where the fence was, and they stayed away from it. They grazed contentedly and became fat and healthy. At the time it seemed to me to be a waste of power to leave the charger running when no animal came near it. My father shut it off and set me to watch.

Within an hour a steer came up to test the fence. He was looking for security. There was no shock. He looked back at the herd. He was confused. He jumped the fence. Had I not been there, others would have soon followed.

This is why I tell the students on the first day of school what I expect of them and what the rules are. Some try breaking the rules just to see if the fence means anything. When they find that things are as they were told, they forget about breaking the rules. They can now work contentedly and happily, secure in knowing that the rules are there and that they can depend on them.

Now and then a potential delinquent tests them just to see. So it is most important that the charger stays on. Nothing must happen to break the confidence, the trust, or the security that has been developed.

Do my students object to being in this state of "rigid control that hampers their zeal to explore?"

One boy, who had been in trouble several times, told me, "I wish everybody were as easy to get along with as you."

"Why?"

"Because I feel so solid here. I know what will happen. I feel free to do things."

No one likes to live in a country where there are frequent revolutions and their accompanying insecurity that make the valued things of today the trash of tomorrow. Insecurity is the detriment to all progressive work. A game is ruined when the referee neglects to enforce the rules—just once.

I recall a parent coming to see me after school one afternoon. As the students left the room at the close of the class, she came up to my desk, an expression of amazement on her face.

"How do you do it?"

"Do what?"

"I've seen all those ruffians hanging around the drugstore at night. I've seen them on the street corners. I must confess I'm afraid to let Tommy out at night for fear that he will be just like them. Yet from the back of the room there, they seemed as nice as you please. They talk, but when it gets too noisy, you look up and they quit just like you had punished them or something. According to my son's references to your strictness, I expected you to be some sort of tyrant. But this I did not expect. How do you do it?"

"They know where the fence is. Inside the fence they are free. But they know they must not cross that fence."

"Well, it is nice to know that somebody can beat these fellows down."

"I don't think I've 'beaten them down,' as you call it. We have a few simple well-understood rules that keep us from infringing on the rights of others and that keep us safe and free. I help them follow those rules. There is no 'beating down' in that. Rather, it is an uplifting to equal dignity."

"Maybe," she smiled. "But I did see some of them chewing gum. I didn't think schools tolerated that."

"I used to refuse permission for gum too, but that was a rule that didn't work too well. When the air was dry and their throats were sore, somehow it didn't seem so wrong to chew gum. So rather than have a useless rule that tempted breaking, we decided to change the rule. But if the chewing annoys anyone, we stop it."

"You say 'we' all the time."

"That's whom the rules are for."

"I see," she nodded and began on her own problem. "You know, Tommy has me worried. Any advice?"

"Tommy is a fine boy. He has a problem or two of his own, you know. To an adolescent like Tom, life is a business of being halfway to nowhere. It's little else but a period of confusion and doubts. He needs firm, dependable security."

"I agree. From now on I'm going to use stricter discipline on him. He's going to be in by eight on school nights and nine on weekends."

"I think that would be a mistake. You are fencing him in too much. He will have no alternative but to jump out. That's not strictness. That is constrictness. You would rebel too if the walls were pushed in on you so close that they stifled."

"I never thought of it that way."

"If I were you, I'd sit down with Tom or, better yet, I'd get your husband and the two of you together . . ."

"My husband thinks Tommy will grow out of it."

"Maybe he will, but in the meantime it will be a very lonesome, unhappy time for him when it ought to be a happy time. And he may not 'grow out of it' before a lot of harm is done and many bad habits are formed."

"You think both of us should talk with Tommy?"

"Yes, that in itself is a pretty good start on a secure fence. Then build the rest of the fence with Tom. Make it comfortable for him—not so big that he gets lost in it and has doubts that it is there; yet not so small he can't move around and grow. Then it is up to you as parents to simply help him stay within those walls. When he is ready, he will build his own fence and live in peace with the rest of his society."

"How will we know when he is ready?"

"If you have helped him with this fence and if he has found that staying inside it is good for both comfort and progress, he will ask you. He will ask because he has learned to trust you as one who helps, rather than detesting you as one who doesn't care where he wanders or hating you because you have fenced him in too tightly."

"I wish I had thought of this years ago."

"It would have been easier, but it's never too late to build a fence. Of course, it's a little harder to get used to, but within his fence Tom will grow up to be a secure, confident, well-adjusted young man. He's worth the trouble!" (Les Johnson, "Looking for a Fence," *Scouting,* December 1964, pp. 14-15.)

What Parents and Teachers Can Do

The family is the most fundamental and significant teaching agency in the Church. President David O. McKay said that the home is the basis for a righteous life and is the best place in the world to teach the highest ideal in the social and political life of man.[1]

Conscientious parents have a profound influence upon a child. Why? Because the parents are so *extensively* and *directly* and *continuously* accessible to the child in face-to-face relationships, particularly during the early formative years of the child's life. This student sits on the same end of the log with his two teachers, and in this ongoing and immediate relationship exists the ever-present reality that these two teachers gave their pupil life itself within the bonds of love and divinely acknowledged matrimony. With instruction about temple marriage and worthiness, the parent-teachers understand and the child-student comes to understand that this family relationship is an eternal one and that the home is the very heart of the school of life. The long-range lesson objective is to lead the child in righteousness to eventual exaltation with heavenly parents.

The meaningful identity of a child with his father and mother, within the framework of God's value system, is most fundamental in Latter-day Saint education. Its importance can hardly be overemphasized.

Considerable responsibility then rests with parents in effectively guiding the child into consistently practicing the revealed doctrines of Jesus Christ. But there is also an important responsibility shared by the parents with the child's classroom teachers in helping the child grow spiritually and intellectually. I speak here of teachers in public school classes as well as in Church classes. In the present society the public school teacher ordinarily attends more to intellectual than to spiritual training of the student. If parents and Church teachers do not provide spiritual training, the student's spiritual development is deprived.

Within the Latter-day Saint community, parents and classroom teachers should never lose sight of this fundamental condition that the child's matriculation with his parents has an eternal dimension in the school of life. Even after marriage and death, the offspring is not fully separated by graduation from his parents' tutelage. With the separation of death, family members who yet remain on earth live in memory of the many learning experiences with the deceased and look forward to a new semester when reuniting for continued educational experiences together. The extent of a student's experience with a classroom teacher by comparison is brief. This of itself makes parents the prime educators.

Any classroom teacher who instructs the child is then an assistant to the prime educators, who are the parents. The parents are not assistants to the classroom teacher. This principle applies to the total education of the child and in some degree at all ages.

With this introduction, I would like to spend some time with you on the parents' responsibility in the child's training and certain specific actions that parents, as teachers of the child, might take. We will then turn to the responsibility of the teacher in strengthening the identity of parents with the child and otherwise assisting parents in the child's training.

Parents as Prime Teachers

Most all of us are aware that an orphan is a child who has lost his parents and that an orphanage is an institution for the care of orphans. Most all of us feel a deep compassion for a little one who is denied the blessing of a home with loving parents and who is committed to an orphanage. Yet when it comes to educational experiences for the child that are initiated by the parents, some homes take on the flavor of an orphanage.

Certainly any parents who are "worth their salt" teach their child to eat, walk, and talk. They toilet train him and teach him to dress himself and interact appropriately with other people. Worthy parents arrange for others to teach the child and guide him into becoming a good citizen in the community and into becoming an active Latter-day Saint. But many parents consider these obligations sufficient. After all, what more might good parents do? And it is at this juncture that many homes take on an orphanage syndrome.

The parents' sin of omission is failing to take hold of their child's hand and walk through his public school and Church classes with him. By this I mean it is failure to go the second mile with the child in assignments, failure to attend PTA functions, back-to-school nights, and extracurricular and religious activities of the child. It is simply failure to take a keen interest in instruction received by the child outside the home. But more than this, the parents' sin of omission is failure to read and share stories with the pre-school child, failure to provide the child of any age with books and instructional devices, failure to challenge the child in intellectual and spiritual discussion.

If the parents are not holding meaningful weekly family home evenings, if the parents do not fast and pray regularly with their children, if the parents do not acknowledge the power of the priesthood and use it in the home, if the parents do not read the scriptures with their children and have meaningful discussions about Christ's teachings, then to that extent of neglect the child is committed to a home that is something less than the Latter-day Saint ideal.

Constructed over every Latter-day Saint home should be a church steeple of spiritual experience and a school bell that rings loud and clear of intellectual training. Let's attend first to the intellectual.

Consider the intellectual training that Henry James gave his children, the two eldest being William and Henry, Jr., who both later attained preeminence. By far the most important part of the education of these boys took place at home. Yet the boys received formal training in some of the finest institutions of learning in this country and abroad.

A common practice at the James' dinner table was for the father to throw out a provocative idea. The entire family would then seize upon it eagerly to prove or refute it. The parents made books available to the children and stimulated the children to read widely. At home the boys experienced the joy of learning for "learning's sake." The father spent many hours with his children teaching them how to think. The two older sons derived from their father his vivid sense of words. Both boys developed literary styles almost unequalled in their fields. Henry, the younger, became one of the most influential theorists of fiction in the English-speaking world. William's contribution was in philosophy and psychology. Because of the theoretical groundwork he laid, William has been acclaimed by some as the "father of psychology." The contributions of these two well-known figures in the latter half of the nineteenth century were generated within the walls of a New England home by a conscientious father.

There have been few parents as committed to teaching their children as was James Mill in the education of his son, John Stewart. John later wrote one of the most detailed and complete descriptions in literature of a father's commitment and technique in training his son.

John Stewart Mill wrote of his father that "a considerable part of almost every day was employed in the instruction of his children." Speaking of his own training, John wrote that his father "exerted an amount of labor, care and perseverance rarely, if ever, employed for a similar purpose, in endeavoring to give, according to his own conception, the highest order of intellectual education."[2]

In his childhood John sat across from his father at the desk reading assigned documents and books as his father wrote and studied. Early mornings the two would take long walks together and discuss what young John had read. John described his training as intense, almost severe. Yet his father's special care gave John "an advantage of a quarter of a century over his contemporaries." He became a distinguished philosopher and economist. As one of the most advanced thinkers of the nineteenth century, John wrote, among other contributions, *System of Logic*, which ranks with Aristotle's work in that field. As with the James brothers, John Stewart Mill had a father who really cared about his education.

I am not proposing that every Latter-day Saint home should produce a generation of preeminent writers, psychologists, and philosophers. But I am suggesting from the two above exceptional illustrations that Latter-day Saint parents teach their children to *think*. No child should be challenged intellectually beyond his mental and emotional capacity to produce. But many parents hardly take the time and effort to stimulate their children's intellectual processes. Probably most of us as parents could do better in this part of our children's training.

As for spiritual training in the home, surely it must take priority over all other subjects. He who is spiritual in the true sense of the word has a close personable relationship with his God and exercises the love of Christ in all dealings with his fellowmen. Spirituality is closely related to one's ability to communicate love to those around him. Intellectual pursuits of the highest order should not supersede spiritual instruction. Weekly family home evenings are not only desirable—they are vital. In 1915 the First Presidency of the Church admonished parents to hold family home evenings regularly with their children. President Joseph F. Smith and his counselors announced: "If the Saints obey this counsel, we promise that great blessings will result. Love at home, and obedience to parents will increase. Faith will be developed in the hearts of the youth of Israel, and they will gain power to combat the evil influences and temptations that beset them."[3] Most teaching techniques suggested in this book are adaptable to family home evening instruction. Again the Teaching Methods Chart on pages 269-71 will give you an overview of methods that can be used in family home evenings.

For a family home evening to be successful, as with a regular classroom lesson, children in the home or students in the classroom must have a meaningful experience. Parents, as well as classroom teachers, must preassess the needs, interests, feelings, and understandings of the children. Much preparation should go into each family home evening lesson to help assure success.

Here is an approach that can be used by parents in family home evenings or in other instructional situations in stimulating children to think. This same procedure is of course also useful with larger groups in gospel classrooms. This technique, which we should seek to adapt to Church teaching, was made popular by Louis Agassiz. As you read the accounts, think of how you as a parent or classroom teacher might apply this technique with those you teach.

There was once an obscure spinster woman who insisted that she never had a chance. She muttered these words to Dr. Louis Agassiz, distinguished naturalist, after one of his lectures in London. In response to her complaint, he replied: "Do you say, madam, you never had a chance? What do you do?"

"I am single and help my sister run a boardinghouse."

"What do you do?" he asked.

"I skin potatoes and chop onions."

He said, "Madam, where do you sit during these interesting but homely duties?"

"On the bottom step of the kitchen stairs."

"Where do your feet rest?"

"On the glazed brick."

"What is glazed brick?"

"I don't know, sir."

He said, "How long have you been sitting there?"

She said, "Fifteen years."

"Madam, here is my personal card," said Dr. Agassiz. "Would you kindly write me a letter concerning the nature of a glazed brick?"

She took him seriously. She went home and explored the dictionary and discovered that a brick was a *piece of baked clay.* That definition seemed too simple to send to Dr. Agassiz. So after the dishes were washed, she went to the library and in an encyclopedia read that a *glazed brick is vitrified kaolin and hydrous aluminum silicate.* She didn't know what that meant, but she was curious and found out. She took the word *vitrified* and read all she could find about it. Then she *visited museums.* She moved out of the basement of her life and into a new world on the wings of *vitrified.* And having started, she took the word *hydrous,* studied geology, and went back in her studies to the time when God started the world and laid the clay beds. One afternoon she went to *a brickyard, where she found the history of more than 120 kinds of bricks and tiles* and why there have to be so many. Then she sat down and wrote *thirty-six pages on the subject of glazed brick and tile.*

Back came the letter from Dr. Agassiz: "Dear Madam, this is the best article I have ever seen on the subject. *If you will kindly change the three words marked with asterisks, I will have it published and pay you for it.*"

A short time later there came a letter that brought $250, and penciled on the bottom of this letter was this query: "What was under those bricks?" She had learned the value of time and answered with a single word: "Ants." He wrote back and said, "Tell me about the ants."

She began to study ants. She found there were between eighteen hundred and twenty-five hundred different kinds. There are ants so tiny you could put three head-to-head on a pin and have standing room left over for other ants; ants an inch long that march in solid armies half a mile wide, driving everything ahead of them; ants that are blind; ants that get wings on the afternoon of the day they die; ants that build anthills so tiny that you can cover one with a lady's silver thimble; peasant ants that keep cows to milk and then deliver the fresh milk to the apartment house of the aristocratic ants of the neighborhood.

After wide reading, much microscopic work, and deep study, the spinster sat down and wrote Dr. Agassiz 360 pages on the subject. He published the book and sent her the money, and she went to visit all the lands of her dreams on the proceeds of her work.[4]

Agassiz was the type of teacher that stimulated students to probe deeply. What the spinster wrote about bricks and ants went far beyond what many people at the time believed could be written on these subjects.

In one of his classes, Agassiz gave a student, Nathaniel Shaler, a dead fish to study. Shaler was to write everything he could find out about the fish without damaging the specimen. No books were used. Shaler was simply to study the fish and write what he learned. After one hour of probing Shaler considered himself finished. But Agassiz told him he had only started. No less than 150 hours were eventually spent with the fish. When the study was completed, Shaler was amazed with his findings. Agassiz was satisfied and awarded Shaler with a "peck of bones" to study for his next investigation. Shaler accepted the assignment with enthusiasm. Shaler later admitted that the time spent with Agassiz offered his finest learning experiences as a student.[5]

Going back to the account of the spinster, Agassiz first identified a common element in the individual's environment—in this case a glazed brick where she placed her feet a few hours in the day (Shaler was handed a dead fish). Agassiz then posed a question to the lady that led her into inquiry: "Would you kindly write me a letter concerning the nature of glazed brick?" Wanting to escape her boredom, the lady began investigating. Escape from boredom was part of her motivation, but not all of it. As with Agassiz, when you put forth a question to your student, you should be sure he is ready for it and that it is the type of question that will engage his interest. When Shaler was handed the dead fish to study, he was in a university class studying natural science. He was eager to learn. He was ready for the challenge.

When the teacher development program of the Church was in its infancy, my secretary expressed an interest in freelance writing. During her first month of service she and I were discussing a particular publication when she mused, "I would like to write an article for a magazine sometime." I responded, "Why don't you do it now?" "Do you really think I could?" she said. "I know you can," I assured her. She wrote the article, had me and a professional editor go over the manuscript, and then promptly sold the article to *Family Circle* for $350. The only claim I can make on this success was that I gave the potential writer encouragement when she was at a point of readiness to learn and contribute. This is a significant key to the Agassiz technique. Build upon an idea that your protegé is ready and able to probe.

Of course the teacher can do a great deal to make the student ready by providing stimulating experience, encouragement, and other positive reinforcement.

I suggest that you think seriously about adopting the Agassiz method of instruction in some of your teaching activities. It was this method of inquiry, among others, that resulted in Agassiz' revolutionizing the methods of study in the natural sciences during the nineteenth century.

I cannot tell you here what are the best questions to ask. The quality of a question for inquiry can only be determined when the nature of the subject matter and materials are identified in relation to the needs, feelings, interests, and understandings of both the teacher and student. Agassiz hit upon the right combination with the woman and the brick and with Shaler and the dead fish. In these cases the teacher used the brick and fish as both subject matter and materials. Questions you use with adolescents or adults might be strictly conceptual, such as "What is light?" or "Does God live?" or "What is truth?" With a child, your questions would be more simple, such as "What is the difference between a dog and a cat?" or "Why do you love Jesus?" Younger people or less motivated individuals will likely need more encouragement and direction than Agassiz gave the spinster and Shaler. One approach you might try at the dinner table is to say to your children, "I am thinking of something." Then have the children use a process of inquiry by asking questions that will help them discover the right answer (see "Inquiry Techniques," page 287, for further help on this approach).

Stimulate your children and students to think, and guide them carefully into spiritual experiences.

How Church Teachers Can Assist Parents

As a Church teacher, you should instruct students "with an eye single to the glory of God" and with the other eye focused on each student's home. You should ask such questions as, "How can I support and strengthen each student's identity with his parents? How might I help students to honor and respect their parents? How might I help build family solidarity? How can I help the student become an outstanding Latter-day Saint in the universal family of God?" The teacher should of course not interfere in family matters. He assists the parents by what he teaches in his lessons and by giving students individualized help both in and out of class. You might plan out-of-class assignments that guide the student into learning activities with his parents in religious performance.

I once challenged a group of fifteen-year-old students to each take the responsibility of doing something to cause family prayer to occur, or to occur more often, or to make family prayer more meaningful. One young lady who had not experienced family prayer at home accepted the challenge. When her father came down for breakfast one morning, he found the chairs turned with backs to the table and his daughter kneeling at one of them. The father stomped out of the house in a huff without breakfast. The mother and other children did better. They knelt and experienced their first family prayer together. The next morning the father entered the kitchen to find the chairs once again with backs turned to the table. But now the wife and children were kneeling. This time the father joined his family. After the prayer, he apologized for his erratic behavior the morning before. Family prayer became a common practice with the family.

Concerning class assignments that link the student substantially to his home in relation to gospel ideals, I would like to share one of the most successful approaches in my observation. I tried this one out when I was a seminary teacher several years ago. I have since seen it used in adapted versions with groups of older children, adolescents, and college-age students in priesthood and auxiliary classes and seminaries and institutes. I have seen the role-play part of this procedure used successfully in family home evenings.

Let me give you a little background and explanation of this approach as it was used in seminary.

The students involved were seniors in high school. At the beginning of the school year I told them that periodically throughout the year they would go into their own homes with a fellow student, as companion, and teach lessons to their parents. They would play the role of missionaries teaching investigators.

George and Bob had no particular desire to go on a mission. Yet some of their buddies were registering for the class, so the two boys committed themselves to the new program.

Weeks passed, and the day arrived when the first home assignment was to be completed. The students had done well—except George and Bob.

"Why haven't you completed the assignment?" I asked.

Bob responded first, "Well, . . . my father is inactive in the Church, and . . ."

George interrupted, "And how can I bear testimony to my inactive father when I don't even know myself that the gospel is true?"

A discussion followed. It was finally decided that the boys would complete their assignments. But Bob would teach George's family, and George would teach Bob's family. I learned later that both meetings were successful.

After teaching three home lessons, the two boys were fired with enthusiasm and were even teaching their own parents. Upon completing four assignments, both fellows expressed the desire in a class testimony meeting to go on a mission.

In March, after seven months with the home approach, I learned that both boys had brought their fathers into Church activity. On a Sunday evening in February, George's family presented the sacrament meeting program in his ward. In this meeting George expressed gratitude for the opportunity of teaching the gospel to his parents. George's father, with tears flowing down his cheeks, then told the congregation of his appreciation to George and Bob for teaching him the gospel and bringing him into activity.

George and Bob both went on missions the following year.

At the end of the school year, we made a survey of the students enrolled in the fourth-year seminary course. We learned that (1) twelve students out of thirty-seven who originally expressed little desire to go on a mission reported that the home approach had stimulated within them the desire to go; (2) twenty-four reported that the home approach had strengthened their testimonies of the gospel (only three out of the total group reported having some doubt that the gospel was true); (3) of the twenty girls, seven acquired the desire to marry returned missionaries; (4) family ties were greatly strengthened, and at least four parents were brought into Church activity.

Four years later a survey was conducted relative to seminary teachers' use of the home approach throughout the Church. We learned that on their own volition fifty percent of the seminary teachers engaged in special units for training students in teaching the gospel used this approach. From this group we heard thrilling success stories that resulted from students teaching the gospel in the home.

One teacher in Idaho reported that through the home approach "many parents became students of the scriptures. I had no parents disagree with the program, and thirty-two of the forty-eight said it was the best program yet." Another teacher indicated, "The only contact with the Church teachings that some parents had was through this program. Men who hadn't been inside the church in years participated and started attending church meetings." A Utah seminary teacher wrote that "some parents stated how it thrilled them to see their students defend and explain the Church. They expressed desires to have their son or daughter go on a mission."

As you will see, this approach can be adapted to almost any

gospel class of older children or youth. Care should be taken in the adaptation not to violate policies of your teaching oganization.

How to Build a "Teaching the Gospel at Home" Program with Your Class

The most desirable lessons for the student to teach in his home, in many cases, are those the teacher feels are most significant to the student himself. Care must be taken to stay away from doctrines and issues that cannot be clearly substantiated from the scriptures—issues that delve into the mysteries or might prove to be embarrassing to the student or his family. A few of the many appropriate lessons are the Godhead, apostasy, restoration, coming forth of the Book of Mormon, faith, repentance, baptism, revelation, prayer, and the present-day prophets. In planning the home approach, you might go through your lesson manual or supplement and choose a number of appropriate lessons that the student can teach to his family. Do not deviate from the prescribed lesson of the course you are teaching.

Letter to Parents

After choosing the lesson to which you desire to apply the home teaching technique, prepare a letter to be sent home with each student a few days prior to the possible date for the cottage meeting. Students and parents should determine an agreeable evening for the meeting when the lesson is presented. The time set for the regular family home evening may be ideal for the meeting. The letter, signed by you, should explain to the parents the nature of the class project. Request in the letter that the parents play the role of interested investigators who are seeking for the truth. In the first meeting they are to pretend, without being facetious, that they have never before seen their son or daughter or heard the message.

Include within the letter a short questionnaire requesting the response of the parents to their son's or daughter's experience. Such items might be included as: Did the students open and close the meeting with prayer? How many times did the students bear testimony? Did the students teach you from the scriptures? Did they shake your hand firmly upon arriving and leaving? Give suggestions or comments that might be helpful to the student in furthering his progress as a future teacher of the gospel.

After the parents have completed the questionnaire and signed their names, the son or daughter is to return the letter to you to receive credit for completing the assignment.

Preparing for the Home Visit in Class

Before the students are sent to their homes to teach, they should study the lesson thoroughly in class. You should present the selected lesson to your students as though you were the student teaching his family. Then give each student the opportunity to practice presenting the lesson to his companion. Encourage the pupils to use teaching aids in their presentations, such as a portable chalkboard, flannelboard, flipboard, or pictures.

It is fun for students to play the role of missionaries. Shaking hands, calling each other brother and sister, presenting lessons, memorizing scriptures, praying together, sharing testimonies, and choosing their own companions with whom they are to study and work are exciting and stimulating experiences for young people. And in role-play situations they do not suffer the humiliation that often comes from error in actual experience.

As in the mission field, adherence to specified methods and rules are vital to the happiness and success of the students and their contacts. In the home technique, the teacher may desire to set up a list of standards for his students. The following rules are suggested. Let the class feel that these ideas are their own, and they will support them much better.

1. Never attend cottage meetings without your assigned companion.

2. Be well groomed and dressed in Sunday best for the cottage meetings.

3. Shake hands firmly with the investigators and introduce yourself and companion.

4. Smile. Radiate joy and enthusiasm. Be alive!

5. Live worthy of your responsibility and pray privately at least twice daily.

6. Give opening and closing prayers in the cottage meetings.

7. While presenting the lesson, bear frequent and sincere testimony after each idea and before going on to the next point. For example, "God the Father has a body of flesh and bones. Brother and Sister Hansen, I know this to be a reality." To be effective, testimonies should be short. Both companions should bear testimony to the principles taught.

8. Teach the lesson with conviction and in simple terms, using appropriate instructional materials.

9. Use the standard works for scriptural reference or quote scriptures from memory to strengthen the lesson.

Summary

The family is the most vital teaching agency in the Church. Parents are the prime teachers of their sons and daughters. Public school and Church classroom teachers play an ancillary role to the parents. This is to say that the teachers assist the parents in the child's intellectual and spiritual training. We have discussed in this chapter certain specific actions parents might take in the intellectual and spiritual instruction of their children. We also discussed procedures that might be used by Church teachers in strengthening the identity of parents with the child and otherwise assisting in the child's religious training.

Chapter 5
NOTES AND REFERENCES

[1]Clare Middlemiss, comp., *Man May Know for Himself: Teachings of President David O. McKay* (Salt Lake City, Utah: Deseret Book Company, 1967), p. 280.

[2]John Stuart Mill, "Unwasted Years" in Houston Peterson, ed., *Great Teachers* (New York: Vintage Books, 1946), pp. 15-42.

[3]*Improvement Era,* April 1915, p. 734.

[4]Marion D. Hanks, "Good Teachers Matter," *The Ensign,* July 1971, pp. 61-62.

[5]Nathaniel Southgate Shaler, "I Became Agassiz' Pupil" in Houston Peterson, *Great Teachers* (New York: Vintage Books, 1946), pp. 203-219 (see particularly pp. 213-14).

TECHNIQUES FOR TEACHING SUBJECT MATTER TO STUDENTS

PART

Organizing for Instruction

We have seen earlier that the teacher, student, subject matter, and materials are elements basic to all teaching situations and that in the gospel instructional setting the Holy Ghost should also be involved. When organizing for instruction, conditions relating to all of these factors should be considered.

At this point it would be well to give *that which is intended to be taught* first consideration and thereby provide a groundwork for discussion of how to set up a plan for teaching. Subject matter suggests of itself clues about how teaching procedures should be planned, as we shall see in that which follows. The subject matter of the gospel has certain distinctive qualities that must not be overlooked by the teacher. After dealing with this, we will consider how to prepare a lesson plan for instruction.

Latter-day Saint Subject Matter

To begin with, Latter-day Saint subject matter is fundamentally made up of the revealed doctrines of Jesus Christ. It is found in Latter-day Saint scriptures and in teachings of the living prophets. These great truths have been pre-defined by God for the teacher. They are divine and are not subject to change by man. It is then your duty as a gospel teacher to transmit these revealed truths in unadulterated form to your students. You may bring many other ideas into your instruction that go beyond that which appears in the scriptures and in the teachings of the living prophets. But whatever you teach should be within the framework of revealed truth, serving as reinforcement to the truth.

Secondly, this revealed truth is common knowledge to most Latter-day Saint students, including adolescents, and even children. Church doctrines are taught to the student in the Church from infancy, and such teachings as the First Vision, faith, repentance, baptism, gift of the Holy Ghost, Word of Wisdom, tithing, and honesty are repeated to the student over and over again. Therefore, no matter the age, most students who have been members for any length of time will already know the basic ideas you will be teaching them. These teachings are easy for students to understand. It follows that you frequently cannot depend on this subject matter itself to provide the kind of intellectual stimulation that is derived by exposing a student to new knowledge. This condition makes it essential for you to devise stimulating strategies to engage the students' attention. You *must* entertain with a purpose.

Interest can of course be generated by providing students with spiritual experiences. There are few ways, if any, for engaging attention of students more securely than when one is relating a deeply meaningful spiritual experience or expressing a sincere testimony or when the spirit of love is profoundly expressed.

Interest can also be attained by social interaction among students and teacher through learning activities such as discussion, role playing, buzz sessions, storytelling, and chalkboard illustrating (see, for example, the teaching methods listed on the chart located on pages 269-71).

You can do much with your personality to stimulate interest (as we have seen in chapter 3) through enthusiasm, humor, smiling, use of your eyes and voice, and by being flexible and spontaneous. Chapter 7 on storytelling will help you develop personal powers of entertainment through dramatizing your presentations.

Notwithstanding the problem we have mentioned in gospel teaching of engaging students' attention intellectually, it can and should be done. Unfortunately many gospel classes function at an intellectual level of a summer camp. Surely the intelligence of God's glory has to do with accurate thinking, reason, and thought control as well as with righteousness. Intellectual stimulation ought to become a more valued commodity within gospel instruction.

There is much literature in the Church that provides in-depth insights to basic gospel teachings—for example, the books *Jesus the Christ* and *Articles of Faith* by James E. Talmage, *Gospel Doctrine* by Joseph F. Smith, and *The Miracle of Forgiveness* by Spencer W. Kimball. There are well-written histories in the Church, including *Comprehensive History of the Church* by B. H. Roberts and *History of the Church*, much of which was written by the Prophet Joseph Smith. Church scholars from the academic community have also made some fine contributions.

Knowledge from outside of the Church, such as great literature, scientific information, historical accounts, and current world and local events, can be integrated into gospel lessons to provide intellectual stimulation through initiation of the student into new ideas. And much can be done to engage attention of students through the power of rational thought with Church teachings as well as with this secular knowledge.

It then becomes apparent that because the fundamental teachings of the Church, which represent the kernel of your subject matter, are common knowledge easily understood by your students, you should build into your teaching ways of engaging students' attention. A caution is not to allow interest-getting devices to become ends in themselves. You should seek to motivate with an instructional purpose spiritually, socially, and intellectually.

A third condition of which you should be aware as you prepare Latter-day Saint subject matter for teaching is that the revealed doctrines of Jesus Christ are not simply ideas to be talked about in lessons. They are teachings of truth that, in the main, are to be *practiced* by teacher and students. In speaking of His revealed doctrines, the Lord instructed that we are "not only to say, but to *do* according to that which I have written."[1] Probably your greatest challenge as a teacher is to practice what you teach and to initiate students into consistently applying these teachings in daily living.

Someone has said, "It is not what we eat, but what we digest that makes us strong; not what we read, but what we remember that makes us learned; not what we earn, but what we save that makes us rich; not what we profess, but what we practice that makes us Christians." You, as a gospel teacher, are in the business of making true Christians of your students.

The fourth and last condition offered for your consideration as you prepare Latter-day Saint subject matter for instruction is how the ideas might be sequenced in the lesson.

Instruction is an activity that takes place through time. The location of ideas within a given time period is the sequence of subject matter. Sequence is the placement of a series of ideas in some form of logical order.

Each idea in a lesson or unit of lessons should build upon those ideas that precede it. This provides the student with a continuity of experience with the collection of ideas. Effective sequencing of ideas is a way of advancing instructional power, because it helps to make the ideas logically meaningful to the student.

Gospel subject matter might be sequenced in several ways:[2]

1. *Chronologically* as in history: Joseph, son of Jacob, received a coat of many colors, was sold as a slave by his jealous brothers, tempted by his master's wife, cast into prison, and fin-

ally made prime minister of Egypt as a result of his faithfulness to the Lord.

From this example of Joseph, we see that each event builds upon the former in the order that they happened.

2. *From Simple to Complex:* This is a book. It is called the Book of Mormon. The Book of Mormon was translated through the power of God from golden plates given to Joseph Smith by Angel Moroni. The golden plates were made up of the large and the small plates of Nephi in addition to the writings of Mormon and Moroni and the abridgment of Ether. Several other prophets contributed writings to this great record.

From this example we can see that an idea expands into an array of ideas. Each former idea contributes to the meaning of the increased number of ideas that follow.

3. *From Easy to Difficult:* These are the Ten Commandments. They are called the decalogue and provide a basis for the Mosaic law that is set forth in the Pentateuch.

That which is understood is developed into more abstract concepts.

4. *From Familiar to Unfamiliar:* Now that we have had the story of Humpty Dumpty, let us go a step further and see how it compares to the fall of man and the atonement of Jesus Christ. Adam fell, and even the kings of the world could not repair what was lost. No man had the power of making restitution for the fall. But through the atoning sacrifice of Jesus Christ, it has been made possible that even the smallest breaks from the right can be repaired to perfection.

Instruction begins with what the student now understands (Humpty Dumpty) and advances into what he does not know (the fall and atonement).

5. *From Specific to General:* "For the want of a nail a shoe was lost. For the want of a shoe a horse was lost. For the want of a horse a rider was lost. For the want of a rider a battle was lost. For the want of a battle a nation was lost."

A detailed idea is presented that is expanded to broader, more universal ideas.

6. *From General to Specific:* The use of drugs is detrimental to a life of peace and happiness. Why is this so? Drugs are habit forming and enslave their user. Drugs cause one to lose touch with reality. Some drugs destroy the mind and cause irreparable damage to the physical senses.

The first idea is of broad quality (the use of drugs is detrimental). From this universal precept, detailed ideas are generated or related. This style of sequencing was used in this book by first presenting in the Introduction the model of teacher, student, subject matter, and materials. Out of this general framework, various specifics about teaching are discussed in subsequent chapters. We went from the general to the specific.

7. *According to Choices of the Students:* There are fifteen topics for discussion. Place these in the rank order of your preference.

The student selects and organizes ideas for study in the sequential order of his preference.

There are many ways of sequencing ideas, and it is likely that no single ideal sequence exists for any group of students.

There are various ways of organizing ideas leading to the same objective.[3] It is up to you as the teacher, as well as the writers of courses of study, to determine which type of sequencing would give the greatest strength in transmitting gospel subject matter to the student. This is done by careful examination of conditions relating to the teacher, students, subject matter, and materials in a given teaching situation.

Preparing a Lesson Plan

He who uses a good map in planning a journey into unfamiliar country is a wise traveler. This traveler will of course first determine where he wants to go. Using the map, he will then decide the most appropriate way to get there.

Cannot the same be said for effective teaching? The teacher must have a good plan as he journeys into the teaching moments, none of which is completely familiar until traversed. Within his plan, the teacher must set forth a predetermined goal—he must define where he intends to take his students. This goal is his point of destination. He will consider the needs, feelings, understandings, and interests of his students, and he will give careful thought to materials that might be employed and to his own skills and personality. He will research his subject matter thoroughly in relation to the above conditions and will be thorough in preparation of all of these factors. The wise teacher will not begin the challenging journey into the teaching moments without supplication to God for guidance of the Holy Spirit. All of these conditions are necessary in bringing the journey of a gospel lesson to success.

There is power in simplicity. Within one of Descartes' four rules of method in scientific inquiry is the notion, "To conduct my thoughts in order, by beginning with the simplest objects."[4] Because I have used this rule as a guideline, you will find nothing elaborate about the ideas for preparing a lesson plan that follow. Most lessons in courses of study are too complex and extensive for direct and unadapted use by a gospel teacher. Such complexity may be necessary in a course of study that is used by many teachers because their instructional needs vary. It is often helpful to the teacher to have a selection of ideas and techniques available in a course of study for local adaptation.

It will therefore probably be necessary as you prepare each lesson plan from a course of study to simplify what goes down in writing under your own hand. In fact, every plan you take into the classroom should be your own—adapted, resequenced, and simplified in writing from other materials.

The approach I am suggesting for the teacher to use in writing a lesson plan is to prepare generally one specific idea for each lesson. Don't try to set your primary focus on the string of ideas you intend to teach students in a lesson. Shoot with a rifle, not a shotgun. Aim directly at the bull's-eye, at the one main idea in which you hope to initiate your students. Plan your journey toward one point of destination. Use supporting ideas to help you get there. This will give you focus, make it easier for you and the students to keep on the subject, and make for meaningful in-depth study. As we have seen in chapter 5, a teaching procedure used by Louis Agassiz was to give a student an object such as a bone, a brick, or a dead fish. He would then ask the student to find out and record in a notebook everything he could about the single specific object under investigation. It was not uncommon for a student to become highly entertained and consequently spend hundreds of hours studying that one single specific item. Try focusing on one main idea as you prepare for a journey with students into a lesson.[5]

On pages 82-86 is a sample lesson plan that is intended to help the teacher focus on a single idea. After studying this plan, try adapting it in your own lesson preparation. If you find another plan that works better for you, then use it. There are many other effective ways of writing lessons. Whatever gives you the most power in changing the lives of students ought to be used. Before the sample lesson plan itself, let's look at its basic outline.

Explanation of Lesson Plan Outline*

The *Lesson Title* and the *Lesson No.* are used mainly to identify the subject of the lesson and the lesson location within a course of study. The lesson title should state succinctly the key idea from the lesson objective.

The *Lesson Objective* is the single idea, point of destination, or goal that we have been discussing. This objective serves at least two functions: (1) to define the boundaries of the subject matter of

---

*This sample plan is not necessarily recommended for a published course of study, although it could be used for this purpose. Instead this sample plan is intended for the teacher in helping him to *simplify* and *focus* in preparing his personal plan for teaching.

Basic Outline of
Lesson Plan

Lesson Title _____ Lesson No. _____

Lesson Objective _____

_____

Special Matters for Consideration _____

_____

_____

_____

      Materials to Be Used in Lesson _____

_____

_____

Outline of Subject Matter and Suggested Teaching Procedures

    1. _____

    2. _____

    3. _____

    4. _____

    5. _____

Enrichment Materials _____

_____

what is intended to be taught within a lesson (this represents the main idea of the lesson), and (2) to identify or suggest intended change that is to take place within the student (this transforms the main idea into a statement of action). Consider the following lesson objective that is presented in the sample lesson on page 82: "Each student will strengthen his personal relationship with God"

This objective has but one idea that, depending on how it is used, is specific enough to be handled in a given lesson. The objective defines the boundaries of the subject matter for the lesson with the idea of improving one's "personal relationship with God." Other supporting ideas will be used during the lesson, such as "What does it mean to have a personal relationship with God?" and "What must I do to have such a relationship?" Ideas on the periphery may or may not be used in the lesson, depending on whether they help to advance fulfillment of the objective. For example, "God is a glorified personage with body, parts, and passions" has only an indirect relationship to the objective. It is not used in the sample lesson, but it might be used. One would of course be completely off target if during the lesson an idea such as "the physical features of the Nauvoo Temple" were considered. Such a thought does not support the lesson objective. The teacher builds a fence around a particular body of knowledge with his lesson objective, within which he and his students are to remain until the knowledge has been adequately explored. This is what is meant by the objective defining the boundaries of the subject matter.

As mentioned earlier, the sample objective we are considering suggests intended change that is to take place within the student. The "student will strengthen" leads the student toward initiating change in his performance. In this particular lesson, the assignment (see p. 85) is intended to serve as a primary catalyst for action by the student in carrying out the objective. The assignment in our sample guides the student into specific action during the week for forming a closer relationship with God as a follow-through to what he has learned in class. (This assignment has qualities of a supporting objective, although here it is not distinctly stated as such.)

Until the prescribed change has occurred with students, the lesson objective is unfulfilled.

Frequently lesson objectives will be direct statements of what change is to take place in the student. For example, in another lesson we might read, "The student will fast for twenty-four hours during the next month."

The following matters should be considered when preparing a lesson objective.

1. As an initial step in preparing a lesson plan, write out the objective in clear concise form. The stated sample objective might have been presented in question form. For example, "At

the end of this lesson each student will have answered the following question: "How can I strengthen my personal relationship with God?" Whether framed as a statement or question, the objective must be clearly stated in as few words as possible. An example of how not to put it would be: "To help the student to come to the understanding, by means of considering what one must do to acquire a personable relationship with God the Father of just exactly where his position should possibly be assessed in relation to God." This may be overstating the issue on what not to do, but the point is to say exactly what you mean clearly and concisely. *You must know precisely what you intend to do.*

2. As you write out the objective, be specific enough that the ideas within its boundaries can be carefully explored. A scuba diver will not attempt to explore the entire Gulf of Mexico in one day. He will probe a small section of one little bay. Focus in on the bone, the brick, or the fish and study its many ramifications. Some lessons will call for the panoramic view, the overview or review of many ideas, but most gospel lessons are appropriately specific in quality. Being specific usually helps to make an idea concrete as opposed to abstract, identifiable as opposed to vague, and manageable as opposed to uncontrollable.

3. Write the objective on the basis of your students' needs, interests, understandings, and feelings. The objective must be relevant to their worlds.

4. Be certain that the objective is within your ability and the students' ability to bring it about. To say, "All nineteen of my students who smoke will be non-smokers within two weeks" might be just a little beyond your ability and theirs. Your lesson goal must be realistic; it must be attainable within the time you have allotted to yourself and students.

5. Do not get caught in the trap of believing that all lesson objectives must be stated in such a way that the outcome of student performances can be measured by the teacher. In the Church we teach feelings, understandings, and attitudes that are not easily measured. How would it be possible to objectively measure love or spirituality, two of the most valued teachings in the realm of Latter-day Saint subject matter? At present we can, at best, infer feelings and attitudes from what we see and hear students do and say.

However, when dealing particularly with intellectual performance or overtly expressed activities, objectives that call for measurable behavior can be very useful in the gospel classroom.

Mager defines an objective as "an *intent* communicated by a statement describing a proposed change in a learner—a statement of what the learner is to be like when he has successfully completed a learning experience." He points out that an objective must be stated in such a way that student attributes can be observed and measured. The objective is to describe an intended outcome rather than to describe simply the subject matter of the lesson. The objective is to be stated in performance terms that show what the learner will be doing when demonstrating his achievement of the objective. It would be better to state the objective "The student will write or recite or identify or solve or construct or list or compare," rather than "The student will know, understand, appreciate, enjoy, believe, or have faith in." The first set of action words is much easier to control and measure. The objective must communicate the instructional intent of the person selecting the objective.[6]

I have taken some examples from the *Teacher Development Basic Course* to illustrate Mager's approach to objectives adapted to Latter-day Saint subject matter:[7]

The student will list four things Joseph Smith learned during the first vision.

Students will attend tithing settlement.

The student will list five external evidences for the authenticity of the Book of Mormon.

The student will sit quietly in church.

The student will tell the story of the Last Supper, mentioning in sequence the four main events.

As you can see, these instructional objectives tend to take the form of learning activities or intellectual (cognitive) discourse. These so-called behavioral objectives certainly have merit. They provide for specific direction and control.

Their use is helping to clear up some of the unclear thinking in Church education—they call for a degree of precision not so evident with most other ways of stating objectives. They are effective for making evaluation of both teacher and student efforts. But for the sake of transmitting certain feelings and attitudes, I believe it is often necessary for the teacher to depart from the requisite measurability of this type of objective, even if a degree of control must be sacrificed.

It is your business and mine to teach such unmanageable subjects as love, faith, and spirituality. Take for example the objective "The student will learn to love the person he dislikes the most" (see page 145 for how this objective might be taught). This objective departs somewhat from the Mager principles in that love is difficult to define or measure. Tight controls cannot be maintained, and accurate evaluation is not as feasible as with the Mager-styled objectives. But is not such an objective to teach love justified in gospel instruction? A teacher should strive for control and precision in every way possible. But simply because we have found greater control in cognitive performances through the behavioral objective, is this any reason to neglect affective aspects of experience that are so much a part of Latter-day Saint doctrine? Efforts are now being made to find ways of writing objectives in affective terms.[8]

      6. Ordinarily, state the objective in terms of specific action or performance by students, with the end in view of helping students practice the gospel idea being taught. This is important. Yet I believe that it would be appropriate to teach some gospel subjects without the specific performance idea. There is merit in simply contemplating, for example, the relationship between light and truth with a group of thinking students. Perhaps here all the teacher needs to do is frame his objective in question form and ask, "What is the relationship between light and truth?" Nevertheless, most gospel lessons should at least point in justification to practicing the revealed doctrines of Jesus Christ, because most gospel subject matter is practicable and is meant to be practiced.

Special Matters for Consideration is a section of the lesson plan where the teacher makes notes to clarify the objective; to preassess the needs, interests, feelings, and understandings of students in relation to subject matter and objective; to note new ideas as they come to him about helping students and improving teaching procedures; and to indicate a specific action he is working on to improve his teaching personality. This section also includes a list of instructional materials that the teacher will need to have on hand before the lesson begins.[9]

The *Outline of Subject Matter and Suggested Teaching Procedures* (learning activities) contains annotations of ideas, methods, and materials in the chronological order that they are to be presented. All of this is written in simple outline style. The teaching procedures are to be specific and complete, rather than generalized and partially explained. You may wish to use the teacher development learning activities of *show, discuss, apply,*[10] or you may wish to simply spell out the methods without this approach. Whatever the approach, if you intend to have a buzz session, don't simply write *buzz session* in your outline. Spell out the specifics of how you intend to carry out the buzz session, including how you intend to structure the problem, a carefully written statement of the problem, time allotment for the group work, how the groups will be organized, the problem or problems each group will be considering, how you intend to summarize, and so on. In this section of the lesson plan you are to set forth the type of sequencing of subject matter that will give the most effective power. Page

83 of the sample lesson uses the general "What does it mean to have a personal relationship with God" to specific (particular answers to this question are considered) sequence.

It may be useful to you for retrieval and emphasis to outline your subject matter in black type. Write out scriptural references and scriptural quotes in red type. Place teaching techniques or procedures in blue.

This section of the lesson plan would indicate time allotments for various activities, out-of-class assignments, and a summary of the lesson. Remember to keep the outline simple.

The *Enrichment Materials* section of the lesson plan is a place for special readings, references, charts, and the like that call for special handling due to size, layout, or indirect relevance to your outline proper.

Sample Lesson Plan*

Lesson No. 1

Lesson Title: Improving My Relationship with God

Lesson Objective: Each student will strengthen his personal relationship with God.

Special Matters for Consideration:

This lesson is intended to assist each student in making realistic evaluation of his personal relationship with God and strengthening this relationship. This topic is of a very personal and sacred nature. The students' feelings should be respected and every possible effort should be made toward a spiritual and reverential feeling in class.

What appears to be the feelings of each student about his relationship with God?

I will talk with George before the lesson to gain further insights into his feelings on this matter.

Bill has a strong relationship with God. I will encourage him to lead out in the class discussion by sharing a personal experience.

When telling personal spiritual experiences, I will speak softly but with intensity.

I will look the students directly in the eyes and let them know I mean what I say.

Materials to Be Used in Lesson:

1. Portable record player or tape recorder.
2. Record or tape of a 3-5 minute sacred musical number.
3. Chalkboard, chalk, easer.
4. A red pencil for each student for scriture marking.
5. A copy of the four standard works in the hands of each student.
6. A sheet of plain paper for each student.

---

*For young adult class

Outline of Subject Matter and Suggested Teaching Procedures:
Lesson 1 (Time: 40 minutes)

1. At the top of the chalkboard write, "What does it mean to have a personal relationship with God?"

2. Say to the students, "Will you please maintain complete silence while this sacred music is playing? We will need the Spirit of the Lord with us today in order to answer the question on the chalkboard effectively."

3. Play the sacred music softly. [With the slightest disturbance, stop the music immediately until silence is restored. Do not play music while the students are entering the classroom or when they are talking or otherwise disturbing.]

4. Tell of a personal spiritual experience. [It is important that this experience bring out your own personal relationship with God. You must express yourself with sincerity and conviction. [To assist you in selecting an appropriate experience, think of a time when you felt particularly close to God. Consider what that feeling was like. Think of a time when your prayers were answered or of a time when you were suffering a hardship and consequently felt humble and close to God.]

5. Say, "Think of the time in your life when you felt closest to God. I would like each one of you to recall such an experience in your mind. Think of the circumstances surrounding the occasion. How did you feel? Humble? Joyful? Edified? Did you feel a oneness with God? Did you have a good feeling?"

6. Have two or three students share their spiritual experiences with the group. [If more than two or three students desire to share experiences in class, give them the opportunity. You might have the prepared students respond spontaneously without announcing that they have been asked earlier to do this. Such an approach may help the more reticent members of the class to respond.]

7. Analyze your experience and the spiritual experiences of the students who responded by asking the question, "What does it mean to have a personal relationship with God?" [At this point, rather than answering the question yourself, engage the students in discussion. Do not place these student responses on the chalkboard, but verbally acknowledge their responses.]

   Say, "What has the Lord said about establishing a personal relationship with God? There are three scriptures I would like to give you for underlining, discussion, and future use." [Annotate these scriptures on the chalkboard under the discussion question.]

   a. Say, "Having a personal relationship with God is like being close to a good friend. You feel almost as though you are a part of Him. You have an understanding with God. You come to think and feel as He does. You love Him with deep reverence and respect.

Have the students open their scriptures and mark with the red pencils John 17:21, 26: "That they all may be one; as thou, Father, art in me, and I in thee, that they also may be one in us. . . . And I have declared unto them thy name, and will declare it: that the love wherewith thou hast loved me may be in them, and I in them."

b. Ask, "How is this unity and love with God acquired?" By keeping His commandments.

Have the students mark in their scriptures Alma 9:13: "Inasmuch as ye will not keep my commandments ye shall be cut off from the presence of the Lord."

Ask, "What does the Lord mean by 'my commandments?' " Possible responses: Church attendance, not smoke or drink, have pure thoughts, honor parents, pay tithing, be honest, love even enemies, be patient with others, serve others willingly.

We cannot have a personal relationship with God without striving to keep His commandments.

c. Say, "A personal relationship with God is made possible through humility."

Have the students mark D&C 112:10: "Be thou humble; and the Lord thy God shall lead thee by the hand, and give thee answer to thy prayers."

If God is leading us by "the hand," we certainly have a personal relationship with Him.

Being humble means to acknowledge the reality of God's power and the reality of our own lack of it and need for it. To be humble is not to be cocky, arrogant, or self-sufficient.

8. Tell the story about George in *Enrichment Materials*.

9. Ask the students to respond individually in thoughts to the following question: "What is my personal relationship with God?"

After each of the following questions, pause long enough for the student to contemplate his past behavior and present feelings:

a. Do I feel close to God, or is He far removed from my thoughts and feelings?

b. What does God in fact mean to me?

c. Have I really considered God much in the past?

d. How many times did I pray last week?

e. Did I feel a close kinship with the Father when I prayed?

f. How faithful have I been in attending Church meetings,

fasting, having clean thoughts, not smoking or drinking, and respecting my parents.

10. Give each student a blank sheet of paper and have him write at the top "My Plan for Strengthening My Personal Relationship with God."

11. Allow students eight minutes to individually prepare a written plan of action for strengthening their personal relationships with God.

12. Summary: Say, "The purpose of this lesson has been to help you evaluate your personal relationship with God and to understand what you must do to be close to God.

13. Assignment for the week: Say, "This week set out with determination to carry out your plan to strengthen your personal relationship with God. Decide now specifically what you are going to do to improve. [Tell the students when and where you will be available to help them with this vital assignment. Let them know that it is significant to you that they accept the challenge.]

14. At the end of the lesson the chalkboard will appear in basic form as follows:

> *What does it mean to have a personal relationship with God?*
> a. John 17:21, 26: Love; unity
> b. Alma 9:13: Keep commandments
> c. D&C 112:10: Be humble and pray
> *Meet your challenge this week with determination.*

Enrichment Materials

GEORGE

(This story was related by a priests quorum adviser who lived in southern Utah.)

One Saturday afternoon my occupation took me on a two-hour drive from home. One of my priests, to whom I shall refer as George, was having difficulty praying. Feeling that this trip might be an opportunity to be alone with George and help him with the problem, I invited him to go along. He accepted.

It was on our return trip home that George and I got into a meaningful discussion about his limited personal relationship with God.

George confessed to me, "I am afraid to kneel and pray to God. Perhaps God is not there and does not answer prayers—or worse still, maybe He will answer and tell me the Church is wrong and my mother is right."

"Is not your mother a Mormon?" I asked.

"No, she believes in pantheism. She tells me that when she dies, she will lose her identity and dissolve into nature. What if I pray, and God tells me she is right. I cannot bear the thoughts of it. I dare not talk to God."

George and I then discussed the matter of trusting in God's goodness. We considered Alma 32:27, which teaches, "If ye will awake and arouse your faculties, even to an experiment upon my words, and exercise a particle of faith, yea even if ye can no more than desire to believe, let this desire work in you, even until ye believe in a manner that ye can given place for a portion of my words."

George said, "I desire to believe." And I responded with further counsel from Alma as to how this desire must be nurtured.

George and I then prayed in his behalf. That experience of prayer brought us both closer to God.

Now through study of the scriptures, Church activity, fasting, humility, faithful prayers, and effort to live in unity with Christ's way of life, George is forming a personal relationship with God. He is now growing in conviction of the reality of the true and living God and of his potential of becoming not an unidentifiable entity in nature, but a glorified son of God.

"And this is life eternal, that they might know thee the only true God, and Jesus Christ, whom thou hast sent." (John 17:3.)

Some Summarizing Thoughts and Conclusions

Subject matter suggests of itself clues about how teaching procedures should be planned. Four conditions concerning subject matter should be considered as you prepare for instruction.

1. In its basic form, Latter-day Saint subject matter consists of the revealed doctrines of Jesus Christ. These great pre-defined truths are not to be changed by man. Whatever you teach in gospel instruction should be within the framework of this revealed truth, serving as reinforcement to it.

2. Students of all ages with any duration in the Church generally have an understanding of the revealed doctrines of Jesus Christ. These teachings are easy to understand and are repeated over and over again to the student. Thus you will often be teaching him what he already knows. You must therefore entertain with instructional purpose. A student's attention can be engaged through spiritual, intellectual, and social stimulation. The latter would include imaginative techniques employed in learning activities as well as how you perform as a teaching personality.

3. Latter-day Saint subject matter is a body of knowledge not simply to be talked about, but teachings of truth that for the most part are practicable. Probably your greatest challenge as a teacher is to guide students into consistently practicing these teachings in daily living.

4. You must take care with the order in which you place a series of ideas within a lesson or series of lessons so as to give the student a continuity of experience with the subject matter. Seven ways of sequencing subject matter were presented in this chapter.

A written lesson plan is a useful and necessary tool for the teacher. Generally in preparing his own lesson plan, the teacher would do well to use a single specific idea for the lesson objective. This objective should define the boundaries of the subject matter that is intended to be taught and ordinarily should identify or suggest change that is to take place within the student. So far as possible, the objective should lead the student into practicing Church teachings, rather than simply generating talk about them.

There are many ways in which an outline of a lesson plan can be written. Acknowledging the power of simplicity, a plan was suggested wherein you would write the ideas to be taught in simple linear form and in the chronological order you plan to teach. Teaching procedures should be spelled out specifically, including the use of instructional materials and overall physical environment.

In planning a gospel lesson, conditions relating to teacher, student, subject matter, materials, and the Holy Spirit should all be carefully considered. A good deal of preparation is necessary in developing the organization of these components for establishing relevancies among them so as to maximize instructional power. Ideally, you should know your lesson plan so well that only occasional reference need be made to it during the lesson presentation. And you should be flexible in how you use the plan during the lesson, spontaneously acting upon the teaching moments to make your instruction most meaningful to the students.

The chapters that follow will provide you with various useful teaching techniques. If these methods are properly built into your lesson plan, having been carefully studied, selected, and adapted to your personality and to your students, you will find that your effect on students will be strengthened.

Chapter 6
NOTES AND REFERENCES

[1]D&C 84:57.

[2]These categories for sequencing ideas have been adapted from Stephen M. Corey, "The Nature of Instruction," in Phil C. Lange, ed., *Programed Instruction,* Sixty-sixth Yearbook of the National Society for the Study of Education, Part 2 (Chicago: The University of Chicago Press, 1967), pp. 18-19.

[3]See Jerome S. Bruner, *Toward a Theory of Instruction* (New York: W. E. Norton and Company, 1968), p. 71.

[4]F. S. C. Northrop, *The Logic of the Sciences and the Humanities* (New York: World Publishing Co., 1966), p. 8.

[5]The Latter-day Saint Church teacher development lesson plan calls for a *main idea, supporting ideas* to the main idea, *major objective,* and *supporting objectives.* You should consider the supporting ideas as vehicles in helping you bring student understanding to the central point of the main idea. Supporting objectives, whenever used, should become a means of bringing students into specified performances and attitudes as stipulated in the overarching major objective. Your primary focus then should be on the *main idea* of the lesson, which defines the boundaries of the subject matter into which student understandings are guided, and on the *major objective,* which sets forth change to be initiated in students.

The simplified lesson plan for teacher use on page 77 combines the main idea and major objective to help maintain focus. In this sample, supporting ideas are found within the body of the lesson plan. Supporting objectives, when used, would also appear only within the body of the lesson plan. This sample lesson plan then might be considered as a simplified adaptation of the teacher development lesson plan that presents a main idea, supporting ideas, major objective, and supporting objectives. In our sample plan, for simplicity and focus, the main idea and supporting ideas, as well as the major objective and supporting objectives, are combined into what is termed "lesson objective." See the *Teacher Development Program Basic Course, Course Directors Materials,* 1971, pp. 151-55, for a discussion of the teacher development lesson plan format.

[6]See Robert F. Mager, *Preparing Instructional Objectives* (Palo Alto, California: Fearon Publishers, Inc., 1962); for further helps, see Robert J. Kibler, Larry L. Barker, and David T. Miles, *Behavioral Objectives and Instruction* (Boston: Allyn and Bacon, Inc., 1970).

[7]*Teacher Development Program Basic Course, Course Directors Materials* (Salt Lake City: The Church of Jesus Christ of Latter-day Saints, 1971), pp. 89, 93.

[8]In their pioneering effort in the booklet *Writing Complete Affective Objectives* (Los Angeles: Wadsworth Publishing Co., 1972), Blaine Nelson Lee and M. David Merrill offer some interesting ideas.

[9]When the teacher plans use of materials, he should think not only about the use of an overhead projector or a picture. He should consider the overall physical environment for instruction: Is the room clean? Is the lighting adequate? Is the temperature of the room at a comfortable level? Is the room free from outside noises? Would a carpet or rug be of value? Is seating appropriate to the method of instruction?

In answer to the latter question, you might give consideration to the chart that follows on page 89, which shows possible seating arrangements according to types of teaching methods used. (*Teacher Development Program Basic Course, Course Directors Materials* [Salt Lake City: The Church of Jesus Christ of Latter-day Saints, 1971], p. 221). With some thought, you might come up with other seating adaptations that might be made.

[10]Ibid., pp. 61-62.

POSSIBLE SEATING ARRANGEMENTS

For Large Group Discussion

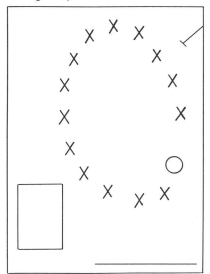

Panel Discussion

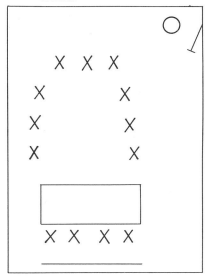

For Lecture and Audiovisual

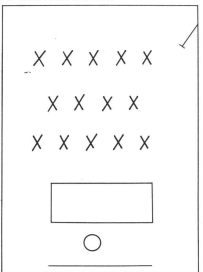

For Small Group Discussion

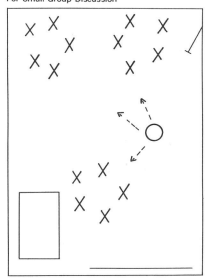

The Art
of Telling
a Story

Anyone can tell a story. Few people tell stories well. It is fundamental that one of the best ways to determine how well a story is told is from the extent of worthy effect produced by the telling.

Walt Kerksiek's storytelling had considerable effect on his listeners. One of his former students told me that she remembered vividly the stories Brother Kerksiek told her in gospel instruction. I asked her, "When did you last receive instruction through stories from Brother Kerksiek?"

"Twenty years ago," was her reply.

Although I was Walt's seminary coordinator, I considered him to be the teaching exemplar and me to be his student. The three years we were together I frequented his classroom, studying his storytelling technique and reaping the harvest of his inspiration.

Walt did not simply tell stories. He dramatized. But his technique had something in it beyond dramatization. He told me that as a young teacher years before, he decided that a primary objective would be to make the gospel live in the hearts of his students. Every story therefore would be filled with vitality, with vivid description, with an impelling sense of reality. "I have been working to this end for three decades," Walt told me.

During our close association, I became aware that Walt had an intense urge to share with others something that moved him deeply—the gospel of Jesus Christ, clothed in stories of the past. And I also observed from the many visits that I made to the Kerksiek farm in the small community of Beaver in southern Utah that Walt lived close to the heart of things—to the earth; to cattle, geese, peacocks, ducks, and dogs; to flowers; to the wind and weather; to his wife and sons; and to his God. Walt loved everything about him, but his most meaningful expressions were for people and the Lord. I never left the Kerksiek farm without a full stomach and an armful of frozen prime beef or eggs or peacock feathers for the children. Walt was town photographer, town florist, town friend, and counselor to all. He had been bishop, and to him people and things were divine.

I believe that Walt's capacity to care, to be moved deeply, to live intensely close to the heart of things and people and his God, were the roots of his power of influence in telling stories.

One afternoon I slipped to the back of Walt's classroom unnoticed. Momentarily he jovially entered the classroom, jesting with students and enjoying himself thoroughly.

When the lesson was to begin, Walt excused himself and left the room. A moment later we could hear scrambling in the hallway. Suddenly the door burst open and Walt came barging through the doorway.

"Captain Moroni! Captain Moroni! The Lamanites are coming!" he shrieked.

Then he was on the other side of the classroom playing the part of Captain Moroni giving orders for battle.

After the battle, victorious "Moroni" Kerksiek marched up the center aisle waving the banner of liberty. We learned that day of the magnanimous character of Moroni. We all left the classroom with vivid imagery of a piece of history taken from two millenniums ago, and we possessed a new identity with a great Christian warrior of ancient times and with a great teacher of the present moment.

On another occasion the crucifixion of Christ was vividly portrayed with a crown of thorns, a large railroad spike, and a hammer. As the large nail was pounded between an acting student's fingers into a wooden plank, Walt gave the students a vicarious experience of Christ's suffering that would cling to their memories for many years to come.

I will never forget Walt's interpretation of Lazarus being raised from the dead. As I entered the classroom, I became intrigued with a tall coffin-like box standing on end in the front lefthand corner of the classroom. A white curtain concealed whatever might, or might not, be in the box. I, along with the class members, was immediately interested in what was ahead for us in the lesson.

Brother Kerksiek told about Lazarus, who was a dear friend of Christ—about Lazarus' illness, about the messenger sent for Christ, about Christ's delay and belated appearance at Lazarus' home four days after Lazarus died, and about the compassionate expressions made to Christ by Mary and Martha, who were sisters of Lazarus. We were caught up in the imagery of Christ weeping along with the others who mourned.

Playing the part of Christ, Brother Kerksiek said, "Where have ye laid him?" Brother Kerksiek walked slowly to the box. Now by the "sepulchre," he said, "Take away the stone." Then Martha called out in the Kerksiek falsetto voice, "But, Lord, by this time he stinketh, for he hath been dead four days." The imagined stone was nonetheless rolled back.

Brother Kerksiek then stretched out his right arm toward the box and called out with a loud voice, "Lazarus, come forth!" And out he came. A student, wrapped in a sheet with a napkin over his face, stiffly emerged with slow halting steps. The class members' eyes were big as saucers.

Now I understood why a former student remembered clearly after twenty years the stories told by this gospel teacher. Brother Kerksiek produced effect.

I am convinced that to be an effective storyteller you must have an intense urge to share with your students that which moves you deeply. And to be moved deeply, you must have the capacity to care, to live intensely close to the heart of things and people. Herein are the roots of power to influence in telling stories.

Notwithstanding the mood of the story, effective storytelling then involves essentially a spiritual experience for both teller and listener. Storytelling is not only an affair of the mind, but of the heart and mind. As Irene Wempey put it in reference to feature writing, "Touch me. Make me laugh. Make me cry. Touch me." This is the appeal made by student listeners to the storyteller. The story must have an impelling sense of relevancy.

Ruth Sawyer, who has written one of the finest books on storytelling, *The Way of the Storyteller,* points out in her book that it is for the most part spiritual experience that makes storytellers. "When spiritual experience is lacking," she says, "all efforts toward expression . . . become but 'sounding brass or tinkling cymbal.' "[1] And for Latter-day Saint teachers, who have claim on the influence of the Holy Ghost, how much more significant spiritual experience in storytelling ought to be.

You may not present your stories as dramatically as did Brother Kerksiek. For most teachers to suddenly adopt this style, which ordinarily takes years to develop, would be unnatural and thus unwise. (We will say more about dramatization later.) But for optimal effect you *must* possess that quality of spiritual experience that is typified in all great Latter-day Saint storytellers. You must have an intense urge to share a living truth that moves you deeply.

Selection

The effective storyteller has a gift for selection. This gift, which I believe is acquired, grows out of the storyteller's sensitivity to preassess his students' needs, interests, feelings, and understandings and out of a sensitivity to his own personal experiences and stories that he has read. Any great artist makes continuous assessments of resources, of his creation, whether his contribution be a sculptured bust, a landscape painting, or a poem. He learns to draw appropriately upon his own experience, as well as on the experiences of others, while evaluating his subject. His contribution thereby takes on a strong flavor of relevance. The stories you select must be relevant to your students' worlds as well as to the defined objective of the lesson.

Some teachers intentionally avoid relating personal experiences. How foolish. So long as a personal experience does not suggest boasting or cause embarrassment, it is one of the best sources for stories at your disposal. Why? Because you know best that which you experience. We are usually most capable of transmitting that which we know best and that which, as indicated earlier, moves us most deeply. If it is awkward for you to tell a particular personal experience, tell the account in third person. But do not deny yourself and your students a personal experience that could be so meaningful to all.

Most of us fail to recognize the countless experiences in our lives that have relevance to ideas taught. Think in retrospect of a time of illness or death in your family, of a time your prayers were answered. Think of common happenings with loved ones or strangers.

I remember so vividly the occasion when my deaf and invalid brother, Klayne, had been beaten by another child. I remember well the time when my three-year-old daughter, Janice, chased after me in her pajamas as I was leaving home in the car for work simply to give me a squeeze and say, "Bye, Love!" Distinct in my memory is an old dirty tramp with greasy beard and tattered clothes approaching me on Broadway and 121st Street in New York City requesting a dime "for a cup of coffee." These experiences and many others suggest to me meaningful stories for gospel instruction.

As you draw from past experience, reach into those happenings that have been most meaningful to you. If an experience has real meaning to you, in the proper context it will have real meaning to your students.

Personal experiences of course are not enough in providing necessary resources for stories. Beyond your own personal experiences are the limitless meaningful experiences of others. You must therefore develop the capacity to listen and to record in your thinking and on file stories shared by others.

Among the most useful stories in the legacy of Mormonism are the faith-promoting ones. These are of much value because the universal spirit of the gospel is to build faith.

Do not neglect, however, the great literature of the ages. Tolstoi's "The Three Questions," Hugo's *Les Miserables,* and Hawthorne's "The Great Stone Face" are but three among the thousands of stories found in great literature that have significant moral messages. These stories offer meaningful entertainment with purpose.

Folklore should not be ignored by the gospel teacher. The *fable* teaches people how they should live. Among the best-known fables is the collection allegedly compiled by Aesop, a Greek slave living about 600 BC. Within this collection the fable of the "Tortoise and the Hare" teaches that he who moves steadily forward with determination will succeed—the race is not always to the swift. We learn from the fable of the "Grasshopper and the Ant" that it is a wise man who prepares diligently for the less prosperous day. The fable of the "Lion and the Mouse" teaches that physical strength and a big noise do not prevail over wisdom.

From the folklore are *legends* of worth in gospel instruction. The story we used in chapter 2 about the dedication of Ivanhoe is a legend. Legends are often partly true. The stories of King Arthur and his Knights of the Round Table are often based on true happenings that can be traced back to events in English history. But the story of King Arthur itself is not true history. As we tell these stories, we should of course be aware of what is true and what is fiction so as not to misrepresent the story to our students. Legends are filled with exciting adventures with moral messages.

Some of the most stimulating gospel lessons I have observed have been based on *fairy tales* and *nursery rhymes*. Fairy tales and nursery rhymes stretch the imagination and provide momentary escape from life's realities as they sweep us into "Never-Never Land." Yet they have a powerful relevancy to the lives of adolescents and adults as well as to children. The tale of the "Ugly Duckling" was told in a class of five-year-olds with such vivid description that the little children could visualize with clear perception just what the naughty little ducks were doing to the "odd one." The children agreed that they would never be unkind to someone else less fortunate, because they now knew how the ugly duckling felt. They could even help the ugly duckling become a graceful swan by being kind to him.

In another gospel class the students were reminded of Humpty Dumpty, who "sat on a wall." The lesson concerned the fall of Adam and the atonement of Jesus Christ. Students learned that Humpty Dumpty had a great fall and that "all the king's horses and all the king's men" could not give redemption from the fall. No mortal could put the "Humpty Dumpty" of man together again. But there was one, Jesus Christ, who, through an atoning sacrifice, made it possible to lift man up and restore him from his sins to a place in the kingdom.

In an adolescent class an open-end story with the three bears and a wolf thrown in was told to structure for a problem-solving discussion session. The open-end story was told up to the point where a character in the story with whom the students identified had a decision to make. The teacher asked the students, "What would you do?" The problem-solving discussion procedures were then used in similar fashion as out-

lined on page 102. After the discussion, the students were told the ending of the story. Whether using fairy tales or real-life stories, the open-
end story leading into a problem-solving discussion can be a powerful
teaching technique.

The adapted story of the three bears and the wolf went something
like this:

> Once upon a time, not too long ago, there were three Baers—Papa Baer, Mama
> Baer, and almost out of high school, Goldi Baer. These three Baers were an average LDS
> family who lived in an average home. The home looked something like this:

> Why is Goldi Baer upstairs in her room and not enjoying family home evening with
> her parents in the living room? Goldi has a problem. And she's trying to decide what to
> do about it. Ten minutes ago Ann called on the phone to report that she heard from
> Mary that Rob Wolf was going to ask Goldi for a date. Rob might even call tonight.
> Rob was six feet of handsome masculinity. With his athletic ability and winning
> smile, he was, as Ann once said, "a walking dream." Yet it had been rumored that Rob

was "a little on the wild side." Once last summer not far from Grandma's house someone had seen Rob smoking. Goldi knew also that Rob didn't attend church meetings.

Suddenly Goldi's thoughts were interrupted by the phone ringing. A shaking hand reached over and grasped the receiver.

"G-Good evening. Goldi Baer speaking!"

"Hi, Goldi. This is Rob Wolf. The gang has been planning a picnic up Left Hand Canyon for Saturday afternoon. We've decided to take dates . . . and well . . . uh . . . I was wondering if you would go along as my date . . ."

What would you do if you were Goldi?

The students tackled the problem with fervor. After the discussion and summary, the teacher gave the ending of the story. Goldi already had a date for Saturday afternoon. She confided in her parents and decided not to go out with Rob if asked again.

All kinds of adaptations can be made with fairy tales and nursery rhymes. Try using your imagination with these as you prepare future lessons.

Being already familiar with characters and events in the fairy tale or nursery rhyme, the students readily identify therewith. Almost any idea you use from a common fairy tale or nursery rhyme is understood and meaningful to your students. With interest, the students readily identify with the familiar ideas and characters. From that which is familiar, you can then move into unfamiliar ideas such as our above example of Humpty Dumpty and the atonement.

In our folklore then are fables, legends, fairy tales, and nursery rhymes that can have considerable utility in teaching the gospel. One would also do well to read broadly in the classics, listen to and observe the experiences of others, and draw upon personal experiences. Such are the resources that are potentially at your disposal in selecting stories for gospel instruction.

Preparation and Delivery

I certainly agree with Ruth Sawyer that "true storytelling" is not story reading. It is not recitation. It is not dramatic reading. This is not to say that story reading, recitation, and dramatic reading do not have a place in the classroom. All of these methods, when appropriately handled, are useful teaching techniques. But our consideration at the moment is *storytelling,* and storytelling is an art unique in its own right.

What you must do as storyteller is bring the student into a vicarious experience. You must provide him with imaginative participation in the experience of others. To do this you must be gloriously alive in forming verbal images in the "mind's eye" of the student. By means of what you say and do and how you say and do it, the student visualizes and imagines. He sees your word pictures. The ideas, happenings, and characters are made relevant to his world. The method of vivid description brings the relevancy alive into an impelling sense of reality. With desired effect, nothing lives in the mind and heart of the listener but the story.

At this point we must consider certain mechanics in the storytelling process. But keep in mind that the mechanics must be clothed with feeling and style of presentation. Don't let your mechanics show.

A storyteller talks at an average rate of 125 words per minute. People think much faster, ordinarily at about 400 words per minute. I happened to mention this to an audience in Atlanta, Georgia. A "dyed-in-the-wool" Southerner raised his hand and said in that colorful Atlanta drawl, "Brutha Hobbs, you all don't have us pegged quite right. Those of us from the South talk at 125 words an *hour.*" Of course, speed of delivery varies from person to person and within each person. But my point is that your students have the capacity to think faster than you speak. What do they do with those extra thought-words beyond the approximately 125 that you are speaking? If you are providing them with vivid imagery, they will be busily attending to imaginative participation in what you say. If you fail to engage their full attention, they will be interjecting into their thoughts, "What am I going to cook for dinner tonight? How can I get George to like me? I'd like some candy." Often their diverted thoughts grow out of ideas you present that are easily associated with other experiences meaningful to them. Beyond what we have already discussed, how can you engage students in vicarious experience so they are with you all the way?

Here are a few techniques. Use detailed description, dialogue, change of pace, and dramatization.

Detailed Description

The trick in the use of detailed description to form the best verbal images is to describe sufficient detail to enable the listener to see word pictures clearly, but not so much detail that key ideas being developed are lost. I have observed that the most violated of the two extremes among gospel storytellers is giving too little detail. In the main, stories are told with too much generalization.

Too much generalization in describing the Prophet Joseph might go something like this: "The Prophet Joseph Smith was tall and quite impressive to look at. He could talk well and seemed to have a lot of influence on people."

Now notice how the imagery becomes more vivid through more detailed description and better choice of words. I am quoting in part from a description of the Prophet Joseph Smith by Parley P. Pratt:

President Joseph Smith was in person tall and well built, strong and active, of a light complexion, light hair, blue eyes, very little beard, and of an expression peculiar to himself on which the eye naturally rested with interest, and was never weary of beholding. His countenance was ever mild, affable, beaming with intelligence and benevolence; mingled with a look of interest and an unconscious smile, a cheerfulness, and entirely free from all restraint or affection of gravity; and there was something connected with the serene and penetrating glance of his eye, as if he would penetrate the deepest abyss of the human heart, gaze into eternity, penetrate the heavens, and comprehend all worlds.[2]

So often the storyteller is in too big of a hurry to get through the story to go into detailed description. But perhaps an even greater neglect is the teacher's being slipshod in preparation, not taking the time to think through the specifics of the images that could be shared with students.

In preparation, think through the story in detail at least three or four times, incorporating words that best describe the ideas. Close your eyes and visualize the transparent yellow in the autumn leaves, the white church steeple penetrating the blue heavens, the carpet of green moss, the lope of the horse, and the laughter of children. Once you have these images in your "mind's eye," it is then a matter of telling what you see and keeping on the track. But you must see the images and happenings deeply and intensely.

But you say, "I don't have the vocabulary to tell what I see!" This is quite possible. The philosopher Polanyi tells us that we "can know more than we can tell."[3] This is why you must read widely, tell stories often, and have a dictionary handy in your hip pocket. It is not easy to tell a story with power. You must be willing to sacrifice time and effort if you intend to do well.

Dialogue

Included within your detailed descriptions should be appropriate dialogue. By use of dialogue I simply mean to express conversation between two or more persons. Dialogue helps promote credibility and imagery. It brings action and variety to play on the characters. It makes living realities of the story characters.

In the story "The Three Bears," Papa Bear said, "Who's been eating my porridge?" Mama Bear said, "Who's been eating my porridge?" And Baby Bear said, "Who's been eating my porridge—and ate it all up?" Isn't this better than saying, "Papa Bear wondered who ate his porridge, and so did the mama and baby"?

Notice how Victor Hugo uses description and dialogue as he approaches the climax in his penetrating novel *Les Miserables:*

> At the knock which he heard at his door, Jean Valjean turned his head.
> "Come in," said he feebly.
> The door opened. Cosette and Marius appeared.
> Cosette rushed into the room . . .
> "Cosette!" said Jean Valjean, and he rose in his chair, his arms stretched out and trembling, haggard, livid, terrible, with immense joy in his eyes.
> Cosette stifled with emotion, fell upon Jean Valjean's breast.
> "Father!" said she.
> Jean Valjean, beside himself, stammered:
> "Cosette! she? you, madame? it is you, Cosette? Oh, my God!"
> And, clasped in Cosette's arms, he exclaimed:
> "It is you, Cosette? You are here? You forgive me then!"

By talking in conversation for your characters in the story, the listeners' vicarious experience will be more vivid and meaningful.

Dramatization

Detailed description and dialogue give you a natural "lead-in" to practice dramatization. To dramatize is to act out the parts as, for example, Walt Kerksiek's demonstrations of Captain Moroni, the crucifixion of Christ, and Lazarus being raised from the dead.

When Papa Bear says, "Who's been eating my porridge?" it might be with clenched fists, an angry facial expression, and a loud gruff voice.

When Jean Valjean speaks, "It is you, Cosette? You are here? You forgive me then!" it would be with a soft compassionate voice of intense emotion and love.

Don't attempt to become a dramatizer overnight. Gradually develop the skill. If you haven't dramatized your stories before, start out by adding variety to your voice inflection and slight body and facial gestures. Don't stand with your hands dangling like a couple bunches of bananas. Begin to let your hands do some of your talking. Be sure all actions are in keeping with what you have to say. Every movement you make should complement the images you are describing and should not detract.

During preparation, think yourself into specific actions that will be used when you tell the story. When telling the story to students, do not concern yourself so much with these predetermined mechanics— let your subconscious take care of this part and put your whole enthusiastic self into the spirit of the story. Do this story after story, and dramatization will tend to become a natural part of your teaching style. Special instruction, practice in front of a mirror, practice with a tape recorder or with a video tape recorder can be useful helps.

Every teacher of course should not be expected to become a dramatic storyteller. In fact, some of the great storytellers use little drama in body gestures. The power for some teachers rests simply in the vital spirit and verbal images they transmit.

Change of Pace

Whether you dramatize your stories or not, you would do well to develop skill in change of pace. There are few practices, if any, as deadly for a teacher as his talking on and on in a dull monotone voice. Change of pace helps to bring life and vitality into the presentation.

If your voice is normal, it has the capacity to function at varying tonal levels. You can speak at high pitch at one moment and low pitch another. You can talk loud or soft, fast or slow, with a "mouthful of mush" or distinctly clear. You have fantastic built-in change-of-pace resources immediately available for use. Why not use them?

In your story a moment of excitement may call for a loud voice;

a moment of sacred expression, a soft voice or even a whisper; necessary but not highly significant details, with fast speeds; the key point to emphasize at a slow emphatic pace; when speaking for Flighty Fae, a high-pitched falsetto voice; when speaking for Baritone Barry, a low-pitched voice; when speaking for Toothless Tony, a less audible voice; when speaking for Polished Paul, clear diction. Listen to others speak. Listen to yourself speak. Observe proficient actors and story-tellers on television. Watch for their change of pace. There is value in pause. Notice how the skilled use the pause for effect in storytelling.

Let your change of pace be done smoothly, and see that your expression reflects the ideas you are relating. Don't say *slowly* fast and don't say *fast* slowly. Rather, say *fast* fast and *slowly* slowly. Think of the meanings of words you intend to use. Then use the type of gesture and voice inflection that the words call for.

Not only do words and ideas suggest moods, but the same can be said for the overall story. Ruth Sawyer tells us that some heroic stories march from beginning to end. Other stories go quickly on light feet. Some stories go clumsily to give certain elemental strength. Many stories go on "bated breath," calling for hesitations and suspense.[4] So you must pace yourself from story to story as well as from idea to idea.

Conclusion

If you want to tell stories well, you must have an intense urge to share with others that which moves you deeply. Your stories must be filled with vitality, vivid description, and an impelling sense of reality. A story well told is essentially a spiritual experience.

In this chapter we also discussed approaches in selecting stories and specific methods of how to bring the student into a vicarious experience through techniques of forming verbal images and dramatizing.

Storytelling is indeed an art, an art that we all could improve upon. I will never forget the stories told in the small gospel classroom in Beaver, Utah. For there I found a teacher who had mastered the art.

It would be well for us all to keep in mind that the Master Teacher told stories often during His earthly ministry. One who has mastered the art of telling a story sits high on the *other end of the log.*

Chapter 7
NOTES AND REFERENCES

[1]Ruth Sawyer, *The Way of the Storyteller* (New York: Viking Press, 1969), p. 20.

[2]Hyrum Smith, *Doctrine and Covenants Commentary* (Salt Lake City: Deseret Book Company, 1950), p. 24f.

[3]Michael Polanyi, *The Tacit Dimension* (New York: Anchor Books, 1967), p. 4.

[4]Op. cit., Sawyer, p. 146.

Problem-Solving Techniques

Let me tell you a story about Sultan, two poles, and a banana. This is a brief account of a popular research in psychology conducted by Köhler a few decades ago.[1]

Sultan was a chimpanzee. Köhler put Sultan in a cage. Also in the cage were two bamboo poles that could be connected at the ends. Outside the cage, beyond Sultan's reach, was placed a banana.

Sultan had used a pole previously to rake in food beyond his arm's length. But in this situation, a single pole was too short to reach his goal. Sultan was hungry and food was within sight. But try as he might with pole in outstretched arm, he could not obtain the banana. He tried one pole and then the other. Frustrated, Sultan then abandoned the enterprise.

After a few moments Sultan returned to his task and continued the struggle. Finally Köhler picked up one of the poles and stuck his finger in an end of it for a clue. Taking a pole in each hand, after a period of trial and error, Sultan finally saw the relationship and slid the end of one pole inside the other. Then, reaching out with lengthened pole, Sultan retrieved his prize.

There are some existing conditions in Sultan's problem-solving effort from which we as teachers can benefit.[2] To see the utility of these conditions, let us first examine Sultan's situation.

1. Certain knowledge from Sultan's earlier experience was necessary but insufficient to acquire what he wanted. Sultan was experienced in locating food, and he had used one pole before to rake in food. His past knowledge brought him close to a final solution but by itself apparently did not make acquisition of what he wanted secure.

2. Necessary properties for solution of the problem were made available to Sultan. These properties included two poles that could be inserted in each other to provide sufficient length to acquire the banana.

3. Köhler had further prestructured the problem for Sultan by placing the ape in a cage without food and by locating a banana in sight but not within reach. Recognizing the existence of a problem, Sultan became interested in its solution.

4. Sultan's behavior became goal-directed. The goal was to solve the problem of hunger by somehow acquiring the banana. He wanted the banana.

5. The problem itself suggested the general dimensions of the solution. Sultan understood that he was hungry, that he was caged in, that a banana was in sight but out of reach, and eventually that two specially prepared bamboo poles could be used as tools to find a solution to the problem. Out of these factors, a solution was feasible.

6. Sultan was unable to arrive at a solution until he established new relationships, thus acquiring new knowledge. All necessary ideas and materials were present in Sultan's environment, but relationships among these ideas and materials were not immediately evident to him. Köhler gave him a clue to a new relationship by inserting a finger in an end of one of the poles.

7. Sultan made uneven advances toward a solution to the problem. He did not progress toward the goal in a series of unbroken steps. He used a process of trial and error, trying one pole and then the other. Some approaches did not take him directly toward a solution.

8. Sultan's appropriate responses to the problem were reinforced. He was provided with satisfying consequences to his efforts, being rewarded with the banana for fitting the two poles together. If Sultan's new knowledge were to be maintained, he would of course need opportunity to repeat what he had learned and receive reinforcement in his repeated performances.

Every student you teach experiences a life filled with challenges. Hardly a day goes by that he does not encounter situations for which he has no ready solution. Much of the growth the student experiences likely comes about as a result of working toward solutions to problems in daily activities. If this is a sound premise, and I think it is, experience in solving problems can be useful in helping students prepare for life. Using controlled synthetic problem situations in the classroom can be an effective method of instruction.

We see from Sultan's experience that a problem is a question raised for consideration and solution. Sultan's question was, "How can I get the banana to satisfy my hunger?" The unsettled question is, to some degree, difficult for chimp or student. What particularly makes a problem difficult to deal with is that the participant's previously acquired knowledge is insufficient or inappropriate to enable him to arrive at an acceptable solution. If he had the appropriate knowledge to deal with the problem, he would not have the problem.

Transferring Sultan's experience to the classroom suggests certain processes. What follows are proposed conditions for action in classroom problem-solving procedures, based on the eight preceding conditions.

In organizing for instruction in classroom problem-solving activities, there are two overarching arrangements that you should keep in mind and practice.

1. *Build upon knowledge students now have* (derived from condition 1, p. 103; *knowledge* is used here to include the students' psycho-motor skills and feelings, as well as ideas that they possess). In the beginning of the problem-solving activity, the problem selected should call for more knowledge than the students possess, but not so much that new relationships for solution cannot be attained in the allotted time. Throughout the problem-solving activity, you should work out of what the students presently know. Draw upon the students' previously acquired knowledge as solution is sought.

2. *Provide students with ideas or materials that are necessary in arriving at a solution to the problem* (derived from condition 2, p. 104). Before instruction, you should carefully prepare materials and ideas that students will need while working toward a solution. It may be necessary for students to read in a textbook or respond on a worksheet, to talk to other students or to you, or to study a physical object or model in which relationships can be established for solving the problem. A file of problems and case studies can be very useful, if not essential, to a teacher who uses the problem-solving method. Write down experiences of others as you hear them. Keep a record of your own experiences. Clip out problems and cases from newspapers and magazines. As one example, consider the value to an adolescent class of the newspaper clipping on page 109.[3] (See also method 4, "Case Study," p. 276, for ways of using the case study in problem solving.)

Build the above two key ideas into the following classroom procedures.

1. *Prestructure the problem with students in ways that will generate interest in working toward its solution* (derived from condition 3, p. 104). Structuring for the problem can be done through such techniques as telling a story in which the problem is inherently based (the open-end story in case study discussion is a useful technique; see p. 276; see also the story of the three Baers and the wolf in chapter 7, pp 96-97), by showing a film or demonstrating other visuals, by explaining ideas in which the problem will be couched, or by presenting a model out of which the problem will be developed.

2. *Define the problem and determine with students that its solution is a goal to be achieved* (derived from condition 4, p. 104). Be accurate in stating the problem. Make the problem continuously accessible to students throughout the problem-solving activity. An effective way to do this is to write out the problem statement in large legible letters across the top of the chalkboard. From time to time throughout the problem-solving process, call attention to the statement on the chalkboard and remind students that its solution is the goal to which the group is working.

The definition of the problem might be the lesson objective or it may simply be part of the objective. Do not allow the problem to be so general that it cannot be studied in depth within the time allotted.

See to it that students clearly understand the problem (derived from condition 5, p. 104). Then as they work toward its solution, they will be able to draw upon the general dimensions of the problem for its solution. If, for example, you are attempting to determine with a group of students how to get better reverence in the chapel, the various dimensions of the problem of irreverence should be explained clearly to the problem solvers. Only when all of the key factors are made clear in the problem itself can appropriate solution be attained.

3. *Guide students toward arriving at a solution to the problem.*

a. *Help students understand new relationships without solving the problem for them* (derived from condition 7, p. 104). If Köhler had connected the two poles for the chimp, the latter would have been denied a worthwhile learning experience. What Köhler did, as mentioned earlier, was provide a clue by inserting his finger in an end of one of the poles. I have observed teachers hand students worksheets with blanks to fill in and then dictate to the students every word as the students filled in blank spaces. This is of course not problem solving.

Guide students to the solution, but do not "spoon feed" them. Provide them with direction, but give them sufficient independence to solve the problem themselves.

b. *Act spontaneously to uneven advances made by students as the students work toward solution to the problem* (derived from condition 7, p. 104). For example, when you are using class discussion as a problem-solving technique, all suggestions students make will likely not be a direct or even useful step toward solution of the problem. When a student makes such an uneven advance, you must act on momentary impulse to maintain group focus on the problem statement and still help the not-properly-directed student save face so he will be willing to try again another time.

c. *Reinforce student responses* (derived from condition 8, p. 104). As a student responds appropriately, use positive reinforcers, such as saying, "That is an excellent contribution" or "Very good" or "You're right on." You might simply give a nod of approval or write the useful response on the chalkboard. If a student makes an uneven advance, use a negative reinforcer, such as saying, "Not quite" or "Try again." Often other students will let the participant know he is "out of orbit." When using negative reinforcers, take care not to alienate the student. As was mentioned earlier, help him save face so he will be willing to try again. Give him the right to make a mistake.

   d. *Summarize* (derived from conditions 6 and 8, p. 104). Once students have arrived at the appropriate solution to the problem, it is generally of value to pull the loose ends together. This provides repetition and helps students see the new relationships in focus. In the summary, point out the useful ideas and ideas considered that were not useful. This gives additional reinforcement to the appropriate solution. Where feasible, relate the final solution to the students' worlds and call for action.

These problem-solving procedures can be used in various ways during a lesson—for example, in problem-solving discussion, case study discussion, spontaneous role playing, brainstorming, and buzz sessions. All of these named methods are explained in forthcoming pages of this book. To illustrate one way these problem-solving procedures can be used in practice, we will turn our attention to problem-solving discussion in the next chapter.

In a Nutshell

We learned from Sultan, the chimpanzee, certain conditions that exist in the problem-solving process. We then adapted these conditions to techniques for action in group problem solving. It was determined that one type of a problem is a question raised for consideration and solution. A student has a problem when his previously acquired knowledge is insufficient or at least inappropriate to enable him to arrive at an acceptable solution.

In organizing for instruction in the problem-solving process, there are two overarching conditions that the teacher must keep in mind and apply:

   1. *Build upon knowledge students now have.*
   2. *Provide students with ideas or materials that are necessary in arriving at a solution to the problem.*

Use the above two ideas while carrying out the following procedures:

   1. *Prestructure the problem with students in ways that will generate interest in working toward its solution.*
   2. *Define the problem and determine with students that its*

solution is a goal to be achieved. See to it that students clearly understand the problem.

3. *Guide students toward arriving at a solution to the problem.*
    a. *Help students understand new relationships without solving the problem for them.*
    b. *Act spontaneously to uneven advances made by students.*
    c. *Reinforce student responses.*
    d. *Summarize.*

These problem-solving procedures can be used with various teaching methods, including discussion, which we will now consider for a more specific example.

Chapter 8
NOTES AND REFERENCES

[1]W. Köhler, *The Mentality of Apes* (New York: Harcourt, Brace and World, 1927).

[2]These conditions are adapted from Bryce B. Hudgins, *Problem Solving in the Classroom* (New York: Macmillan Company, 1966), pp. 1-8. I have taken the liberty of expanding, readjusting, and deleting some of the ideas proposed by Hudgins to establish an appropriate basis for subsequent ideas in this book.

[3]Following is an example of a newspaper clipping from the "Dear Abby" column that might be used in an adolescent class as a case in dealing with the problem "Should a girl 'prove' her love to a boy friend?"

DEAR ABBY: My boyfriend has been after me to prove my love. I tried to tell him what you said in an article about this, but it didn't come out right.

If you can remember what you said, I would very much appreciate seeing it in your column. I am 15. Sign me . . . "WEAKENING"

DEAR WEAKENING: Here it is: Girls need to "prove their love" through illicit sex relations like a moose needs a hat-rack. Why not "prove your love" by sticking your head in the oven and turning on the gas? Or playing leapfrog out in traffic? It's about as safe.

Any fellow who asks you to "prove your love" is trying to take you for the biggest, most gullible fool who ever walked. That proving bit is one of the oldest and rottenest lines ever invented!

Does he love you? It doesn't sound like it. Someone who loves you wants what is best for you.

But now figure it out: He wants you to surrender your virtue. Throw away your self-respect. Risk the loss of your precious reputation. And risk getting into trouble and hurting yourself and hurting your family.

Does that sound as though he wants what's best for you? That's the laugh of the century. He wants a thrill he can brag about at your expense.

Love? Who's kidding whom? A boy who really loves a girl would rather cut off his right arm than hurt her.

If you want my opinion, this self-serving so-and-so has already proved that he doesn't love you. (P.S. It wasn't an "article," it was from my book "Dear Teenager.") [Used by permission of Abigail Van Buren.]

How Effective Are Your Discussion Techniques?

Albert Schweitzer was being interviewed in London when a reporter asked him, "Doctor, what's wrong with men today?" The great philosopher was silent a moment, and then he said, "Men simply don't think."[1]

What is wrong with many teachers in the Church is that they simply don't stimulate students to think.

How often have you heard teachers present such unthought-provoking discussion questions in class as, "What did we talk about last time? If you have anything to say while I give the lesson, raise your hand and I will call on you. Are there any comments on this thought?"

How many lessons have you experienced where only two or three students out of fifteen or twenty were involved in the discussion? Or how many classes have you attended where there was no discussion or student participation at all? I have attended hundreds of classes where students' thinking was not stimulated. In many classes I have observed teachers present a thought-provoking question and then let nature take its course. This type of teaching is comparable to a fellow jumping in his car, starting the engine, getting the auto rolling down the road in high gear, and then bailing out to let the outfit go its own undirected way. No discussion would often be better than uncontrolled discussion. Both car and lesson usually end up confused wrecks.

Every teacher in the Church should have a way and order of guiding student minds into thinking through organized group conversation.

In the last chapter we considered processes for classroom instruction by which solutions to problems might be found. Group problem solving through discussion, when skillfully guided, is a way of stimulating students to *think* in terms of unsettled questions that they have encountered or will encounter in life.

We will deal in this chapter with discussion techniques, particularly in terms of guiding students into seeking solutions to problems. Many teachers have difficulty in forming a good problem statement for discussion. We will take up this matter first. Then we will spend some time on procedures, or the *how-to,* of carrying out a problem-solving discussion session. In the development of these ideas, we will of course not ignore what we learned from Sultan in the last chapter.

Preparing a Problem Statement for Discussion

A problem statement might begin with, or at least include, such words (among the many) as:

> *Give evidence . . .*
> *Explain . . .*
> *Demonstrate . . .*
> *Define . . .*
> *Compare . . .*
> *Correlate . . .*
> *Illustrate . . .*
> *Find . . .*
> *Trace . . .*
> *Classify . . .*
>
> *How . . . ?*
> *Why . . . ?*
> *What . . . ?*
> *Where . . . ?*
> *When . . . ?*
> *Is . . . ?*
> *Should . . . ?*

You will note that the first group of beginning problem statement words lend themselves to ending with a period rather than a question mark. The latter group lend themselves to ending with a question mark. What is common to both groups of words is that they suggest inquiry. A problem statement for discussion is an idea that is unsettled in the minds of the students that leads them into investigation. It can be presented strictly as a statement or in question form. Here are two sample problem statements respresenting each group (both of these examples present basically the same idea). *"Give evidence* that the Bible prophesies of the coming forth of the Book of Mormon." *"How* does the Bible prophesy of the coming forth of the Book of Mormon?" What is important to inquiry is that a problem clearly exists for the students within the problem statement.

It is apparent from chapter 8 that in order for a problem to exist, the statement must, for one thing, *build upon knowledge students now have.* The problem must be relevant to the students' needs, interests, feelings, and understandings. It would be ludicrous to present a problem about retirement for discussion to a group of five-year-olds. Nor would it be wise to raise the question to a group of senior citizens, "What can I do to make Mother happy?" Such extremes are unthinkable. Where most of us have difficulty is with the less easily defined irrelevancies such as bringing up a social drinking issue when the students are preoccupied with the drug problem or asking young students to explain Paul's difficult definition of faith in Hebrews 11:1 when they are not yet capable of grasping the meaning of *substance, evidence,* and *hope,* which are all part of that definition.

A problem statement would most appropriately deal directly with the reality of student experience. For one little child, a relevant issue might be, "How can I get my friend to willingly share his toys with me?" An issue for a particular adolescent might be, "I am afraid that friends will pressure me to drink alcohol. What should I do?" For a young adult, a significant matter might be, "How can I know when I have found the right person to marry?"

We have seen in chapter 8 that the problem must call for more knowledge than students possess, but not so much that new relationships and solution to the problem cannot be attained in the time allotted. Under one arrangement where a Bible concordance would be used, for example, students would need a working knowledge of the concordance to deal with the problem statement considered earlier, "How does the Bible prophesy of the coming forth of the Book of Mormon?"

At the time the question is raised, the students should not have sufficient knowledge to give direct answers. If students possessed the complete knowledge called for, they would not be dealing with a problem. They would be simply involved with recitation of what they already know.

Recitation is of course a useful teaching technique, but it is not problem solving. Many teachers think they are engaging students in problem solving when in reality the students are simply reciting what they already knew in the first place.

Problem solving calls for such skills as analyzing relationships, putting together ideas, interpreting, applying principles, and evaluating —not simply reciting from memory. Dewey wrote that the initial step in inquiry is "to see that a situation requires inquiry."[2] A problem statement that suggests nothing more than a rehash of old ideas does not generate investigation that of course is the crux of inquiry. All too many teachers in the Church are not only fitting the poles together for Sultan, but they are raking in the banana and peeling it for the onlooker who sits at the other end of the log.

We can then say that if a statement for discussion is firmly relevant to the students' worlds and causes the students to stretch in finding new relationships for solution, then a problem clearly exists.

A problem statement must of course be supportive of the revealed teachings of Jesus Christ. Consider, for example, the statement "Give six reasons why the New Testament is outdated." Such a question would probably stir up the thinking of students, but in my estimation it would be totally inappropriate to the ideal of Latter-day Saint education. It is non-supportive of the mission of Jesus Christ.

A useful problem statement would also of course meet criteria for a well written lesson objective (see chapter 6, pp. 78-79). In addition to defining the boundaries of the subject matter to be investigated, it should initiate change in students. The problem statement should be written out in clear, concise, and specific form in as few words as possible.

Procedures in Conducting a Problem-Solving Discussion Session

Ideally, a problem statement is the pivot around which all ideas and learning activities take place during the problem-solving session. For almost every rule in teaching there is an exception, however. And it is necessary to qualify here that occasionally departure from the problem statement would be appropriate. This exception particularly applies as new dimensions to student needs are discovered by the teacher as he acts spontaneously to each new teaching situation during the problem-solving session. But in most all instances, you as teacher would do well to maintain direct focus on the problem statement for discussion.

One of the most effective techniques I have found to maintain focus, as suggested earlier, is to put the problem statement before the students in printed form. Chalkboard, overhead projector, poster, or flannelboard are but a few of the various materials that might be used. But when the problem statement is introduced, *get it visible before the students and keep it there.*

Effective prestructuring will also help maintain focus and interest. Before the problem statement is introduced, present a related story, filmstrip, diagram, physical model or object, or whatever to engage the students' attention on what is to come.

One of the many techniques that might be used in structuring for discussion is called "priority."[3] The students are to rank given alternatives on an issue according to such criteria as fair, good, better, best;

bad, worse, worst; hard, harder, hardest; or easy, easier, easiest. This might be carried out through discussion, individual written responses, or both.

An example of such an approach in structuring for problem solving might be with the subject of the Sabbath day. Suppose you gave the students the following alternatives:

What would be the best thing for you to do on a Sunday afternoon?

1. *You arrive home and are invited to play croquet with the family.*

2. *Some of your friends suggest that you take a nature hike up in the mountains.*

3. *A friend wants you to play tennis with him in the city park.*

4. *There is a good football game on TV that you have been wanting to see.*

The students now rank the above according to what they consider to be fair, good, better, and best (or bad, worse, and worst) to do on the Sabbath. There are many factors to be considered in this decision, and there are no necessarily right or wrong answers to these priority situations.

Here is another example that might be used as a springboard for discussion, this time using a positive approach with priority:

What would be the best performances for you to do on Sunday afternoon?

1. *Visit the sick.*

2. *Do genealogical work.*

3. *Do your home teaching.*

4. *Prepare your Sunday School lesson for next Sunday.*

Here is a third example:

A young teenager has been invited out by his friends on Saturday evening. They have not made special plans—just an evening to associate together with good company. However, the parents have planned an evening cookout and desire that all the children be there. Here are your three choices:

1. *You can go with the crowd. (Your parents will be angry with you, and you may be grounded for ten days.)*

2. *You can stay at home for the cookout. (Your friends may get disgusted with you and say, "This has happened before. We want no more part of you.")*

3. *You can go with your friends for the first half of the*

evening and come home to be with your parents for the second half. (Then both groups may become angry with you.)

The emphasis in the technique of priority should not be on what is right and what is wrong, but rather on what attitudes motivate the decisions that are made. If a person chooses to go with his friends instead of his parents, does that necessarily mean that he loves his friends more than he loves his parents? It is easy to determine through discussion that, though it may look as if such is the case, in reality it may not be so. Priority can therefore be used as a technique to help students see the reality of issues clearly.

A useful technique is to let students help you formulate the problem statement. You would have the problem clearly identified in your own written plan before the lesson starts, but you would give students the feeling that they were developing the statement as a result of your careful guidance. And again you must be flexible to adapt your predefined statement to newly discovered student needs.

Once the problem statement is clearly defined and displayed before students, make it clear to them that solution to the problem is a goal to be achieved and that it would be well for every person in the group to take part in discussion, each accepting personal responsibility for achieving the goal.

Be certain at this point that everyone clearly understands the many ramifications of the problem. If the problem statement is "How can I keep from quarreling with my brothers and sisters?" and you are working with several students, you might use a case study that presents a particular situation about siblings quarreling. The case should of course typify experiences of students in the group. By using the case, various ramifications of the problem statement will be exposed to the students. Other types of problems may call simply for an explanation of the various issues inherent in the problem.

During the problem-solving discussion session, as you provide students with ideas in helping them to see new relationships for solution, you will almost automatically form many of the ideas into questions. It is not uncommon for thirty to sixty questions to be asked by the teacher in a forty-minute problem-solving session, not to mention the many questions raised by students.

The questions the teacher asks are supporting questions to the central problem statement. Each question should have a direct or indirect relevance in helping students find solution to the problem statement.

While supporting questions are, or should be, thought out before instruction, they usually are not given the careful preparation in construction and wording as the pivotal problem statement. They are necessarily dealt with spontaneously in class. Frequently supporting questions will actually be formulated "on the spot" by the teacher. As a result, supporting questions are seldom thought out as thoroughly as they ought to be.

In preparation you may find it useful to write out some of the supporting questions in detail and consider whom you will call on to answer each question. Anticipate possible answers and prepare "back-up" questions.

Following is a useful activity to check certain aspects of your skill in the use of supporting questions.

Before your next class, ask a student to write down every question you ask during the problem-solving session. Instruct the student that he is to write down *every question* you ask with the exact wording in which you present it. It might save confusion if other students are not aware of this project. At the end of the class period, obtain the list of questions.

Evaluate your questions against the following criteria:

_____ 1. *Did the sequence of questions display a logical development of ideas leading students directly to the heart of the problem and to its solution?*

_____ 2. *Was each question related in some useful way to the problem statement?*

_____ 3. *Was the question accurately stated—specific and to the point?*

_____ 4. *Was the question in harmony with revealed truth?*

_____ 5. *Was the question, if calling for direct student response, within the ability of the student to whom it was addressed?*

_____ 6. *Was the question relevant to students' needs, interests, and feelings?*

_____ 7. *Was the question of the type to stimulate students to think and investigate?*

If you are interested in making a careful analysis of your list of supporting questions, evaluate each question against the seven criteria above. Place a check ($\sqrt{}$) for each "yes" response. After doing this with all of your supporting questions, examine the number of checks on each of the seven items. Those items with the most checks indicate your strong areas. The least checked items indicate areas where you probably need most improvement. Item 1 is of course a general question to cover the entire list, but it is extremely important.

A function of the supporting question, in addition to communicating information, clarifying, and guiding students toward solutions to problems, is its lead in to evaluation. You should be alert to how students respond to each question you ask. Each student response gives you some feedback as to certain needs, feelings, interests, and understandings of the student. Discussion is a useful technique for evaluating students.

Building partly upon what we have thus far considered, a problem-solving discussion session might well include the following procedures:[4]

1. Prestructure the problem with students in ways that will generate interest in working toward its solution.

2. Define the problem and determine with students that its solution is a goal to be achieved. Present the problem in printed form, such as on the chalkboard.

3. See to it that students clearly understand the various ramifications to the problem.

4. When presenting a question for discussion about the problem statement—

   a. Present the question to the entire class.

   b. Pause to allow reasonable time for response.

   c. Accept volunteer responses or call on a particular student.

   d. Listen to answers given by students, rather than concentrating on what you are going to say next.

   e. As you use questions and ideas, be natural and spontaneous.

   f. Avoid giving more information than the students need for solution.

   g. Avoid allowing one or two students to monopolize the discussion. Do this by ignoring, by calling on those who have not raised their hands, or by stating that you would like to give others opportunity to express themselves.

   h. So far as possible, involve every student in the class.

   i. Adjust questions to the students' abilities to answer. Ask more difficult questions to the more alert students and easier questions to the less able.

   j. Although some useful questions call for yes-no responses, generally call forth responses that are stated in complete sentences. As a rule, do not settle for fragmented responses from students.

   k. Encourage students to direct answers to class members as well as to the teacher.

   l. Allow only one student to speak at a time.

   m. When a student asks a question you know the class can answer, reflect the question back to the class and let students give the answer.

   n. As a discussion progresses, build effective questions spontaneously out of questions students raise. Questions raised by students often suggest their needs in relation to the objective being discussed. Be sensitive to student questions.

o. In large classes, have students stand as they participate in a discussion. This provides the student with opportunity to learn to think on his feet. Standing gives him more recognition and he can better be heard. Imagine a ward testimony meeting where all sat to bear their testimonies.

p. *Never* stimulate an argument by defending an untruth. If an argument does arise, stop it by bringing out points of agreement and ignoring differences. Thank the contentious and assure him you will think carefully about his idea.

q. As stated in chapter 8, p. 104, reinforce student responses. Recognize appropriate student responses by saying, "Excellent" or "Very good" or "That's exactly what we were looking for," or write the response on the chalkboard. Expressing appreciation for students and their ideas is a way of providing positive reinforcement. When a student makes inappropriate or uneven advances, use negative reinforcers such as "Very close, but not quite" or "Perhaps you will have it in the next try," or do not write the inappropriate response on the chalkboard. Help the student who is in "left field" save face so he will try again.

r. Summarize by pulling the loose ends together and giving direct focus to the solution attained. Show students how the solution can be applied in their lives. Call for action.

Hill and Hill have suggested that there is considerable advantage in teaching students the procedures of effective discussion.[5] Once students learn the process, they tend to maintain focus on the problem better. There also tends to be less domination of a few students during discussion. If you are involved with a class very extensively in the discussion method, it would be well for you to consider giving the students a special lesson on discussion techniques.

As the Lord one time asked, "What think ye?"

Chapter 9
NOTES AND REFERENCES

[1]Earl Nightingale, "The Strangest Secret" (recording from Success Institutes, Inc.).

[2]John Dewey, *Logic, the Theory of Inquiry* (New York: Holt, Rinehart and Winston, Inc., 1964), p. 107.

[3]By permission of the Department of Seminaries and Institutes of Religion, The Church of Jesus Christ of Latter-day Saints.

[4]Some of these procedures have been adapted from *And Ye Shall Teach Them* (Provo, Utah: Department of Seminaries and Institutes, The Church of Jesus Christ of Latter-day Saints, 1968), pp. 163-66.

[5]Ida Stewart Hill and William Fawcett Hill, *Learning and Teaching Through Discussion* (Chicago: Center for the Study of Liberal Education for Adults, 1958).

CHAPTER 10

Teaching the Gospel with Music

There is considerable merit in providing students with a satisfying emotional experience during a lesson. Music is a way of expressing ideas clothed with feeling. It can be a useful means of initiating students into gospel subject matter. It has been said, "He prays twice who sings well." It may be that he *learns* twice who sings well.

Using Music to Teach Gospel Subject Matter

Sometime ago in a small community in southern Idaho a gospel class was studying the martyrdom of the Prophet Joseph Smith. The story of this memorable day in history was vividly described by the teacher. In the account, students learned how Joseph loved to hear the beautiful singing voice of John Taylor. While in Carthage Jail, the Prophet, knowing that he was soon to die, said, "Brother Taylor, would you sing 'The Poor Wayfaring Man of Grief?' " Brother Taylor gladly responded, being aware of how the Prophet enjoyed this hymn.

The teacher went on, "Students, I have asked Ross to sing this song just as Brother Taylor might have sung it to our beloved Prophet on that day. Listen carefully to the words. They typify the Prophet's life and his death."

Ross slowly rose to his feet and walked to the front of the classroom. With a lovely tenor voice, he sang all seven verses of the hymn without accompaniment. As the melody came to a close, students were weeping. Each had learned, through music, the inspiring message of the life and death of the Prophet Joseph Smith.

In lessons that followed, the class as a group sang "The Poor Wayfaring Man of Grief," sometimes at the students' request. Each time the strains of the hymn filled the air, students recalled the martyr-dom lesson. Occasionally during the singing a tear would appear on the cheek of Ann, Bill, or June as they remembered the sacrifice of the Prophet. The students studied the martyrdom with their hearts as well as their minds.

Our hymnbook is filled with songs that can be sung by an indi-vidual, a small group, or a class to help teach a lesson. The time dur-ing the lesson for students to sing is not necessarily at the beginning or closing of the lesson, but *where it best fits the mood of the occa-sion.* Here are a few examples of the many songs that can be used to teach various gospel subjects. Use the topical index of the hymnbook as a guide in preparing your lessons with song:

Love at Home: "There Is Beauty All Around"
Atonement: "I Stand All Amazed"
Prayer: "Sweet Hour of Prayer"
Destiny: "The Spirit of God like a Fire Is Burning"
Sacrament: "How Great the Wisdom and the Love"
Plan of Salvation: "O My Father"
Prophets: "We Thank Thee, O God, for a Prophet"
Israel and Zion: "O Ye Mountains High"

Another type of instructional singing that appears to be effec-tive in the classroom is singing an assignment to be memorized.

In some of the old Bible schools, students were compelled to memorize the books of the Bible through rigid drill. Grudgingly stu-dents would write long lists of the sixty-six books of the Bible or suffer through embarrassing recitation periods in order to squeeze through a final examination. Certainly the books ought to be learned, but there is a more interesting and stimulating way of doing it—by putting the books to music.

Following are the names of the fifteen books of the Book of Mormon put to the music of a familiar song, the thirty-nine books of the Old Testament to the tune of "Praise to the Man," and the twenty-seven books of the New Testament also to the tune of "Praise to the Man."

The following procedures can be used to teach any of the three scripture songs. We will use the books of the New Testament to illus-trate.

Before class, write the books of the New Testament on the chalk-board. To introduce the song, sing it or have a student sing it to the group. The second time through, have the group sing along with you as you point to the syllables of the words on the chalkboard. As the pupils become acquainted with the words, erase them from the chalk-board. When the students become acquainted with the song, divide the group into two sections and sing it in rounds. When the pupils become proficient with this, divide them into four or five groups and

BOOKS OF THE OLD AND NEW TESTAMENT

(Music "Praise to the Man," page 147, *LDS Hymns*)

Genesis Exodus Le - vit - i - cus   Numbers Deu - ter - on - omy Joshua Judg-es
Mat - thew Mark Luke and John   The Acts of A - pos - tles Epistle to the

Ruth Sam - uel Sam - uel Kings Kings Chronicles Chronicles Ez - ra Ne - he - mi - ah
Ro - mans, Cor - in - thi - ans, Cor - in - thians Gala - tians E - phe - si - ans

Esther Job Psalms Pro - verbs Ec - cle - si - as - tes The Song of Sol - o - mon
Philip - pians Col - os - sians Thes - sa lo - nians and Thes - sa - lo - ni - ans

Isaiah Jer - e mi - ah Lamen - ta-tions E - zek - i - el Dan - iel Ho-
Tim - o - thy Tim - o - thy and Ti - tus and Phi - le - mon Epistle to the

se - a Joel A - mos Ob - a - di - ah Jonah Mi - cah Na - hum
He - brews E - pi - stle of Ja - mes Peter Pe - ter John John Joh - n

Habakkuk Zeph - an - i - ah Haggai Zech - a - ri - ah and Mal - a chi
Jude Rev - e - la - tion. These are the books of the New Test - a - ment.

sing in more rounds. Use student song leaders. See that they exert enthusiasm and get others to sing out.

The final test is to have each student carry a round by himself. Your classroom will sound like a giant hornets' nest, but don't let that trouble you—your students are learning the books of the New Testament.

Another way to stir up a hornets' nest is to have a race seeing who can sing all of the books first.

Advanced students, who have learned the books of both the Old and New Testament, can sing both songs at the same time in rounds, because both are to the music of the same song.

There is no need for putting pressure on the students to have the books learned in a given time. When pupils have learned the song, they have become acquainted with the books.

BOOKS OF MORMON Composer Unknown

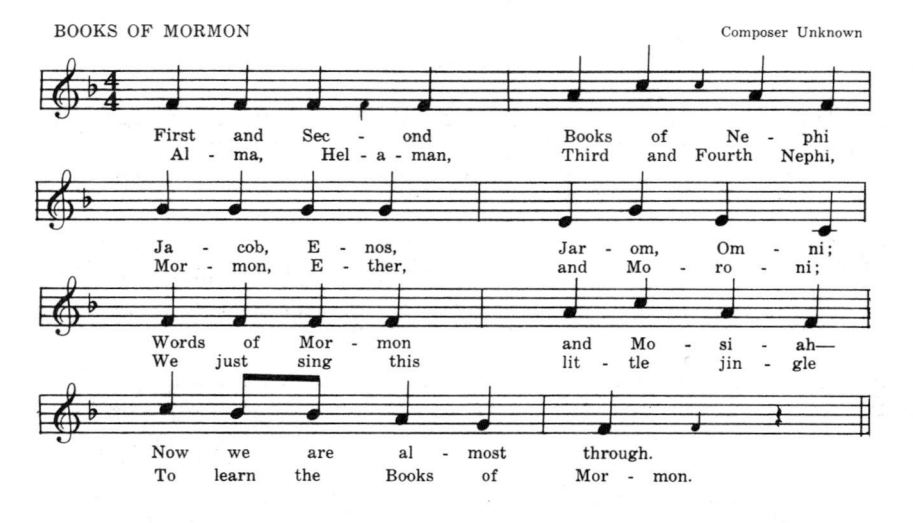

First and Sec - ond Books of Ne - phi
Al - ma, Hel - a - man, Third and Fourth Nephi,

Ja - cob, E - nos, Jar - om, Om - ni;
Mor - mon, E - ther, and Mo - ro - ni;

Words of Mor - mon and Mo - si - ah—
We just sing this lit - tle jin - gle

Now we are al - most through.
To learn the Books of Mor - mon.

After the song is learned, try singing it on those days when students seem to be bored and when the lesson isn't going over. A couple of enthusiastic rounds of the books of the New Testament is a pretty good guarantee to wake students up—and with a type of educational entertainment.

Teaching Students to Conduct Church Hymns

The success of class singing depends a good deal on the skill of the song leader. Encourage students to lead the singing, but a class member should conduct a song only after receiving instruction and after practice.

Have you ever been in a group where the song leader stood as motionless as a cedar post waiting for the group to start *him* singing? This often results from an individual's being pressured into leading the singing when he does not know how. The other alternative for this unfortunate person is to stand before the group waving his arm as a barn swallow flying with a broken wing. Don't you think it is desirable that students have opportunity to conduct a group in song. It is appropriate that they receive the basic fundamentals in leading.

If you do not feel qualified to teach students how to conduct, and a qualified instructor is not available, you might choose a student who has had experience conducting. Have him study the following pages. Then have him instruct his classmates. Here are the instructions.

When conducting a hymn, smile and be enthusiastic about what you are doing. Stand before the group with an air of confidence. Let the expression of the music be reflected in your facial expression. Look directly at pupils who might be inattentive. Just before the cue beat, you might say, "Everybody sing!" or "Let's put real spirit into this!"

or "This is a sacred song. Let's sing it softly with real feeling" or "Think of the words as we sing this song. They are truly inspiring."

If you are using a piano, remember that the song leader, not the pianist, is to set the tempo. Let your accompanist know the tempo you want to follow *before starting to sing.* You might do this by going over to the piano and saying, "Let's take it about this speed—1-2-3-4, 1-2-3-4." Don't let it drag. On spirited songs it is better to go a little fast than too slow. However, usually try for the exact tempo that is indicated in the hymn. When conducting, stand where the accompanist can see you and follow the speed of your beat pattern.

At the upper lefthand corner of the music, you will generally find a note and a number such as ♩ = 76. The 76 indicates that the music is to progress at the speed of 76 beats a minute. The quarter note indicates that each quarter note receives one beat. In practice, count the number of beats in one minute as the music is playing to determine whether the music is progressing at the right speed.

Another good way to determine tempo is by the words in the hymn. What do the words tell you? Music is written to help bring out the meaning of the words. Decide the tempo by the feeling you want the song to have. For excitement and enthusiasm, speed up the tempo. Where reverence and spirituality are desired, go more slowly. Beat with small patterns for soft music. Use larger patterns for forceful dramatic singing.

Basic Beat Patterns

The beat pattern of a hymn is determined by two numbers (one above the other) always placed at the beginning of a musical staff. The top number indicates how many beats in each measure. This is the number that tells you which beat pattern to use. Here are the beat patterns.

Two-Beat Pattern

Place your leading hand in front of your face. Bring your arm straight down, making a fish hook at waist level. The hook goes away from the body to the right when using the right arm (see figure 1). If a piano is available, have students practice beating the pattern in unison while hymns are played on the piano.

Time Signature to Be Used with
the 2-Beat Pattern

Practice this pattern with "Praise to the Man" and "Master, the Tempest Is Raging."

Figure 1

Three-Beat Pattern

Make a triangle by placing your leading hand in front of your face. Bring your hand down to the waist, out away from the body, and back up to the original position in front of your face (see figure 2). (When using the right hand, the swing on the second beat is always to the right and away from the body.) Now add a slight twist on beats 1 and 2 (see figure 3). Avoid back lashes as in figure 4.

Time signature to Be Used
with the 3-Beat Pattern

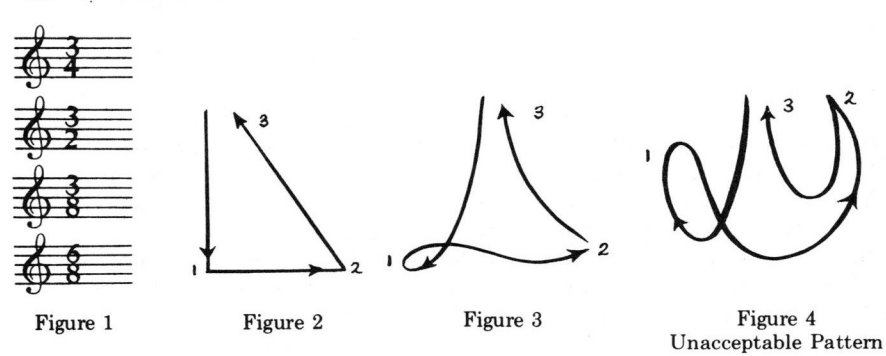

| Figure 1 | Figure 2 | Figure 3 | Figure 4 |
| | | | Unacceptable Pattern |

Practice this pattern with "America." On the 6/8, 9/8, and 9/4 time signatures, when the music is slow, use two 3-beat patterns for each measure, emphasizing the first beat in each measure.

Four-Beat Pattern

Place the leading hand in front of your face. When using the right arm, bring the hand down to the waist, across the body to the left, back across the body to the right, and up to the original position (see figure 5). Now add a slight twist in beats 1, 2, and 3 (see figure 6). Avoid back lashes as in figure 4 of the 3-beat pattern above.

Time Signature to Be Used
with the 4-Beat Pattern

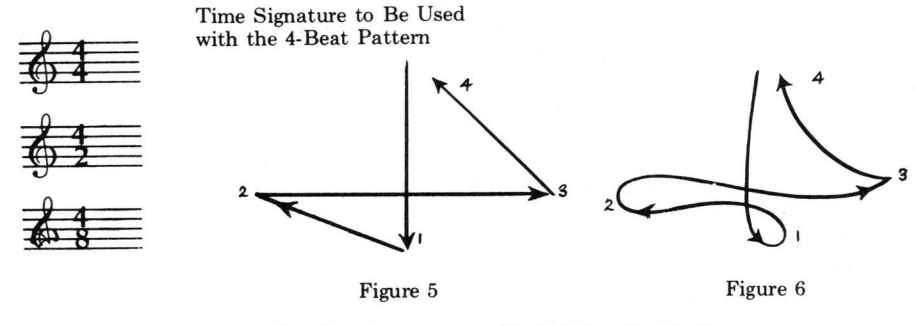

Figure 5   Figure 6

Practice this pattern with "Abide with Me."

Cue Beat

To start a group singing, it is necessary for the conductor to cue them in. If the song begins on the first beat of a measure, the preliminary movement (cue) will be the last beat of the pattern, as in figure 7.

If the song begins on the last beat of a measure, the leader's preliminary movement will be on the first beat of a 2-beat pattern, second beat of a 3-beat pattern (see figure 8), or third beat of a 4-beat pattern.

Figure 7   Figure 8

Cutoff

When approaching the end of a hymn, stop beating time on the very first beat of the last word, no matter where it may fall in the beat pattern. From that position, slowly extend your hand upward and to the right until you want the group to stop singing the last word. Then quickly bring your hand down, indicating the group is to stop singing (see figure 9).

Figure 9

Letting the Record Player or Tape Recorder Help You Teach

Teacher A was presenting a lesson on dedication. She decided to let recorded music help teach her message. Sister A obtained a record player from her meetinghouse library and brought a record from home. To summarize the lesson on dedication, she played a recording of "Invictus" sung by a great vocalist. Sister A asked the pupils to listen to how the singer put his heart and soul into his singing. Sister A pointed out, "This man is an outstanding singer because he has dedicated himself to becoming a great singer. When this man sings, he *really tries.*" Teacher A added, "As you listen to this song, think of a noble goal you have in life to which you desire to become dedicated.

Listen also to the words of the song. If you are committed to your goal, surely it will be fulfilled."

As the strains of "Invictus" filled the air, the students gained greater insight into becoming dedicated to a righteous goal—all by listening to an idea "clothed with feeling."

Teacher B used a tape recorder during study periods. He selected orchestrations and choir music that had a consistent restful tempo. During the study period, he would play the music very softly so as not to distract, thus setting the proper mood for study. He found that this technique was useful in maintaining order during study periods.

For family home evenings, Teacher C taught appreciation for the classics. He used judgment in introducing the classics, knowing that some members of the family did not fully appreciate this type of music. The first record chosen to be played was one he knew all would enjoy hearing—"On the Trail" from the *Grand Canyon Suite.* Brother C studied the brief biography of the composer and what to listen for. This information he obtained from the back cover of the record album. Before playing the record to the family, he explained the conditions under which the music was written. Family members were instructed to listen for the donkey going down the trail, for the rock that dislodged from the trail and hurled into the immensity of the canyon depths below, and for the colorful sunrise. They were to listen for the different kinds of instruments used to obtain various musical effects. Can you see how a family would learn to appreciate good music presented in Teacher C's family home evening?

One should be highly selective with classical records presented to a group of students. If the music is not uplifting to students, more harm than good can be done. Handel's "Hallelujah Chorus" from the *Messiah* would ordinarily be more edifying to the average student than the "Alemande" from Bach's *Sixth French Suite.* As in Teacher C's class, this type of music should be presented only after verbal orientation giving pupils incentive to want to hear the record and helping them understand the music.

When involved in gospel instruction, ordinarily only part of class time should be used in music appreciation, and it should take place only periodically. When larger works are presented, such as Grieg's *Piano Concerto in A Minor,* Tchaikovsky's *Fifth Symphony* or Robertson's *Book of Mormon Oratorio* usually only a part of the work should be presented to the class at one time. Choose first that movement or section of the work that has greatest appeal to students.

Be careful in your selection of music. Edifying music causes one to associate himself with the things of God, with noble goals and righteous endeavor. And isn't this accomplished with such music as "The Lord's Prayer," "Battle Hymn of the Republic," or "Temple by the River"? Do you not also find such music as "Clair de Lune" and Chopin's "Fantasy Impromptu" inspiring?

Music with a constant strong beat is usually undesirable in the gospel classroom. It may appeal to certain emotions, but usually it does not edify. When using music in the gospel classroom, use that which inspires and brings one closer to God. Students get plenty of the other type of music in their everyday lives.

Do you know of any greater music of inspiration than the Mormon Tabernacle Choir's renderings of our Church hymns and works of the great masters? Let's not neglect this great source of inspiration in our lessons.

Summary Outline

Music in the gospel classroom is a way of initiating students into gospel subject matter by expressing ideas clothed with feeling. Some of the ways it can be done are by—

1. Having the class sing an inspirational hymn during a lesson.
2. Requesting talented students to sing vocal solos, duets, trios, and the like, the words of which give students further insight into the lesson objective.
3. Teaching students to conduct Church hymns, thus preparing them for future opportunity to conduct in classes and in other Church organizations.
4. Using the record player or tape recorder—
   (a) In presenting soft background music in study periods.
   (b) In teaching appreciation of the classics.
   (c) In playing religious music, such as the Tabernacle Choir, for spiritual edification.

The teacher should be highly selective in his choice of records to be used in the gospel classroom. Only that which is upbuilding is of God.

Instructional Games
Can Be Packed
with Fun
and Learning

One time just before I visited a gospel class, a fourteen-year-old boy came up to me and said, "Brother Hobbs, I just can't wait for this class to get started."

I responded, "What's all the excitement about, Jimmy?"

"Well, we're having a game of football in Brother Able's class. In our last lesson the other team was winning. So I've been cramming for today's game."

"Football in a gospel classroom?"

"That's right! And when we get started, you'll want to play too."

Jimmy was right. I would have liked to join in the game. It turned out to be an instructional game on gospel questions, but it appeared to be almost as much fun as real football.

There are many games with instructional value that we can use in the gospel classroom. These are excellent for student motivation and instruction. Instructional games might be used by missionaries in teaching investigators. Family home evenings and regular gospel classes of all ages can be enhanced by using appropriate instructional games.

Preliminary Suggestions

Do not consume valuable class time in choosing sides for team competition.

Slow students are almost always the last chosen, which is embarrassing. Use rows or sections of the class for division of teams.

To stimulate competition, divide the teams so as to get a balance of equal ability on each side. Occasionally you will find nearly equal competition by having the females stand the males. If you have a slow learner, let him be scorekeeper. But keep it from being obvious that he is a slow learner.

Let the teams name themselves rather than referring to team 1, team 2, and so on.

In one class of young people I was visiting, one team called themselves "The Good Lookers." The other team chose for themselves "The Intelligences." Another group of students were the "Black Goats," who were competing against the "White Sheep." Don't spend much time on team naming, although it does add to the interest of the game.

Highly active and hilarious games should not be played in the gospel classroom. If necessary, students can be controlled by giving demerits on a score when one does not follow the rules. Students might even help formulate the rules before starting the game.

Another suggestion of importance is that games used in the classroom should have educational value. They should be used as an approach to learning and not just for fun. They must entertain with a purpose and not simply entertain. Instructional games are particularly useful as overviews, reviews, testing, evaluating student knowledge, and getting acquainted.

Football

Draw a football field on the chalkboard as below. On a sheet of paper draw and cut out a football three inches long. Place masking tape on the back of the ball so it will stick on the chalkboard (the chalkboard must be free of chalkdust).

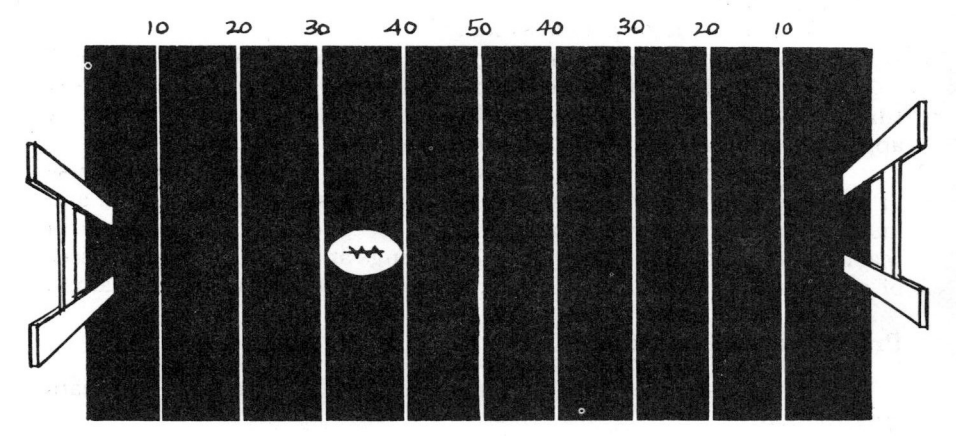

Prepare five yard, ten yard, and twenty-five yard questions. Five yard questions are easy to answer. Ten yard questions are of intermediate difficulty. Twenty-five yard questions are difficult to answer.

The ball is placed on the fifty yard line. Have a representative from each team guess the number of pages in a book to determine who will be in possession of the ball first. Each team member takes his turn answering the questions. He may choose either a five, ten, or twenty-five yard question. If he misses the question, his team loses the ball and the question then goes to the opposing team. If he gives the correct answer, the ball is placed toward the proper goal line the number of yards he has won.

If a student speaks out of turn or violates the rules, a penalty of so many yards is given to his team. Scores are computed as in regular football.

This game is of course most relevant during football season when people are thinking about football.

Clue

Divide the class into three to five teams with three to eight students on each team. Appoint a captain for each team. The captain should sit behind his team so he can see the members and call on them when they raise their hands for opportunity to give the answer.

Before the class the teacher is to prepare a minimum of fifteen sets of clues that are about the lesson material to be reviewed. In each set are four clues. The first clue is most difficult, and each of the following three clues becomes progressively easier.

To begin the game, the captain of the first team confers with his members to decide how many clues to request. If a team asks for one clue and gives the proper answer, it wins four points. Two clues are worth three points, three clues are worth two points, and four clues are good for only one point. The team has fifteen seconds to respond after the number of clues has been requested and the teacher has written the number on the chalkboard.

When a teammate thinks he has the right answer, he raises his hand and the captain calls on him. If the wrong answer is given, the same set of clues goes to the next team. Because two clues have already been revealed, the next row must take at least the two clues that have been given. If this second team prefers to try for fewer points, feeling inadequate with the clues that have been given, the members can ask for three or four clues. A set of clues is to go from one team to the next until the right answer is given.

After each team has had opportunity to answer a set of clues but has failed to give the correct answer, the teacher gives the correct answer. The next team in line is then offered a new set of clues. The members request the number they would like to try for. And thus the game progresses. At the end of the period, the team with the most points wins.

Clues can be written by the teacher so as to call for responses on names of people, cities, rivers, mountains, dates, and even Church doctrine and principles of truth. Here are four sets of clues as examples in writing your next lesson review.

1. *Our spirit brother.*
2. *Our father.*
3. *Is perfect.*
4. *Member of Godhead.*

   Answer: Jesus Christ

1. *The lowest one can get.*
2. *A body of water.*
3. *It receives, but never gives.*
4. *It is the Dead _____ .*

   Answer: Dead Sea

1. *Give the day, month, and year of the restoration of the Aaronic Priesthood.*
2. *Give the month and year.*
3. *Give the year.*
4. *Give within five years.*

   Answer: May 15, 1829

1. *A word describing something unseen.*
2. *We develop it through good living.*
3. *It is associated with confidence.*
4. *It is the first principle of the gospel.*

   Answer: Faith

Picture Identification

Number a series of such visuals as maps or pictures of Church presidents, General Authorities, and historical sites, and place them on a wall in the classroom or display them one at a time to the students. If there are twenty pictures in the series, pass to each student a sheet of paper with twenty numbers and blanks. The student is to write the name of the country, Church leader, or historical site next to the corresponding number on his sheet of paper. As soon as his list is completed, he is to stand and receive recognition for being the first to complete his sheet. When less than half of the class members have stood, ask them to be seated so as not to embarrass the slower students.

When played in teams, the students in each team confer with each other on what they feel are the correct answers. An appointed reporter for each team writes down the answers as they are given. The team that obtains the largest number of correct answers in the least amount of time is the winner. The teacher then reviews the correct answers with his students.

I Have It!

Select twenty-five names of people or places that have been studied. On the teacher's master copy, list these twenty-five names and an identifying statement for each name. With scissors, cut each name with its identifying statement into separate units as below:

5. Nephi—Righteous son of Lehi.

1. Enos—Received manifestation while in forest.

· 3. Zarahemla—Capital city of Nephites.

Provide each student with a sheet of paper. On the paper he is to draw five lines vertically and five lines horizontally, all of equal distance apart, in order to make sixteen squares.

The twenty-five names are written on the chalkboard, from which each student selects sixteen. He writes these sixteen names in any order in the squares he has prepared.

The teacher scrambles his twenty-five slips of paper in a box. He then draws a slip from the box and reads only the identifying statement. If the student knows the answer and has it written in a square, he places a small piece of paper on that square. The teacher draws another slip of paper and reads the identifying statement. When a row of squares on a student sheet is covered with small pieces of paper either across, down, or diagonally, he calls out "I have it!" indicating he is the winner. The bits of paper are cleared from the student sheets, and the game is played again using the same materials.

Tic-Tac-Toe

Tack nine envelopes on a board. Within each envelope place three to five questions or statements, each on a separate slip of paper. Place the more difficult questions in the center and corner envelopes.

Divide the class into two teams—the Xs and the Os. The first student on team X steps to the front of the room and draws a slip of paper from the envelope of his choosing. He is to read what is on the paper. If a question, he is to answer it. If a statement, he is to discuss it. If he answers to the satisfaction of the teacher, he is privileged to place an X on the tic-tac-toe scoreboard that the teacher has previously placed on the chalkboard. (The envelopes can be used for the scoreboard by placing acetate over them and using a grease pencil for scoring.) If the student fails, no mark is given.

The teams alternate on the questions as they would alternate in a regular game of tic-tac-toe. The first team to make the three Xs or Os in a row wins.

Word Recall

Write on the chalkboard the name of an important person who has recently been studied, leaving space between each letter of the word. Each student does the same at the top of a plain sheet of paper. When the teacher says "go," students are to write, for example, names of people, cities, countries, rivers, mountains that have been studied during the year. The names are to be written under each letter of the main word, and the word must start with that letter. For example:

C	H	R	I	S	T
Christ	*Haran*	*Ruth*	*Isaiah*	*Samuel*	*Terah*
Chaldea	*Habakkuk*	*Red Sea*		*Solomon*	
Chronicles	*Haggai*			*Sinai*	
Canaan	*Horeb*			*Samson*	
Cainan					

The student who produces the most names within a given time limit is the winner.

Know Your Bible

A Bible should be available to each student, and the class should be divided into two teams. After giving instructions on how to use the Bible concordance, write a scriptural verse on the chalkboard such as, "Where no counsel is, the people fall: but in the multitude of counselors there is safety."

Students are to keep their Bibles closed until the teacher gives the signal to go. Pupils then turn to the concordance, seeking key words in finding the scriptural reference. Key words in the above verse might be *counsel, people, or safety.* As soon as a student finds the scriptural reference and locates book, chapter, and verse in the text, he raises his hand. If teammates help each other, they are disqualified. Not until all members of the team have their hands in the air does the team receive a point. The point is given to the winning team. The teacher then asks one of the winning students to read the scripture he has found, which in this case is Proverbs 11:14.

The teacher then writes another scripture on the chalkboard and the procedure is repeated.

For still another variation, write a familiar verse or statement identifying a scripture on the chalkboard such as "The Lord is my shepherd," "The Lord's Prayer," or "Find the story of Samson," and then have a race to see which team can find it first. The student who knows his Bible will not refer to the concordance this time. He will remember that "The Lord is my shepherd" is Psalm 23. He will recall that the Lord's Prayer is in the Sermon on the Mount and that this sermon includes Matthew 5-7. When looking for the story of Samson, the alert student will recall that Samson was a judge. The story therefore must be in the book of Judges. Upon finding this book, the student flips through the pages, watching for the word *Samson* in the heading at the top of the pages.

Know Your Scriptures (For More Advanced Students)

For a review of scripture locations, have students sit in a circle. One student stands within the circle. He points to one in the circle, quotes or identifies a scriptural passage that has been studied, and counts to twenty-one. The sitting student should then give the book, chapter, and verse of the scripture within the count of twenty-one. If he fails, he trades positions with the center man.

When reviewing scriptural memorization, the student in the center gives book, chapter, and verse as he points to a sitting student. The sitting student then quotes the scripture verbatim.

Association

The class is divided into teams of three to five students. On the chalkboard the teacher writes twenty words such as *gum, book, candy, water, and glass.* Above these words, in bold type he writes a keyword pertaining to that which has been studied, such as *faith, gospel, love,* and *dedication.* Students are then to associate each of the twenty words with the keyword. Each team consults privately. As ideas are developed, they are written by the team reporter on a sheet of paper. Here is an example:

GOSPEL (the keyword)

1. *gum*
2. *book*
3. *candy*
4. *water (etc., to twenty words)*

The first four items on a team list might appear as follows:

1. *The gospel is like gum; it is something to chew on.*
2. *The gospel is like a book; it should be studied often.*
3. *The gospel is like candy; it is sweet and gives energy.*
4. *The gospel is like water; it cleanses and purifies.*

In the beginning a time limit should be agreed upon by the teams. The team that creates the most effective associations within the time limit wins.

Charades

Students pantomime a word, idea, or story for others to guess what it is.

Divide the class into two teams for competition. Consulting one another, the teams decide themselves what to pantomime (it must relate to material that has or is being studied in class). Each person writes an idea to be pantomimed on a slip of paper and deposits it in his team's box. A member from team A draws a slip from team B's box and acts out the charade for his own team members to guess. Thus, team B knows the charade and enjoys watching it dramatized while team A tries to guess. The teams then alternate.

Seven Up

Seven students are chosen from the group and stand before the class. The sitting students place their heads on the desks and cover their eyes. The seven standing students then circulate throughout the class, each touching the head of one student. They then return to the front of the room.

The sitting pupils raise their heads. Each person touched, in turn, guesses who touched him. If he guesses correctly, he is privileged to ask that person at the front of the room a question about the lesson. If the wrong answer is given, the two trade places. If the answer is correct, the student answering remains at the front.

Getting Acquainted (The Unique Accomplishment Approach)

A blank piece of paper is handed to each student, who then writes two or three of his "unique" accomplishments, things he feels he has done or achieved that probably no one else in the class has done (for instance, a student might write, "I walked fifty miles in one day" or "I met the president of the Church." The entire exercise[1] need not take more than three to five minutes.

When class is over, the teacher compiles the responses and duplicates them, omitting student names. In the next class period, using only five or six minutes, the teacher can involve his students in an interesting verbal guessing game as to which accomplishments belong to which students. It is a fascinating way to learn much about people in a short time, and the conversational carry-over after class is excellent. This information is invaluable to you in adding to the "interest inventory" of each student (see p. 290).

Thumbs

In this technique[2] the students are requested to indicate their feelings by either putting their thumbs up or down. There are four responses possible on the part of the student:

1. Agree by putting thumbs up.
2. Strongly agree by putting the thumbs up vigorously.
3. Disagree by turning thumbs down.
4. Strongly disagree by putting thumbs down vigorously.

An example dialogue of this technique follows (note that generally the approach to thumbs up and thumbs down is one of requesting responses to areas in which students would not be inhibited to indicate their feelings. They are gradually taken into areas requiring greater responsibility on their part and commitment of themselves in order to respond):

Thumbs up questions

1. *Our town has a football team (or team from another appropriate sport).*
2. *Our town has a good football team.*
3. *Our town is going to win its next game.*
   (These are motivational fun-type questions to get your class enthused about the process of thumbs up and thumbs down. You may add as many of this type of question as seems appropriate.)
4. *Parents are important.*
5. *I appreciate the wisdom of my parents.*
6. *I usually agree with my parents.*
7. *My parents can make my decisions better than I can make them myself.*
8. *Parents should be consulted in all important matters.*
9. *My parents could probably pick a better marriage companion for me than I could pick for myself.*
10. *It is easier to be a parent than a child.*

Now let's consider another subject. Let's say that the subject is "decision making." Here are some sample questions:

1. *Opportunity sometimes passes me by because I am so slow in making decisions.*

2. *I sometimes do the opposite of what I decide I should do.*

3. *Most of my decisions are already made.*

4. *My parents could make my decisions better than I can.*

5. *Sometimes I can't make a decision.*

6. *I am impetuous (too quick) when making decisions.*

7. *Decisions are easy to make.*

8. *God can help me make decisions.*

9. *God often does help me make decisions.*

10. *I usually ask God for help in all decisions.*

11. *I am making many decisions now.*

12. *The decisions that I make today will have little effect on the decisions I will be required to make tomorrow.*

Summary Outline

Instructional games presented in this chapter are:

Football
Clue
Picture Identification
I Have It!
Tic-Tac-Toe
Word Recall
Know Your Bible
Know Your Scriptures
Association
Charades
Seven Up
Getting Acquainted
Thumbs

Chapter 11
NOTES AND REFERENCES

[1]Paul H. Dunn, *You Too Can Teach* (Salt Lake City: Bookcraft, Inc., 1962), p. 76.

[2]Used by permission of the Department of Seminaries and Institutes of Religion, The Church of Jesus Christ of Latter-day Saints.

Helping Students Practice Gospel Ideals[1]

How well I remember the Christmas when my eldest daughter, Christi, was five years old. As she and her younger brother, Mark, scrambled over each other to get to the presents, Christi let out a high-pitched squeal, of which only little girls are capable, exclaiming, "My dolly!" Yes, Santa Claus had received her letter, and a talking doll under a tiny stuffed stocking was the evidence.

My wife and I had mused to ourselves that the plastic doll would be fine entertainment for a little girl. Now as we observed Christi with her new toy, we came to realize that the doll was teaching her to be a good mother.

Christi pulled the string hanging out of the doll's back, and her baby said, "Please brush my hair." Promptly the little mother ran for the brush and groomed her dolly's hair.

The string was pulled again, and the toy baby said, "Where are we going?" The mother said, "For a walk," and off they went.

Again the string was pulled. "Tell me a story." With doll in lap, this tiny mother rocked back and forth in a little rocking chair as the piece of plastic learned about the three bears.

The baby then said she was sleepy. As the mama tucked her little one into bed, the string was pulled again to hear, "I love you."

I thought, "That little piece of plastic is doing more to guide Christi into practicing desired values than some of the teachers are accomplishing in gospel classes." The talking doll asked the role-playing mother to become a "doer." As a talking teacher, do you lead your students into becoming doers? Are you pulling the right string?

To be an effective teacher of the gospel of Jesus Christ, you must literally change the lives of your students. When they leave the classroom, they must not go alone with increased knowledge of the truths that have been taught, but they must leave with the desire and capability to practice that knowledge in their everyday living. Not until this latter goal of "doing" is achieved does a teacher realize optimal effect in teaching the gospel.

Remember the basic question? "How can I increase my power to influence students to consistently practice the revealed teachings of Jesus Christ?" You would of course do well to go to class prepared for each lesson in the subject matter with a variety of stimulating methods that guide students into understanding and committing to ideas in the pre-planned objective. But the end to which you usually should be working is presentation of procedures, both in the classroom and out, that will promote practice of the principles taught. The use of methods that lead to student involvement should appropriately receive much of your attention.

In his lessons, the average teacher of the Church guides pupils toward carrying out a very limited amount of student application. Generally the practice of the principle taught is left to the student to figure out for himself and to do on his own initiative. On the other hand, the successful teacher provides ways and opportunities for his students to experience a principle of truth being taught through direct involvement with the principle. One approach in helping students realize this purpose is through use of what I would term the "linking assignment."

What is a linking assignment and how is it used? Basically, it is a well thought-out and clearly defined task suggested by the teacher or students wherein students are to practice the truths they have come to understand and accept through instruction. For the students, this type of assignment links the classroom with the outside world of reality. It brings students to perform, usually out of class, the principles studied in class. The students are led into becoming doers of the ideas taught them.

A linking assignment is not to be confused with a behavioral objective. In a strict sense, a behavioral objective describes a proposed change in the student that can be measured. It is a statement of purpose that is often achieved by students in class. A linking assignment is a specified procedure that leads the student into practicing in daily living an idea being taught. It is a designation of procedures for action. A linking assignment is not always directly measurable, because it may take days or weeks to complete and it may deal with feelings, attitudes, and spiritual experience that are not clearly manifested in student performance. A linking assignment provides for explicit follow-ups week after week on proposed change in student performances. In a sense, a linking assignment might be considered as an extended process objective. In its most formal use, it specifies not only what is to be done, but how it is to be done and finally how it was done.

An example follows of how a linking assignment can be used in a lesson. This is an actual account of the situation that developed as a class discussed the principle of love.

Brother Will Masters had taught a stimulating lesson to his twenty students on "How Can We Learn to Love Our Enemies?" His single idea lesson objective was "Each student will learn to love the person he dislikes the most." Feeling assured that the students had a good understanding and conviction of the principle of love, he said to the class, "How many of you are willing to make an effort to love everyone with whom you work from day to day?" All hands went up.

Brother Masters then passed out a slip of paper to each student and said, "Would you now think of the person you dislike the most, or love the least, whom you see almost every day." When all had someone in mind, he said, "Place a symbol at the top of your paper that will serve to remind you of that person. You must avoid letting others know who this individual is unless you have a friend who, in confidence, will help you with this assignment. Now that you have someone in mind, you are ready for your challenge. It is *learn to love this person you have in mind.*"

With this Mary cried out, "Oh, no, Brother Masters. We can't do that."

Bill said, "It's too hard. The kid I have in mind is just no good. We have words practically every day."

Brother Masters calmly said, "You can do it, and I am going to help you. Let's make a list on the chalkboard, which you can copy on your sheet of paper, of ways one can learn to love an enemy."

As the discussion progressed, Carla suggested, "When I pass this person in the hall, I guess I could smile at her."

Another item placed on the chalkboard was "Decide, first of all, why you dislike this person and list these reasons on the paper. Then try to find a solution to each reason."

Joan suggested, "Ask yourself what you might have done to cause ill feelings with this individual."

After a few general approaches were listed and discussed, Brother Masters informed the students that in one week he would ask them to write an evaluation of their progress. Two questions would be presented for student response:

1. What have you done this past week in learning to love this ˆperson you have selected?

2. What was his reaction to your efforts?

This follow-up procedure was to take place at least three or four times at one-week intervals. The students became enthusiastic about the project, and they left the class ready to meet the new challenge.

As the days and weeks passed, it was found that every student who tried made remarkable progress.

Bill reported in the third follow-up evaluation that he and his once bitter enemy were now pals.

Joan had decided on the day the assignment was given that Suzanne, who had been snubbing her for some time, perhaps was not really "stuck-up." Through self-analysis, Joan decided that she was partly at fault herself; she therefore set out with a plan to find out why Suzanne acted as she did. Through an occasional smile at Suzanne and by passing a sincere compliment to some of Suzanne's closest friends, the two girls began to enjoy warmer relations. Joan finally found a close friendship with Suzanne, and she later testified in class that this came about through an effort to look for and talk about Suzanne's good qualities rather than her weaknesses. This attitude became contagious, and Suzanne began to appreciate Joan for her consideration.

Mary and many of the other students enjoyed similar successes.

Through effective structuring of the linking assignment and through consistent follow-up, Brother Masters not only gave the students an understanding of the principle "love thy neighbor," but he helped them to live accordingly. Thus they became "doers of the word."

During his ministry, Christ gave considerable emphasis in linking his instruction to his students' daily experience. He taught them to practice gospel subject matter.

To those who walked with Christ and found a degree of understanding and conviction in His message, He said, "Therefore, whosoever heareth these sayings of mine, and doeth them I will liken him unto a wise man" (Matthew 7:24). After intensive instructions to the Twelve, Christ declared, "Go ye therefore, and teach all nations . . . to observe all things whatsoever I have commanded you" (Matthew 28:19-20).

The Lord's instructions to these Church leaders did not end with the admonition merely to teach others, with understanding to the point of attaining conviction. He emphasized, "Teach all nations . . . *to observe* all things whatsoever I have commanded you." This, that so far as possible, all should become "doers of the word."

The apostolic teachers were instructed to assign their students to literally apply the principles of truth presented. They were taught to help students link their immediate learning experience with the world of reality. This was also the Savior's final charge to Church leaders before His ascension into heaven.

Christ's students were instructed by Him, after obtaining sufficient understanding and conviction of His teachings, to be baptized and "sin no more." To the receptive student, such assignments may be followed with promptings of the Holy Ghost, leading to increased insight into the Lord's laws and the prophetic teachings of the scriptures.

To the rich young ruler who announced that he kept all of the commandments, Christ said, "One thing thou lackest; go thy way, sell whatsoever thou hast, and give to the poor, and thou shalt have treasure in heaven" (Mark 10:21). In this case the young ruler turned away, refusing an assignment that would have truly made him a doer and would have linked him to the Master and eternal life. With the Savior, an understanding or even a testimony of the law was not sufficient— His students were to apply the assigned principles of truth in their everyday lives. As with the rich young ruler, your students should not be forced to carry out the assignment. Your job is to motivate and persuade.

The greatest of all teachers has assigned to us, as His pupils, many other laws of doing, of application, and of personal involvement. To the Church member, He gave the sacrament as a means of reminding them of their obligations relative to the atoning sacrifice. He requires *doing* by all who would claim to be His students. Along with other acts of doing He desires that all have a Church responsibility and that members go to the temple, on a mission, attend Church meetings, pay tithing, live the Word of Wisdom, donate work on the welfare farm, and help the unfortunate. Thus, the receptive student is constantly reminded of the assignments he has been given, and the day will come when every individual will stand before the Savior for a grade on how well he has listened to and applied His linking assignments. To teachers of the gospel, He could very well add, "How have you helped *your* students apply my doctrine? Are your pupils 'doers of the word, and not hearers only'?"

I would suggest that in preparing for the next lesson, you utilize a large part of the time in developing stimulating methods that will lead students to practice the subject matter. Try to create procedures that will link students in the classroom with their outside worlds or reality.

Following are a few examples of other linking assignments that might be developed.

1. For teaching the third commandment, have students carry a slip of paper on their person and write swear words they might say over a twenty-four hour period. In the next class, discuss how swearing might be overcome. Repeat the above assignment and encourage each student to compare his first slip of paper with the second. This assignment might be repeated one or two weeks later. The non-swearing students could be given assignments in other areas.

2. In a lesson on prayer, suggest that students who do not have family prayer in their homes carry out a plan to encourage it with their families. How approaches may be made should be drawn from the students and not dictated by the teacher. Undue pressures must not be placed on the students to carry out this project.

3. Teach a lesson on the divinity of the mission of the Prophet Joseph Smith with the assignment for students to go into their own

homes and play the role of missionaries, teaching the lesson to parents (see p. 62).

4. With permission from the proper officials, have students print and post a highway sign on the pitfalls of drinking or smoking after a lesson on the Word of Wisdom.

5. After a lesson on self-control or goals, suggest that each student plan to be alone in the evening and write every thought he can remember from his waking hours of the day. After a careful self-evaluation, the student should destroy the paper and, on another sheet, establish a set of goals upon which he will begin working immediately.

6. When students are taught about obtaining a personable relationship with God, help them create within themselves the desire to be alone and have an extended talk with the Lord.

7. During a lesson on the sacrament, assign students to memorize the sacramental prayers. During the sacrament, students are to repeat the prayers to themselves and think of the requirements and blessings involved. For follow-up, remind students weekly of this project and discuss individual progress.

In structuring a linking assignment, it is often preferable to have students themselves suggest ways in which they may adapt the day's lesson to a situation where actual practice may be experienced. "Man convinced against his will is of the same opinion still." After students have achieved understanding and reached conviction of the principle taught, you might say, "Now what are you going to do about it?" Students may then be guided into suggesting and determining their own linking assignments.

One day while observing an outstanding lesson on dating taught to a group of adolescents, I saw this principle in practice. After a stimulating discussion the objective "What Makes a Good Date?" was summarized. Then came what I saw as the groundwork for a linking assignment. The teacher gave the assignment verbally and then wrote it on the chalkboard thus, "Decide on one thing you are going to start doing to improve your dating habits. Write in detail exactly what you are going to do and how you plan to do it." Of course completion of the assignment calls for each student's carrying out his plan of action and ongoing follow-up by the teacher until the new habit is secure in the student.

Here are a few other ideas that you might develop as linking assignments. Students thought these out for themselves while in various gospel classes throughout the Church. These grew out of lessons where students were confronted with the question "Now what are you going to do about today's lesson?" Here are the practicable projects that are adaptable to various age levels and that you might try developing into linking assignments:

1. On a card indicate each time you catch yourself making excuses for something you have done that is not right.

2. Have a children's class make a popsicle-stick tree. When a member of the group does a good deed, he is to write his name on the stick and add it to the tree. Watch the tree grow.

3. Carry a copy of the Book of Mormon to invite discussion about the book.

4. Make it a project to help each member of your family build a stronger testimony of the Book of Mormon.

5. List your five most important goals in life. Then ask yourself, "Which friends are leading me closer to my goals? Who is leading me away from these goals? What must I do with myself to attract the type of friends who will help me attain my goals?"

6. Select a friend who needs help. Fast and pray with him to assist in finding a solution to the problem.

7. On a sheet of paper outline your own program that will prepare you for a mission. Consider such areas as living the Word of Wisdom, moral cleanliness, tithing, active Church attendance, physical fitness, understanding of the scriptures, mission savings plan.

8. Look for opportunities to tell an inactive or nonmember friend about something happening in the Church that is edifying.

9. Make it a point to tell a friend of a time your prayers were answered or of another spiritual experience that is close to you.

10. Lead out in encouraging a reverence campaign in your home ward. Carry out a campaign with reverence posters, telephone calls, and slogan buttons to get better reverence.

11. Make it a point to put yourself out for a lonely classmate. Smile at him, walk to school with him, talk with him, introduce him to friends, and eat lunch with him.

12. Dare to be different. Defend the unfortunate being abused by others, even if you stand alone in the defense.

13. Make a commitment to yourself that you will take a stand against cheating in school. Discuss this commitment with friends and determine what to do when someone cheats.

14. Save money and obtain the missionary edition of the standard works. Study these scriptures using a systematized plan of marking.

15. Visit your bishop. Express appreciation and your love for him. Pledge your support to him and indicate that you will be willing to assist in whatever activity in which help might be requested.

16. If you really want to know that the gospel is true, fast and pray and study the scriptures with an intense desire to know.
17. Encourage someone from a minority group to participate with you in social activities.
18. In a class or with a group of friends decide on a plan of action to stop an improper practice of rowdiness, marking up school or Church property, and littering.
19. Discourage friends from joining secret organizations.
20. Bear testimony in the next fast meeting in your ward.
21. Team up with a friend. Each is to agree to check up on the other for evidences of pride. After a designated period of time, notes are to be compared and discussed.
22. Agree with a friend to resist together any group pressure of breaking the Sabbath, stealing, smoking, drinking, and the like.
23. Help someone in need without revealing your identity.
24. Write out the different techniques Satan uses to control our bodies. Next to each technique write out a plan of counter attack.
25. If you haven't done so already, prepare yourself for a patriarchal blessing. Then seek an interview with your bishop for a recommend for a blessing.

A linking assignment should not be made for every lesson presented. A good rule to follow is to make a few linking assignments, with follow-ups being conducted for weeks and even months on these assignments. Adam S. Bennion said, "There may be just a little danger of cheapening the process of application if it is insisted that for every ideal impressed upon the minds of pupils there must be a corresponding immediate response in daily actions of the pupils taught."[2]

Such lessons as "Geography of Palestine," "How Ancient Records Were Kept," and "Construction of the Salt Lake Temple" may not call for moral action by students. Yet these ideas may be used to change student behavior in terms of new understandings.

Also, it is often wise to teach such a personal subject as repentance without directly leading students into practicing that principle. In such a lesson, however, students should be inspired toward repenting on their own volition.

Points to Remember

Success with linking assignments tends to be in proportion to preplanning the assignment and prestructuring it in class through an effective lesson, followed by significant and consistent periodic checks on individual student endeavor. Two follow-up questions to the students are germane to the linking assignment: (1) What action did you carry out in fulfilling the assignment? (2) What were the results of your efforts?

To be optimally effective as a teacher of the gospel of Jesus Christ, you must literally change the lives of your students. The challenge is that they become doers of the will of Him who is the Master of all teachers.

Let's pull the right string and get the dolly talking.

Chapter 12
NOTES AND REFERENCES

[1]Adapted from Charles R. Hobbs, "Teachers, What About Your Lesson Application," *Improvement Era,* September 1962, p. 648.

[2]Adam S. Bennion, *Principles of Teaching* (Salt Lake City: Deseret News Press, 1958), p. 119.

SPECIAL TECHNIQUES USING INSTRUCTIONAL MATERIALS

How to Create a Graphic Art Worksheet

Clarence A. Schoenfeld tells of an old hunter pal who was regaling him about his exploits in the mountains of Colorado. The friend enthusiastically reported, "I was working along this narrow trail on the side of a canyon when up ahead I spotted as fine a rack of horns as ever you'll see. But a big boulder was in the way, and I couldn't get a clear shot. . . .

"I figured if I could just get the right angle, maybe I could ricochet a bullet off the opposite canyon wall and hit that buck. So I sighted away carefully and fired."

"Well," said Schoenfeld, "did you get the deer?"

"Heck, no," came the reply, "I missed the canyon wall!"[1]

That tale bears a resemblance to how close many teachers in the Church come to hitting the bull's-eye with student worksheets. I speak of the teachers who don't use student worksheets at all. They go hunting without taking a gun. Then there are those teachers who do use worksheets but present to students an uninteresting sheet loaded with meaningless problems and questions and thus miss the canyon wall.

Whether teaching a Primary class in Key West, Florida, or an adult Sunday School class in Anchorage, Alaska, principles upon which students learn remain unchanged. Students tend to learn best when doing. Of course, seeing an idea illustrated pictorially or graphically can help students comprehend its meaning. Hearing the same idea can be useful. Put *doing, seeing,* and *hearing* together in one meaningful learning activity, and we have the possibility of an effective learning situation.

This, in essence, is accomplished in the *graphic art worksheet.* Each student makes written response to thought-provoking questions. This he does on a picture or graph that symbolizes the idea he is developing. He receives verbal instructions along with individual help from the teacher. Thus, these three conditions of learning are employed. A graphic art worksheet can be appropriate in all classes of gospel instruction, including family home evenings. A group of adults would naturally be presented with advanced concepts and illustrations, while children would be given simplified problems to work out on simple illustrations.

To create graphic art worksheets for your students, you will need:

Master dittos on which the master copies are made (sell for about 10¢ per ditto).

Ball-point pen or stylus to draw the illustration on the master ditto.

Ditto paper (ream of 500 sheets generally sells for less than $2).

Hectograph or duplicator machine (Simple instructions on making your own hectograph are given at the end of this chapter on page 163 for those who do not have access to a duplicator. A hectograph can be made for a few cents or purchased commercially at a nominal price. A good quality duplicator runs from $150 up.)

All of the above items are available in most school supply stores.

What Makes Good Questions for Student Worksheets?

Each of the questions or problems you prepare on student worksheets should meet at least one of the following criteria:

1. Does the question meet a *student need?* Does the question ask for a solution to a problem that students might have faced yesterday or will face tomorrow, next week, or next month?

    Good example: "What basic rules should a boy remember when asking a girl for a date?" (For a class of sixteen-year olds.)

    Poor example: Ask the above question to a group of twelve-year olds.

2. Does the question *relate to the students' lives?*

    Good example: "Write the story of the Good Samaritan as though it happened last Saturday night two miles south of town."

    Poor example: "Write the story of the Good Samaritan."

3. Does the factual question ask for recall of *meaningful facts* on which students can hang great ideas?

> *Good example:* "What great quality of leadership does King Benjamin bring out in Mosiah 2:11-17?" or "Why is April 6 such a significant date in our Church?"
>
> *Poor example:* "How old was Brigham Young when called on his first mission?"

4. Will the question obtain a *commitment* from the students on the principle being studied?

> *Good example:* "At what age do you think you will let your children date? Why?" or "If you are willing to read 1 Nephi during September with the rest of the class, sign your name on the dotted line."
>
> *Poor example:* No question at all or "Someday when you get the chance read the Doctrine and Covenants. . . ."

5. Will the question *lead students to practicing* the principle being studied?

> *Good example:* "What action do you plan to take as a result of this lesson? Write out your plans in detail" or "Write specifically the steps you plan to take in bringing a nonmember friend into the Church."
>
> *Poor example:* "Now, students, I want you to listen to what I have to tell you." (An idea is then presented that is irrelevant to the students' needs.)

6. Will the question cause the students to dip into their reserves of *creative thought and reason?*

> *Good example:* "After reading 3 Nephi 12-14, write a diary that covers the three days of destruction and two days of Christ's appearance to the Nephites. Write the entries as though you were actually there. Make your descriptions specific, stimulating, and meaningful to the reader" or "Describe the relationship of mercy and justice to the atonement of Jesus Christ."
>
> *Poor example:* "Was Moses 120 years old when he died?" (Calls for only yes or no response.)

7. Is the question stated in an *understandable* manner?

> *Good example:* "What must one do to sin against the Holy Ghost?" (Use short sentences and simple vocabulary. Watch sentence construction for ambiguous statements.)
>
> *Poor example:* "In what sinister practice must one indulge to commit the unpardonable sin?"

How to Illustrate a Graphic Art Worksheet

Creating a graphic art worksheet calls for a little imagination, but I have seen teachers with no art talent create effective worksheets.

A friend gave me the picture of the happy little man in figure 2 several years ago. One day while preparing a lesson on life's trials I ran onto the long-forgotten picture in my files. As you can see, it would be a simple matter for anyone to add the instructions on the bottom of the picture, making it into a graphic art worksheet.

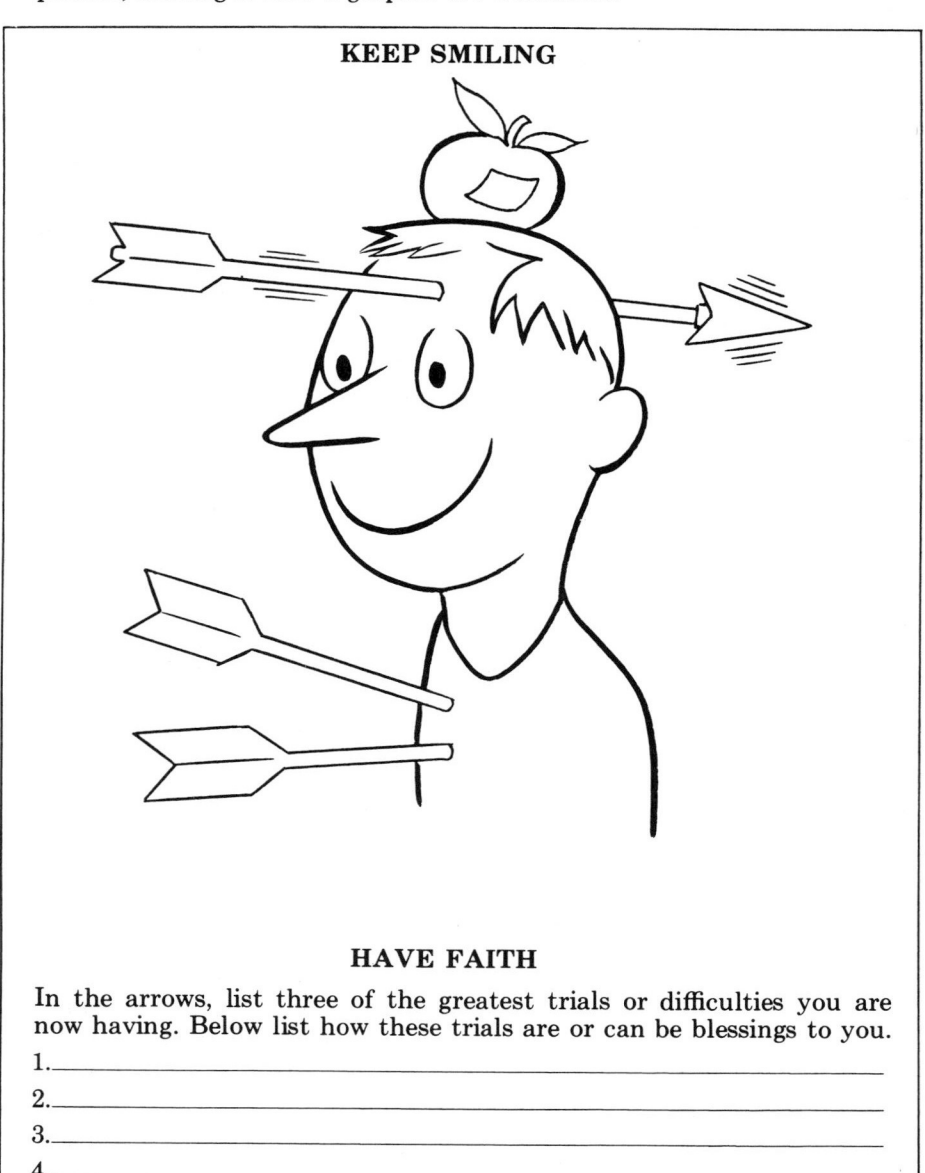

KEEP SMILING

HAVE FAITH

In the arrows, list three of the greatest trials or difficulties you are now having. Below list how these trials are or can be blessings to you.

1._____

2._____

3._____

4._____

Figure 1

Example of a Graphic Art Worksheet

Figure 2

On the billboard above, make an advertisement of your own creation on the adverse effects of smoking or drinking.

As you start gathering pictures from the Sunday funny papers and magazines to build a reserve of material for graphic arts that you will be creating, write on them names of lessons and concepts that come to mind. Later when preparing lessons, go through your morgue (file of pictures) searching for a picture that will help build the lesson objective. Upon finding the appropriate illustration, proceed as follows:

1. Trace and simplify the picture on a plain sheet of paper. Perhaps you have a student who is an artist who would be happy to help you out.

2. Arrange the written instructions, problems, or questions in such a way that the students give responses *directly on the illustration.* If this can't be arranged, place the picture above, below, or in the middle of the questions or problems.

3. The illustration should be symbolic or descriptive of the idea to be taught. The propeller in figure 3 is not symbolic of the degrees of glory. Figure 4 with the sun, moon, and star is more relevant to the idea of the degrees of glory. The graphic arts in figures 5 and 6 should be helpful in seeing how the principles are applied.

4. With a ball-point pen or stylus, trace the illustration on a master ditto. Then type or print the instructions, problems, or questions on the ditto.

5. With a duplicator or hectograph, run off enough copies to provide each student and yourself with the finished product.

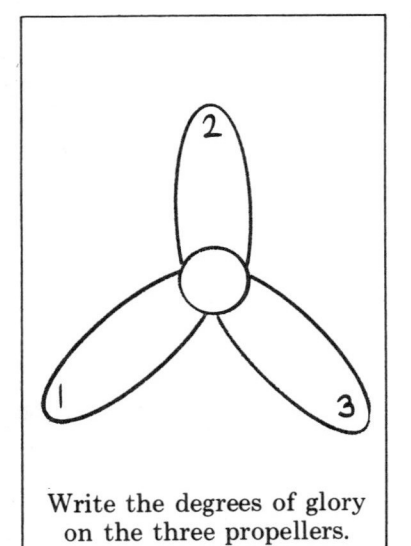

Write the degrees of glory on the three propellers.

Figure 3

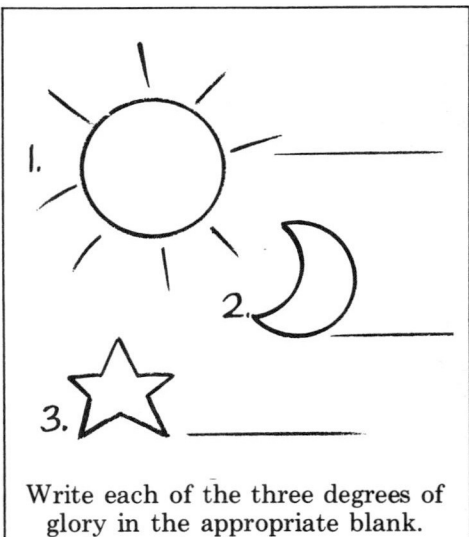

Write each of the three degrees of glory in the appropriate blank.

Figure 4

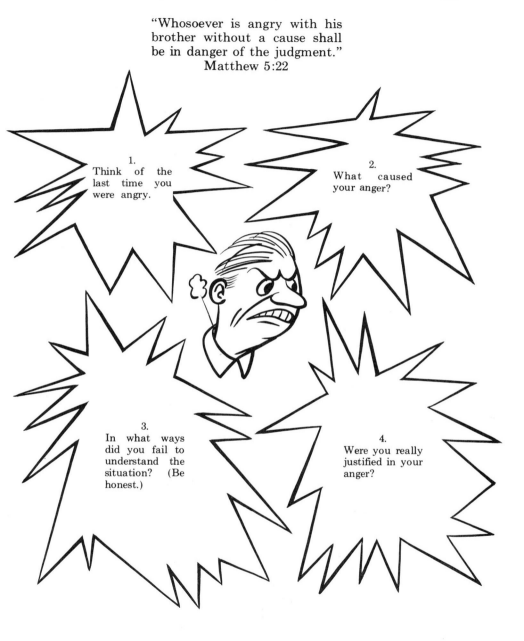

Figure 5

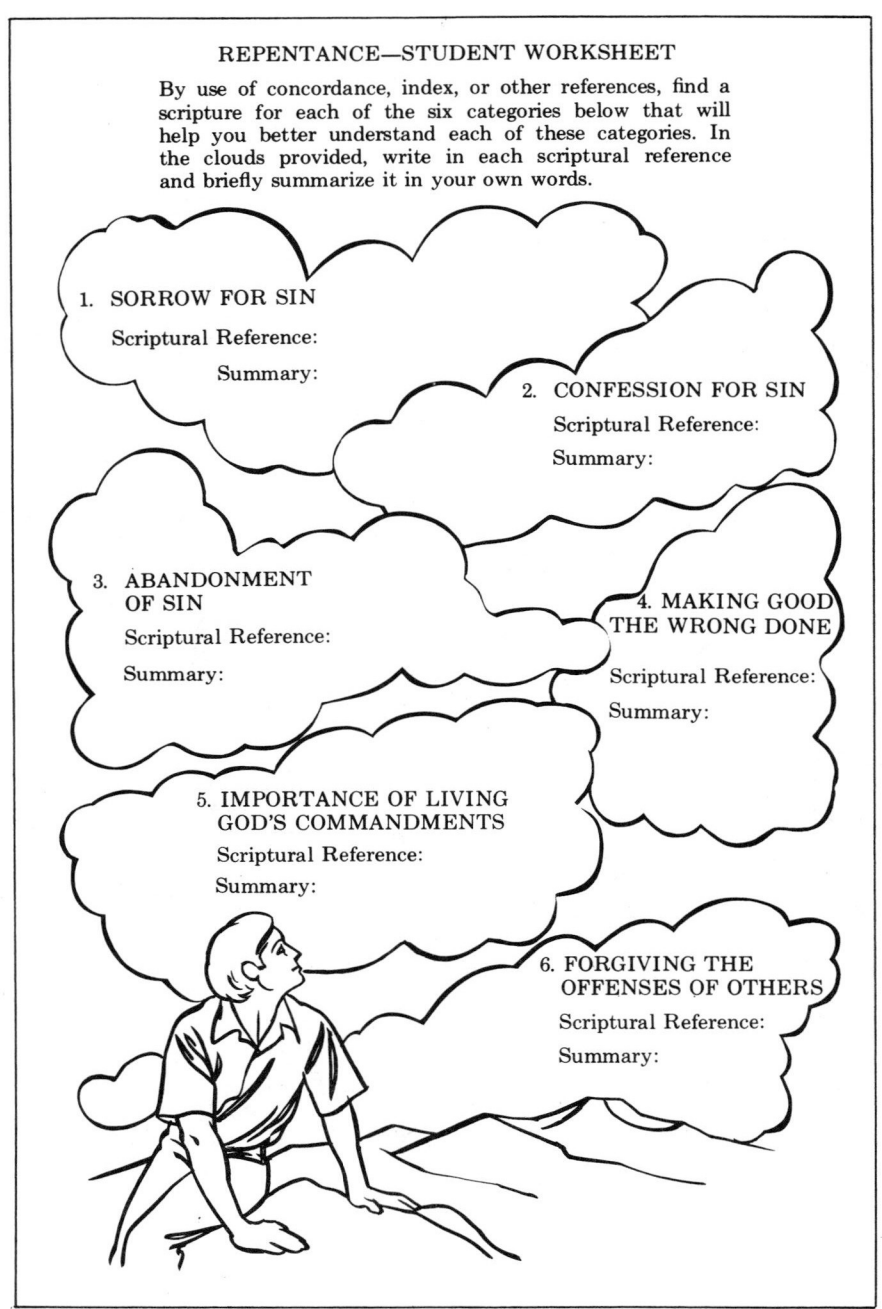

Figure 6.

How to Make a Hectograph

You can make your own hectograph by using a small cake pan large enough to accommodate an 8½-by-11 inch sheet of paper. Hectograph refills can be purchased in cans, melted, and poured into the cake pan, or you can make your own mixture by using the following recipe and boiling for seven minutes:

1 pkg. (4 envelopes or 4 tablespoons) clear gelatin
3 tablespoons of sugar
1 pint of cold water
1 pint of glycerine
Boil the mixture for seven minutes, and then place in a shallow pan and allow to cool for twelve hours. It is then ready for use.

Suggestions for using: First dampen the substance with cold water and then dry with about three sheets of paper, rubbing gently with the palm of the hand. Use hectograph pencil, ink, or hectograph carbon paper when making your master copy. You can get pencils and typewriter ribbons in several colors. With this equipment you can prepare the master copy of any material, of which many copies are desired, be it outline, story, picture, program, map, diagram, or music.

The master copy, whether prepared with hectograph pencil, ink, carbon, or typewriter ribbon, must be placed face down on the gelatin and smoothed out with the palm of the hand to assure every part's coming in contact with the gelatin. The master copy should remain in this position from three to seven minutes, depending upon the number of copies desired. The longer it remains on the gelatin, the more copies (maximum 70) can be made.

After the copies are made, sponge the gelatin with lukewarm water, and then drain off to remove as much of the hectograph ink as possible. The residue will in time be so completely absorbed into the gelatin that it will not appear on copies of material subsequently made. If hectograph ink is used, do not turn the master copy face down on the gelatin until the ink is dry.[2]

Perhaps with these few ideas you will better be able to hit the canyon wall.

Chapter 13
NOTES AND REFERENCES

[1]Clarence A. Schoenfeld, *Effective Feature Writing* (New York: Harper and Brothers, 1960), p. 69.

[2]A. Hamer Reiser. *A Reader for the Teacher,* p. 220; Hazel West Lewis, "Making and Operating a Hectograph," *Instructor* (April 1953), 88:119.

CHAPTER 14

Have You Tried Student Projects with Objects?

I would like to refer you once again to the story of Christ and the tribute money that we considered in chapter 3:

Is it lawful to give tribute unto Caeser, or not?
But Jesus perceived their wickedness, and said, Why tempt ye me, ye hypocrites? Shew me the tribute money. And they brought unto him a penny.
And he saith unto them, Whose is this image and superscription? They say unto him, Caesar's. Then saith he unto them, Render therefore unto Caesar the things which are Caesar's; and unto God the things that are God's. (Matthew 22:17-21.)

This is one of the many profound object lessons presented by the Master Teacher.

At another time He pointed out that the eyes are the light of the body. Drawing attention to the lilies of the field and fowls of the air, He taught that God provides. Possibly Jesus held a tiny mustard seed in His fingers and observed a mountain while teaching the principle that the faith of a mustard seed can move mountains. In His lessons the city gate became the way of eternal life; bread and water, His body and blood; an oxen yoke, the easy burden of the gospel. His immortal parables tell of wheat representing the righteous, and weeds the wicked. The gospel was likened to a pearl, again to a treasure, and another time to a fishing net. The lost sheep became a lost soul; fishermen became fishers of men. The Master Teacher frequently taught with objects.

There is substantial evidence that effective teaching is not merely "telling" information to students. It also involves stimulating pupils to think through and create for themselves. Object lessons can be used to help accomplish this end. One of the ways is to teach students how to create their own object lessons and give them the opportunity to present these to each other in class. I have found that students with the proper instruction often produce superior object lessons to those developed by teachers or presented in books. So, along with your becoming proficient with the instructions that follow, teach your students to do the same.

How to Create an Object Lesson

On a plain sheet of paper write down the lesson objective. Beneath this objective list familiar objects that in some way relate to the objective. For concreteness and utility, from this list choose the object that is—

1. Most related or adaptive to the objective.
2. Most familiar to the students.
3. Most easily available.
4. Most visible.

In choosing an object, it may help to scan the following list. As you can see, the object could be almost anything.

air	chain	faucet	matches	scale
baby	chalkboard	flashlight	mountain	scissors
beans	clean fluid	flower	nail	spark plug
bell	coin	glass	paper	stamp pad
board	comb	hair	paper clip	stapler
book	dirt	hammer	pencil	stone
box	doll	heater	pencil	telephone
bread	door	house	sharpener	twig
cake	elastic	ink	poster	wagon
candle	electrical	leaf	radio	weed
candy	current	letters	ring	
carrot	fan	light	rope	

Often an effective object is one that is unusual but not unfamiliar —for example, great-grandfather's pocket watch might stimulate more interest than an ordinary wristwatch. At times an exaggerated object is preferred. Occasionally a reduced or tiny object is more effective, such as the mustard seed.

Use objects that convey a positive upbuilding point of view. At one time I was sitting with a group of teenagers in a Sunday evening fireside listening to a guest speaker talk on chastity. With a hope to teach the youth what not to look at, he held up a pornographic picture with the emphatic statement, "Don't you ever look at an immodest picture like this one!" The effect was electric but highly negative.

When you have chosen a major object, write down other objects that might be used in the object lesson. Next to each object write what it is to represent. When teaching the object lesson, you might list these parts on the chalkboard, each followed by what it represents, even though you may be holding the object before the class. This will help onlookers to hold the train of thought and readily see the transfer from object to principal idea. This will also assist in keeping the idea being taught in focus, rather than placing overemphasis on the object. Probably the most frequent error in object lesson presentations is giving overemphasis to the object.

Let's look in on how Brother Wood followed the rules above in developing an object lesson. His objective was, "At the end of this lesson the students will be able to answer the following question: 'How does sin drive people out of the Church?'"

After making a list of objects, Brother Wood chose a magnet. He could also see how the drawing power of a magnet would make a good transfer to sin. The magnet was easy to see, and was of course well known to the students. He then wrote on a sheet of paper, "Magnet = Sin." At this point he could see that other objects were needed in the list. So he added:

Magnet = Sin
Metal Knife = Students
Book of Mormon = The Word of the Lord

Book of Mormon = Study of Scriptures, Prayer, Holy Ghost.

Obtaining the three objects listed, Brother Wood worked with them, testing their various physical possibilities, while thinking of various ways of relating these to his objective. As they came to mind, he wrote out ideas he wished to compare and emphasize as follows:

Physical Traits of Objects	Transfer to Students' Lives
1. The magnet draws the knife to it if the knife is not anchored.	1. Sin attracts unanchored people.
2. The magnet has no power over the metal knife as long as the knife is kept a safe distance away.	2. Students are less susceptible to sin if they keep a safe distance from it.
3. The magnet becomes comparatively ineffective when the Book of Mormon is placed between it and the knife.	3. Sin becomes ineffective when we study the scriptures, pray, and receive the guidance of the Holy Ghost.
4. Rubbing the knife on the magnet partially transfers the magnetic pull to the knife.	4. When in direct contact with sin, evil powers rub off and the evil influence spreads.
5. The metal knife is sharp.	5. I will give my students the reputation of being sharp enough to stay away from sin.

Brother Wood used this object lesson in teaching his class how to create their own object lessons. He took the students through the steps he went through. For practice and to test their knowledge, he gave them the assignment sheet on the following page to complete.

After checking the assignment, Brother Wood selected Bill to present his well-planned object lesson to the class on a day they were studying about the fall of Adam. After the class observed Bill's success with his three-minute lesson, Brother Wood said, "I desire to give each of you students an opportunity to enjoy the type of experience Bill has had today." Brother Wood then assigned a lesson objective to each student. The class members were told what day their lessons were to be taught. Another assignment sheet similar to the above was given to each student on which he could create his object lesson.

Students were enthusiastic, and they experienced much personal development in creating and presenting their *projects with objects* in Brother Wood's class. These students were teaching each other as Christ taught—with objects that were near.

In a Nutshell: How to Create an Object Lesson

1. Write down the lesson objective.

2. Make a list of familiar objects that in some way relate to the objective or answer the question raised in the objective.

3. From this list, choose the object that is:

PROJECTS WITH OBJECTS

Name of Student _____ Date _____

Lesson Objective: At the end of the lesson the students will be able to answer the following question: "Did Adam fall upward?"

List one or more familiar objects that relate to the objective above:
1.
2.
3.
4.
5.

The object I have chosen from the above list is _____.

This object is to represent _____.

Other objects, if any, I plan to use in the object lesson are:		These objects are to represent:
1.	=	1.
2.	=	2.
3.	=	3.
4.	=	4.

Physical Traits of Objects		Transfer to Students' Lives
1.	=	1.
2.	=	2.
3.	=	3.
4.	=	4.

    a. Most related or adaptive to the objective.
    b. Most familiar to the students.
    c. Most easily available.
    d. Most seeable.

4. List other objects that might be used effectively with the major object.

5. Next to each object on the list, indicate what it is to represent. (This list might well be written on the chalkboard when the object lesson is being presented so students can readily see the transfer.)

6. Obtain and study the objects chosen. Then write out the physical traits of the objects. Next to each of these, write out how these traits transfer to the principal idea being taught and to the students' lives.

Remember

1. The object should be unusual but not unfamiliar.

2. The object should convey a positive upbuilding point of view.

3. Give the principal idea being taught major emphasis rather than the object.

4. Don't stretch the comparison to the point of being ridiculous.

5. Don't present anything that would cause embarrassment to yourself or others.

6. Don't use an object that has been used recently in class. Use variety. Be different.

7. After the object lesson is presented, build on the ideas brought out in the object lesson throughout the remainder of the class period.

8. Relate the object lesson to the lesson objective.

9. In your daily activities be object conscious.

10. Let your object lesson preparation be *detailed preparation.*

The Stick Figures in Chalk

(For Teachers Who Cannot Draw Straight Lines)

More than eighty-five million people in the United States attend motion pictures weekly. At least five hundred million comic books are published annually.[1] The rocketing television industry has dwarfed the radio industry. This ought to tell us something about the significance of pictures in the lives of people. Confucius is credited with the saying, "One illustration has the learning value of a thousand words." This is a rather broad generalization, but I think this wise sage had the right idea—that pictures can be of considerable value in the learning process.

The chalkboard is perhaps the most common of all instructional materials in classrooms. Many homes have chalkboards. If a teacher in the classroom or home doesn't have access to a chalkboard, he can easily obtain one at minimal cost. It is not difficult to make a chalkboard.*

The chalkboard has multiple uses. On it we might write words, numbers, or other symbols. We might draw charts, graphs, and maps. And we might draw *pictures*. Because of its commonness and versatility, and because you probably don't know a great deal about chalkboard illustrating, we will take the next four chapters to help you learn to make "chalk talk." After you have practiced the ideas in these forthcoming chapters, you should be able to prepare some of

---

*Obtain a piece of masonite (minimum size 3' x 4') and a small can of chalkboard paint (most lumber yards have both of these items available). It is then a simple task to paint the board and hang it in the classroom or family room.

your own chalkboard-illustrated lessons, we will begin by assuming that at the present moment you are unable to draw—even a straight line.

Anyone can illustrate on the chalkboard who possesses the "I want to" and the "I am going to" attitude. As missionaries in Holland, Ray Duffin and I learned this lesson from a factory worker who was investigating the gospel.

Elder Duffin and I were conducting our second cottage meeting with the Pete Kabel family in their Zaandam home. Upon completing the gospel lesson, Elder Duffin looked up and exclaimed, "Where did you get that splendid windmill sketch?"

I glanced at the wall behind me to see a large beautiful pencil sketch of a Dutch windmill and canal.

"I just drew it myself," beamed Pete.

"How many years have you studied art?"

"None at all. I just picked up drawing on my own. In fact, this windmill is one of the first sketches I ever drew."

"How could you possibly have done it without training?"

"Oh, I was able to sketch this picture because I wanted to. One time an artist told me that all I needed were three things in order to sketch—drawing paper, drawing pencil, and desire. I had the desire, and shortly thereafter came the pencil and paper. Excitedly I planted myself on a canal bank with these essentials, and the windmill sketch you are now viewing was the result."

Pete then turned to me and added, "If you have the desire to sketch something, all you need is the drawing tools."

We applied this lesson of desire and realized many satisfying results.

To paraphrase Brother Kabel's words, "If you have the desire to increase your effectiveness as a teacher through chalkboard illustrating, all you need to start is a piece of chalk and chalkboard."

When you get your hand on the chalk, you must remember that simplicity is important. Elaborate chalkboard illustrations stifle student response when the pupils try to reproduce them in their notes. In contrast, simplified teacher sketches result in more student participation because students asked to participate tend to reproduce that which is within their realm of accomplishment more than that which appears beyond their ability to do.

One of the most simplified forms of art is the cartoon. And the fact that at least five hundred million comic books are published annually substantiates exceptional interest in the cartoon medium.

The stick figure is perhaps the most simplified of all cartoon types. Contrary to some opinions, the stick figure can be very active and expressive, because it contains the basic parts of the human figure that connote action.

By the time you finish this chapter, you will be able to draw the eight basic positions of the stick figure that appear on the following page. You will also begin to see how these stick figures can be used to illustrate ideas in lessons. However, you may not be able to create your own chalkboard-illustrated lessons until you have at least completed the instructions in this chapter and the following three chapters.

With slight adaptations of the eight basic positions of the stick figure, you should be able to draw the human figure in almost any conceivable position. However, we will leave the adaptations to your own experimentations and concern ourselves here only with the fundamentals.

In learning to illustrate on the chalkboard through the instruction that follows, you will have a step-by-step walk through experience. At this point you must obtain a pencil. If you do not wish to write in the blank areas provided in the right column of each page, lay a plain sheet of scratch paper over the righthand blank column and draw on the scratch paper. Don't simply read the following pages, but practice as instructed. **On the righthand side in each frame, completely redraw everything that appears in the adjoining lefthand frame.** As soon as you have learned to reproduce the illustrations on paper, practice on the chalkboard.

1. **STANDING**

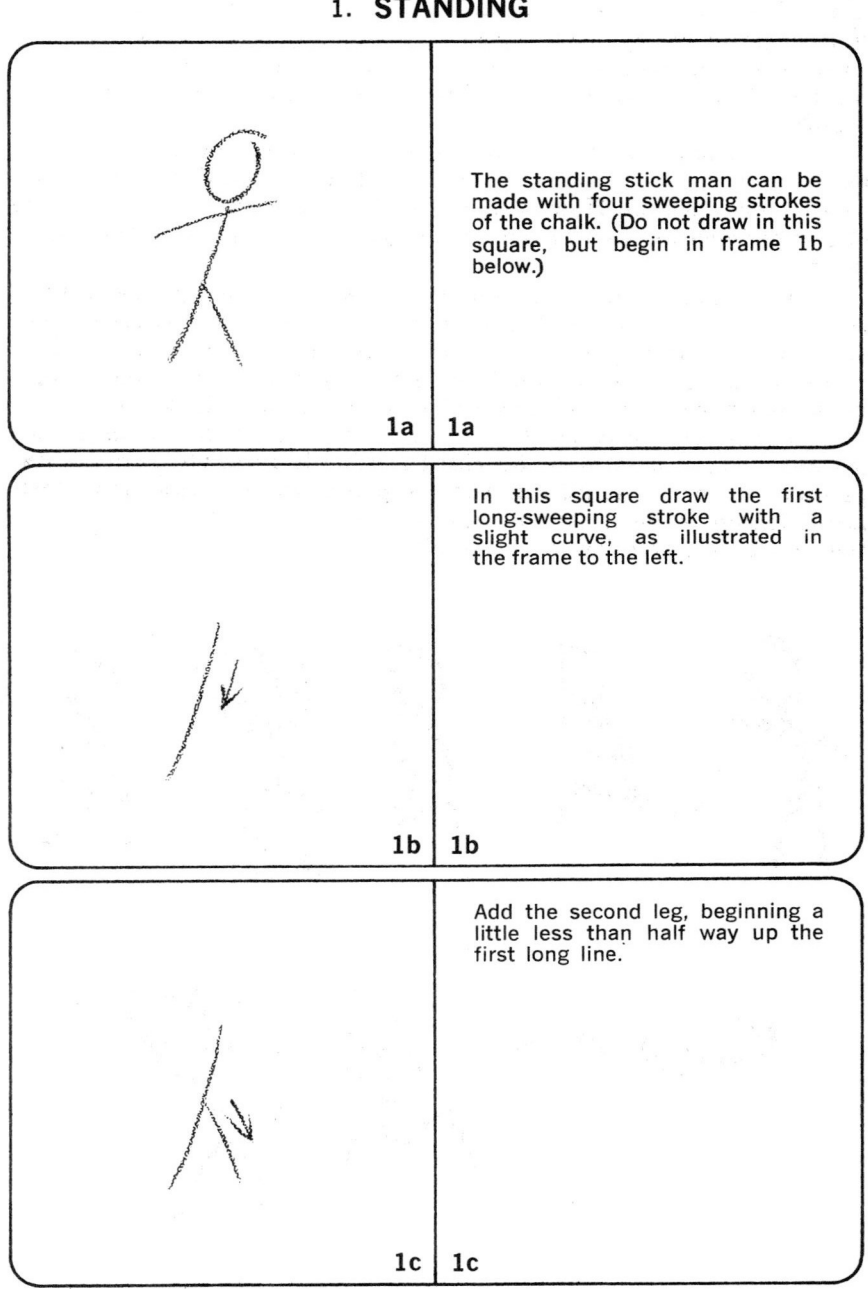

The standing stick man can be made with four sweeping strokes of the chalk. (Do not draw in this square, but begin in frame 1b below.)

1a | 1a

In this square draw the first long-sweeping stroke with a slight curve, as illustrated in the frame to the left.

1b | 1b

Add the second leg, beginning a little less than half way up the first long line.

1c | 1c

Draw the head in the shape of an egg or balloon. Extend one end of the oval for hair.

1d

The fourth stroke makes the arms and completes the body. Add the arms.

1e

Now draw Apostle Paul preaching on Mars' Hill.

1f

Practice the standing figure on the chalkboard. Break the chalk into a one-inch length. Pinch the chalk at the middle with thumb and index finger so you can use the full one-inch surface of the chalk to make a wide line. Use the wide line for body, legs, and arms.

2. RUNNING

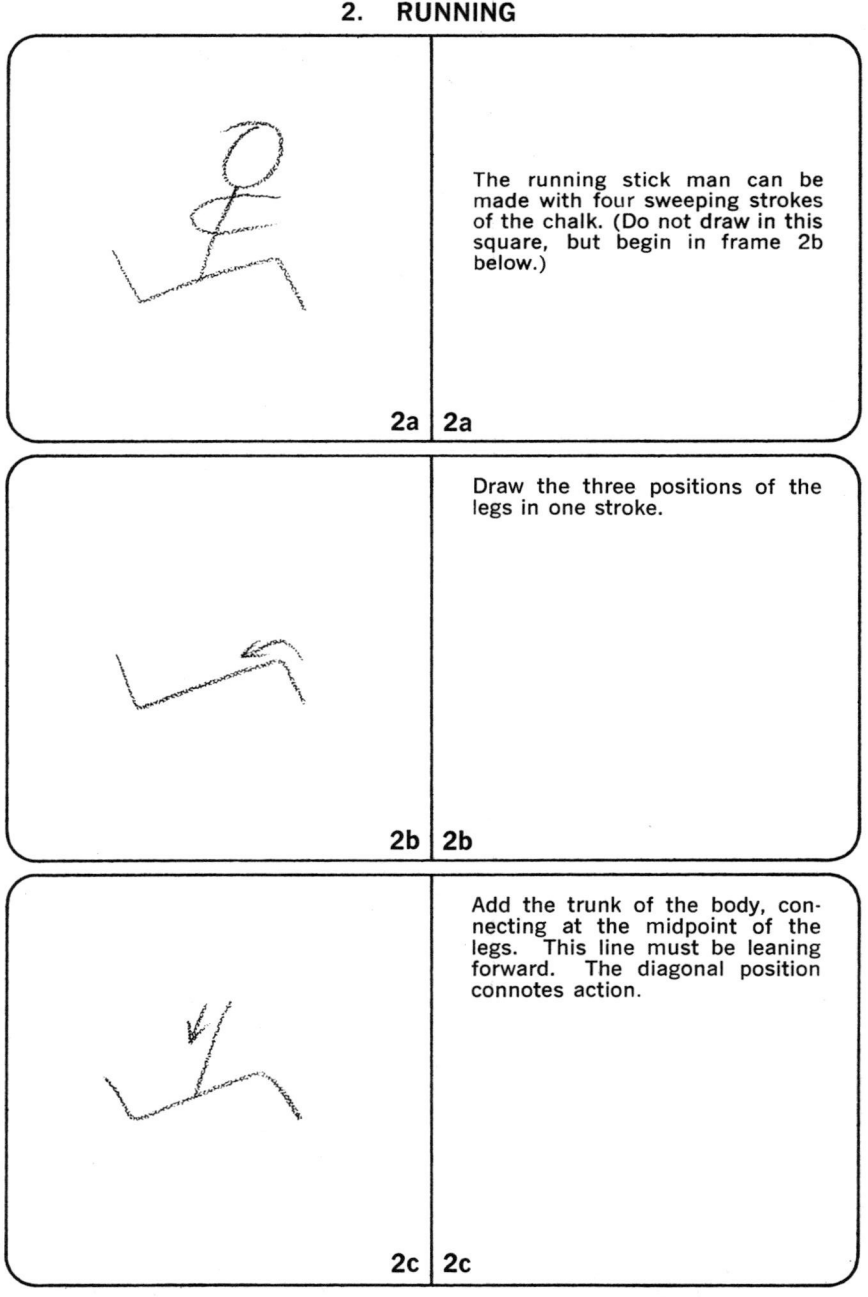

2a

The running stick man can be made with four sweeping strokes of the chalk. (Do not draw in this square, but begin in frame 2b below.)

2b

Draw the three positions of the legs in one stroke.

2c

Add the trunk of the body, connecting at the midpoint of the legs. This line must be leaning forward. The diagonal position connotes action.

Add the egg-shaped head in one stroke, with hair flowing away from the direction he is running.

2d

The fourth stroke makes the arms. Make them reach out as though he is going somewhere.

2e

Draw Jonah running away from the Lord.

2f

Practice the running figure on the chalkboard. Remember to use the full one-inch surface of the chalk for body, arms, and legs.

3.   KNEELING

3a | 3a

A profile of a kneeling stick man can be made with three simple strokes. (Do not draw in this square, but begin in frame 3b below.)

3b | 3b

Think about bending a coat hanger to the shape at the left.   Avoid tipping the body forward too far.

3c | 3c

Add the arms and head.

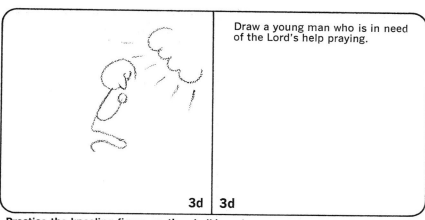

Draw a young man who is in need of the Lord's help praying.

3d | 3d

Practice the kneeling figure on the chalkboard.

4. JUMPING

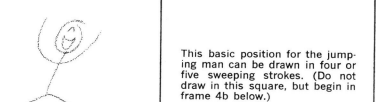

This basic position for the jumping man can be drawn in four or five sweeping strokes. (Do not draw in this square, but begin in frame 4b below.)

4a | 4a

Draw the trunk of the body.

4b | 4b

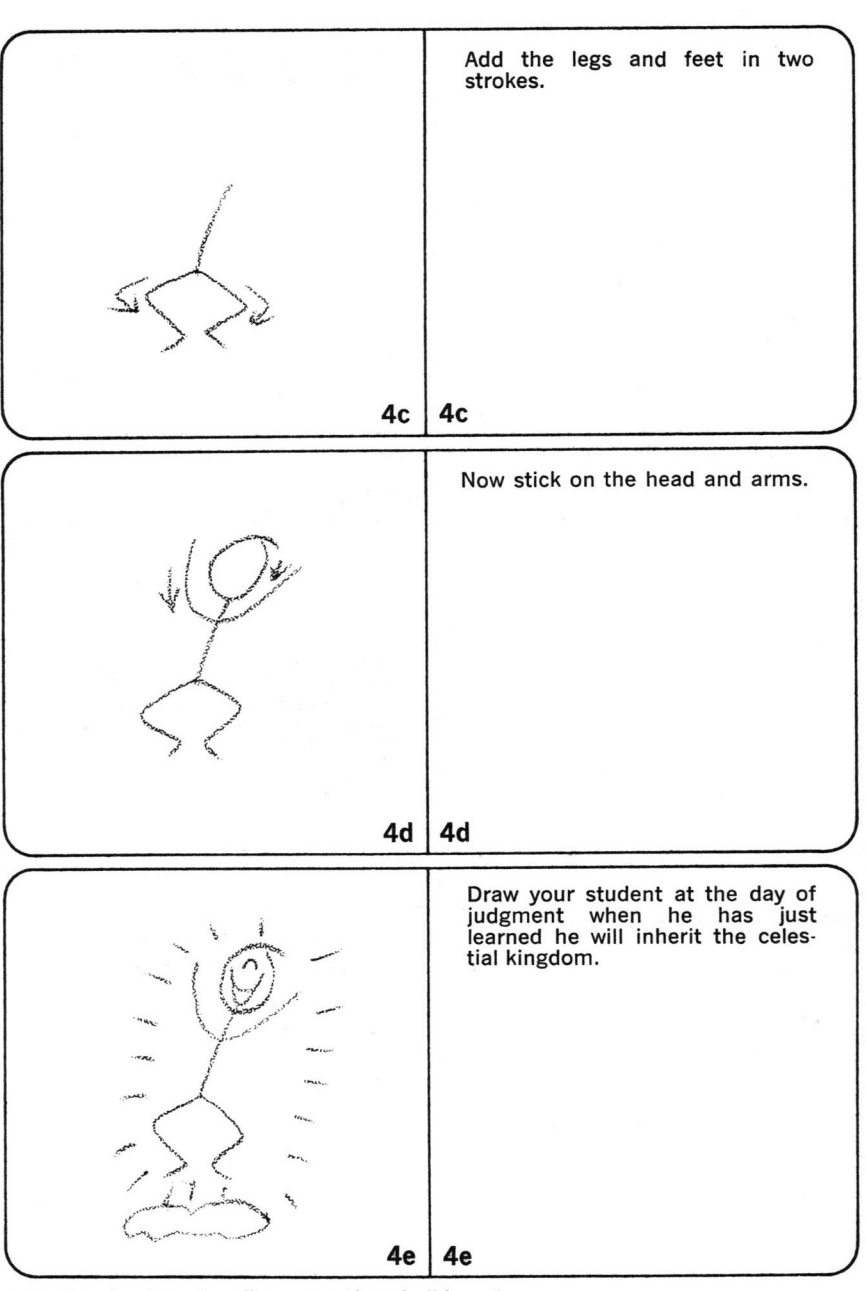

Add the legs and feet in two strokes.

4c | 4c

Now stick on the head and arms.

4d | 4d

Draw your student at the day of judgment when he has just learned he will inherit the celestial kingdom.

4e | 4e

Practice the jumping figure on the chalkboard.

5.   SITTING

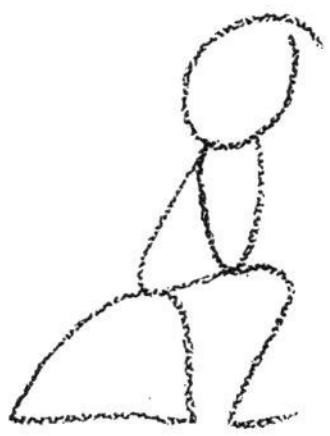

In three simple strokes you will be able to come up with a sitting individual. (Do not draw in this square, but begin in frame 5b below.)

5a

The trunk of the body is similar to the praying position, except the knees are higher when sitting. Draw this part of the sitting position.

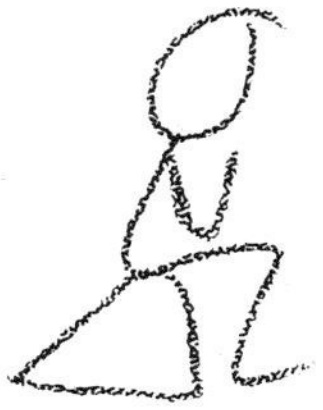

5b

Add the head and arm.

5c

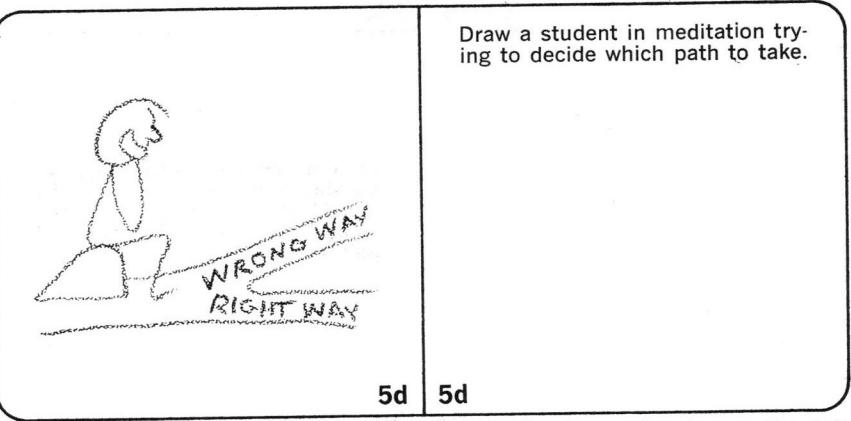

| | Draw a student in meditation trying to decide which path to take. |

5d | 5d

Practice the sitting figure on the chalkboard.   Remember to use the full surface of a one-inch piece of chalk for body, leg, and arm.

6. LYING

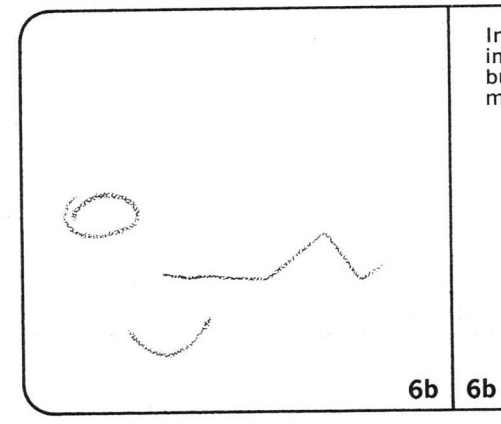

| | The basic lying position for a resting, sleeping, or dead man is easily done in three strokes. (Do not draw in this square, but begin in frame 6b below.) |

6a | 6a

| | In this box draw the three strokes in the shape indicated at the left, but connect your lines to form the man in the 6a lying position. |

6b | 6b

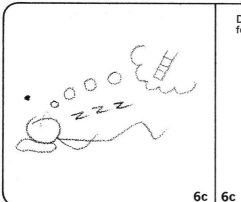

Draw Jacob sleeping, using a rock for a pillow, while having a vision.

6c | 6c

Practice the lying figure on the chalkboard.

7. FALLING

This is one way to illustrate the falling position. (Do not draw in this square, but begin in frame 7b below.)

7a | 7a

Draw the trunk of the body, legs, and feet.

7b | 7b

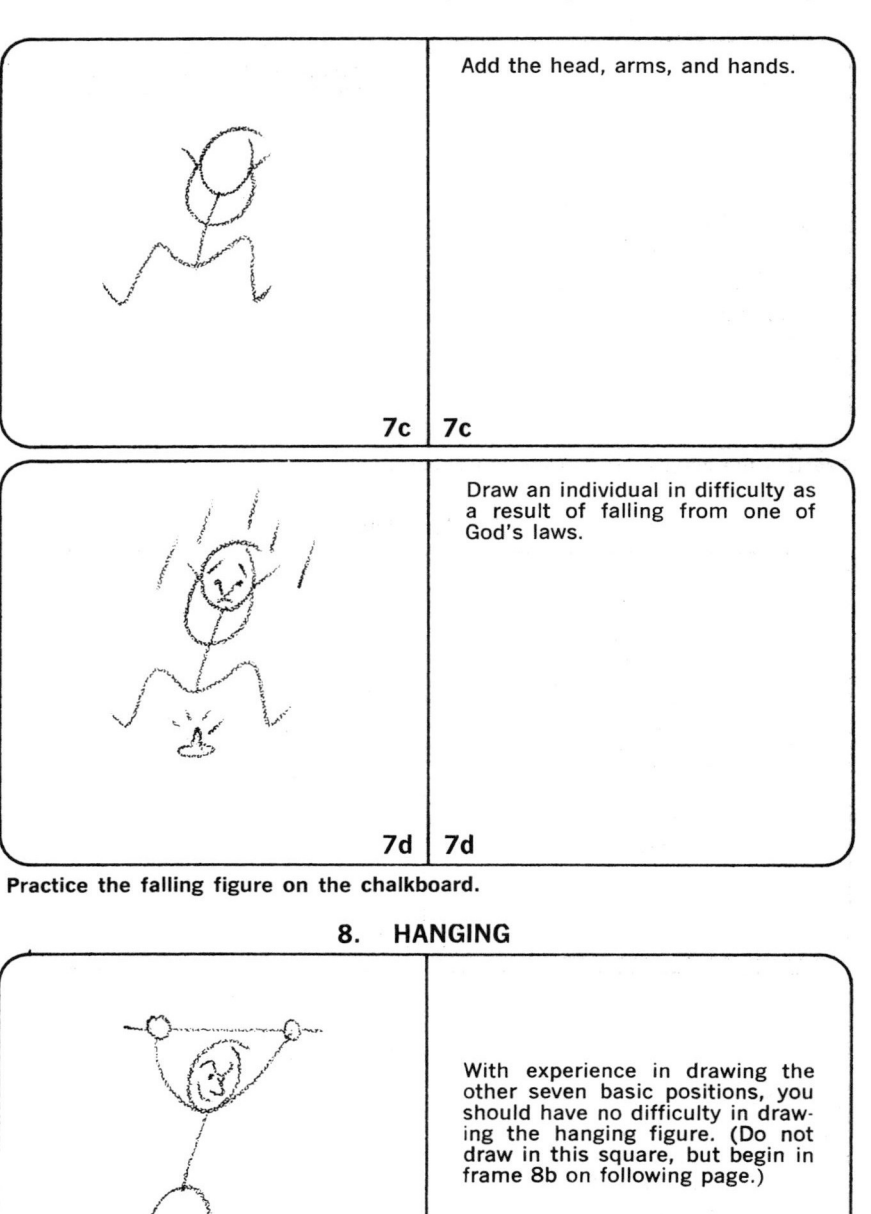

Add the head, arms, and hands.

7c | 7c

Draw an individual in difficulty as a result of falling from one of God's laws.

7d | 7d

Practice the falling figure on the chalkboard.

8. HANGING

With experience in drawing the other seven basic positions, you should have no difficulty in drawing the hanging figure. (Do not draw in this square, but begin in frame 8b on following page.)

8a | 8a

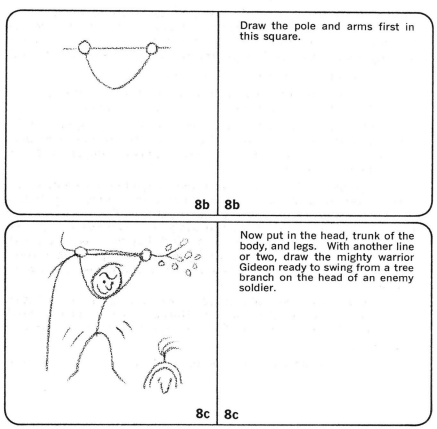

Draw the pole and arms first in this square.

8b | **8b**

Now put in the head, trunk of the body, and legs. With another line or two, draw the mighty warrior Gideon ready to swing from a tree branch on the head of an enemy soldier.

8c | **8c**

Practice the hanging figure on the chalkboard.

When you can reproduce these eight basic positions fairly well, try drawing the stick figure in other variations. If you want a female body, simply give the stick man a skirt and more hair. If you want a child, simply make the head larger and round rather than egg shaped.

Here are a few other tips to keep in mind:

Use the side of the chalk for wide heavy lines and the end of the chalk for more detailed work such as on the face.

When drawing with chalk, make long sweeping strokes by swinging the entire forearm. Do not make the sweeping lines with finger or hand movement. Use movement of finger and hands for more detailed work.

A general rule when drawing the complete stick figure is not to clutter up the illustration with unnecessary buttons, eyelashes, fingers, shoelaces, or other distracting detail. These are costly in time and divert student interest away from the lesson objective. In your practice, however, you will find that the eyes and mouth are the most useful parts of the figure in bringing out expression. Yet even they must be simple and are not always necessary. Keep it simple.

Do not be afraid of making an awkward illustration before your students. It adds interest. Rather than be embarrassed, laugh with your students. They do not expect you to draw as Schulz does.

Now let's consider what you might do about using your head.

Chapter 15
NOTES AND REFERENCES

[1]A. Hamer Reiser, *A Reader for the Teacher,* p. 257; Marion G. Merkley, "Using Pictures in Teaching," in *Instructor,* September 1952, 87:266.

On Using Your Head

One of the most remarkable objects on earth is a medium-sized bony structure located above the human's shoulders called the *head*.

Many uses have been found for this sphere. It tells the rest of the bodily attachments how to act. Looking, speaking, hearing, smelling, and even thinking are all functions peculiar to this orb.

A head is something no one can do without, and something everyone should have more to do with. Outside of normal uses, this upper story attachment can be a useful object for presenting ideas in lessons.

In the last chapter you were introduced to the idea that anyone can illustrate on the chalkboard who possesses the *I want to* and the *I am going to* attitude. And you were given opportunity to practice drawing the stick figure in eight basic positions.

After completing this chapter, if you follow instructions, you should be able to draw at least eight different facial expressions in balanced dimensional form. If you are a second miler and are willing to practice, you will also be able to reproduce many other facial expressions.

Now turn the page and you will be provided further experience toward learning to present your own chalkboard-illustrated lessons.

As in chapter 15, on the righthand side in each frame completely redraw everything that appears in the adjoining lefthand frame.

1. DRAWING THE HEAD

You will draw this head first, with the purpose of learning to put the parts of the head in the right place, and to get a round dimensional look rather than flat look. (Do not draw in this square, but begin in frame 1b below.)

1a   1a

People's heads are basically in the shape of a balloon. Draw a balloon in this box. Do not press hard with the pencil, but use a light swinging stroke as illustrated at the left.

1b   1b

Draw a light vertical line **around** the front and back of the balloon as illustrated in the box to the left.

1c   1c

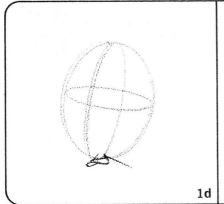

Divide the top and bottom halves of your balloon with a fine line going *around* horizontally, meeting the other lines at right angles. The horizontal line is to be equal distance from top to bottom of the balloon.

1d | 1d

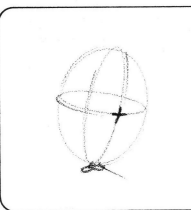

Select one of the four points where the guidelines cross. This will be your point of reference for all parts of the head. Place a + at the point of reference.

1e | 1e

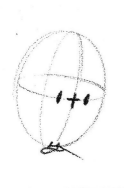

Now ignore the two lines that go around the back of the head. The eyes are halfway down on the horizontal line. The point of reference is always between the eyes.

1f | 1f

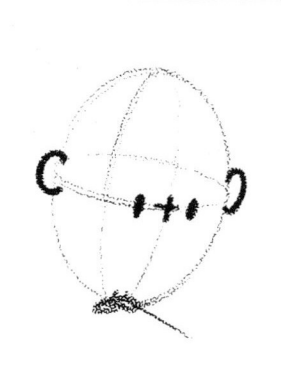

The ears are on the same horizontal lines as the eyes, and each ear is halfway back on the head. The ear to your right does not show as much because the head is slightly turned. Put on the ears.

1g | 1g

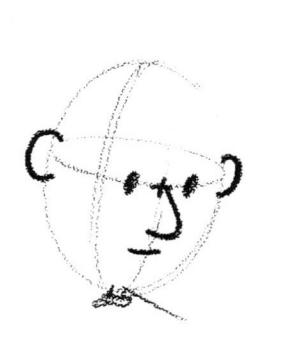

Place the nose on the vertical line beneath the point of reference. Place the mouth somewhere under the nose.

1h | 1h

Whatever you do with the hair, make it go around the balloon head. Give the hair a solid look rather than trying to draw every hair. Keep it simple as you now draw it.

1i | 1i

As you practice the above steps on the chalkboard, think about the balloon being round. Draw the guidelines lightly all the way around the balloon. Always work from the point of reference you select on the guidelines.

Using all of the steps you have been through, draw the head in the space provided in this box, using the man at the left as a model.

1j | 1j

2. HAPPINESS

The head can be placed in any position. Use whatever position that will help put over the expression. In the happy expression at the right, the head is tilted way back to allow plenty of room for the mouth. Perhaps you have noticed that the eyes and the mouth carry the expression. (Do not draw in this square, but begin in frame 2b below.)

2a | 2a

Because the head is tilted way back, the horizontal line around the balloon has been raised in front and lowered in back. Draw the open horizontal line in a balloon below.

2b | 2b

Now draw in the vertical line, which is in about the same position as the first head you sketched. Remember, the vertical line should always meet the horizontal line at right angles.

2c | 2c

Select a point where the lines cross for a point of reference. Place the eyes on the horizontal line on each side of the point of reference.

2d | 2d

Place the ears halfway back on the horizontal line. Notice how the ears are lower on the head. Draw the mouth to fit the roundness of the balloon. Do not draw it flat.

2e | 2e

Practice these steps on the chalkboard.

3. SADNESS

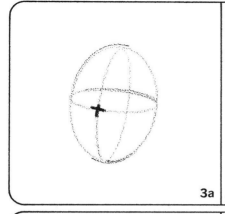

Draw in the guidelines for the regular front position. Select one of the four points where the lines cross for a point of reference.

3a | 3a

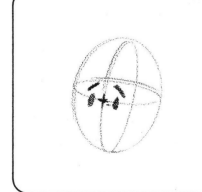

Place the sad eyes on each side of the reference point of the horizontal line. Notice the position of the eyebrows.

3b | 3b

Place the ears halfway back on the same line as the eyes. Add nose, mouth (turn corners of mouth down), and hair.

3c | 3c

In the box at the right, try drawing a sad looking fellow in your own style by using the steps and principles you have practiced.

3d | 3d

Practice drawing a sad face on the chalkboard.

4. SURPRISE

For surprise, the eyes are big with pupils "dead center." Place the mouth in a round "Oh!" position. Remember, how you use the guidelines is important to show dimension and to help get the parts in the right places. (Do not draw in this square, but begin in frame 4b below.)

4a | 4a

In this box draw only the balloon and guidelines for the above expression.

In this box draw the surprised expression in completed form.

4b | 4b

5. STUPIDITY

You will be asked to practice the stupid expression here in a pro-file position. When the balloon is turned far enough around to get a profile, the vertical merges into the outside line of the balloon. The horizontal line remains in regular position. (Do not draw in this square, but begin in frame 5b below.)

5a | 5a

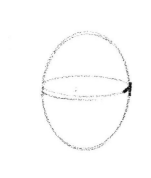

In light pencil draw the balloon and horizontal line. Indicate the point of reference.

5b | 5b

Place the one visible eye at the reference point on the horizontal line. Place the ear halfway back on the horizontal line. Shape the mouth. Add nose and hair.

Practice the stupid look on the chalkboard!

6.   LOVE

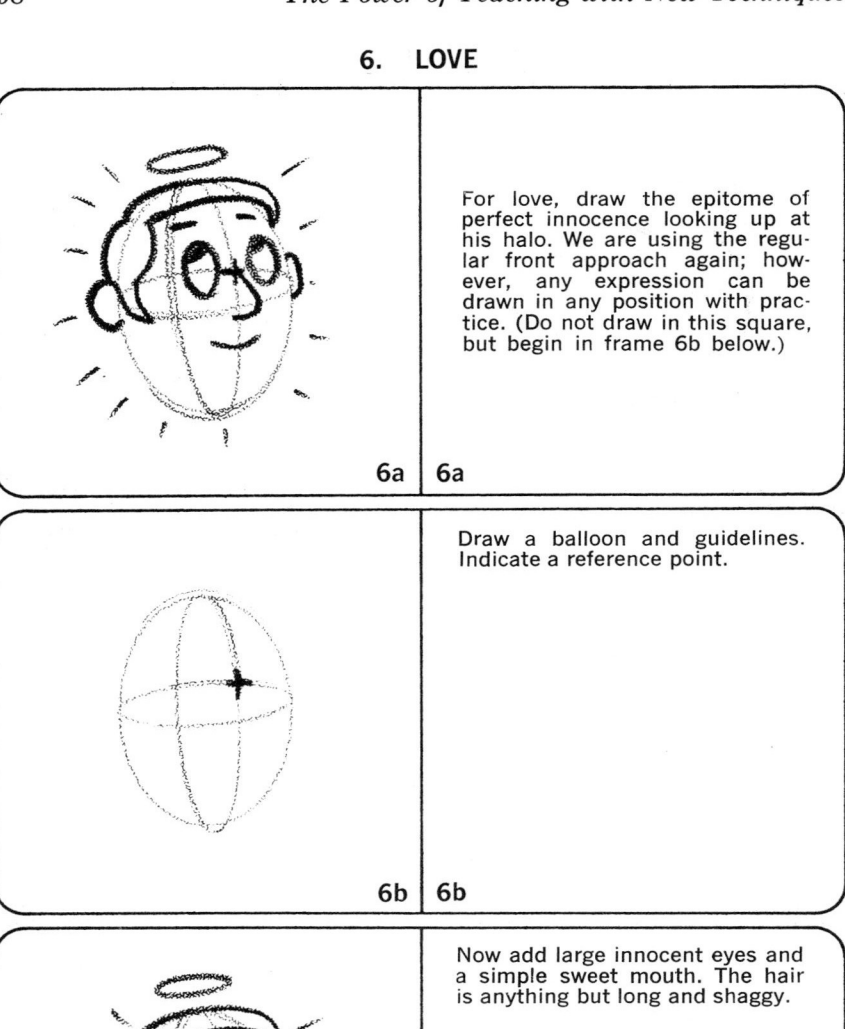

For love, draw the epitome of perfect innocence looking up at his halo. We are using the regular front approach again; however, any expression can be drawn in any position with practice. (Do not draw in this square, but begin in frame 6b below.)

6a   6a

Draw a balloon and guidelines. Indicate a reference point.

6b   6b

Now add large innocent eyes and a simple sweet mouth. The hair is anything but long and shaggy.

6c   6c

7. HATE

The balloon of a head can be squeezed into almost any conceivable position. If you use a different shape, be sure that the guidelines follow the shape of the balloon. Let's try a hateful look in the shape of a bean. (Do not draw in this square, but begin in frame 7b below.)

7a | 7a

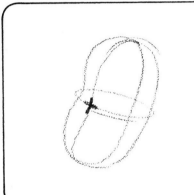

Notice how the guidelines still intersect at right angles. Draw the bean and guidelines. Add a point of reference.

7b | 7b

Hate is expressed in the scowl of the brow and mouth. Over-accentuate the key parts you want to emphasize. Draw the entire hateful head in this box.

7c | 7c

8.   WOMEN AND CHILDREN

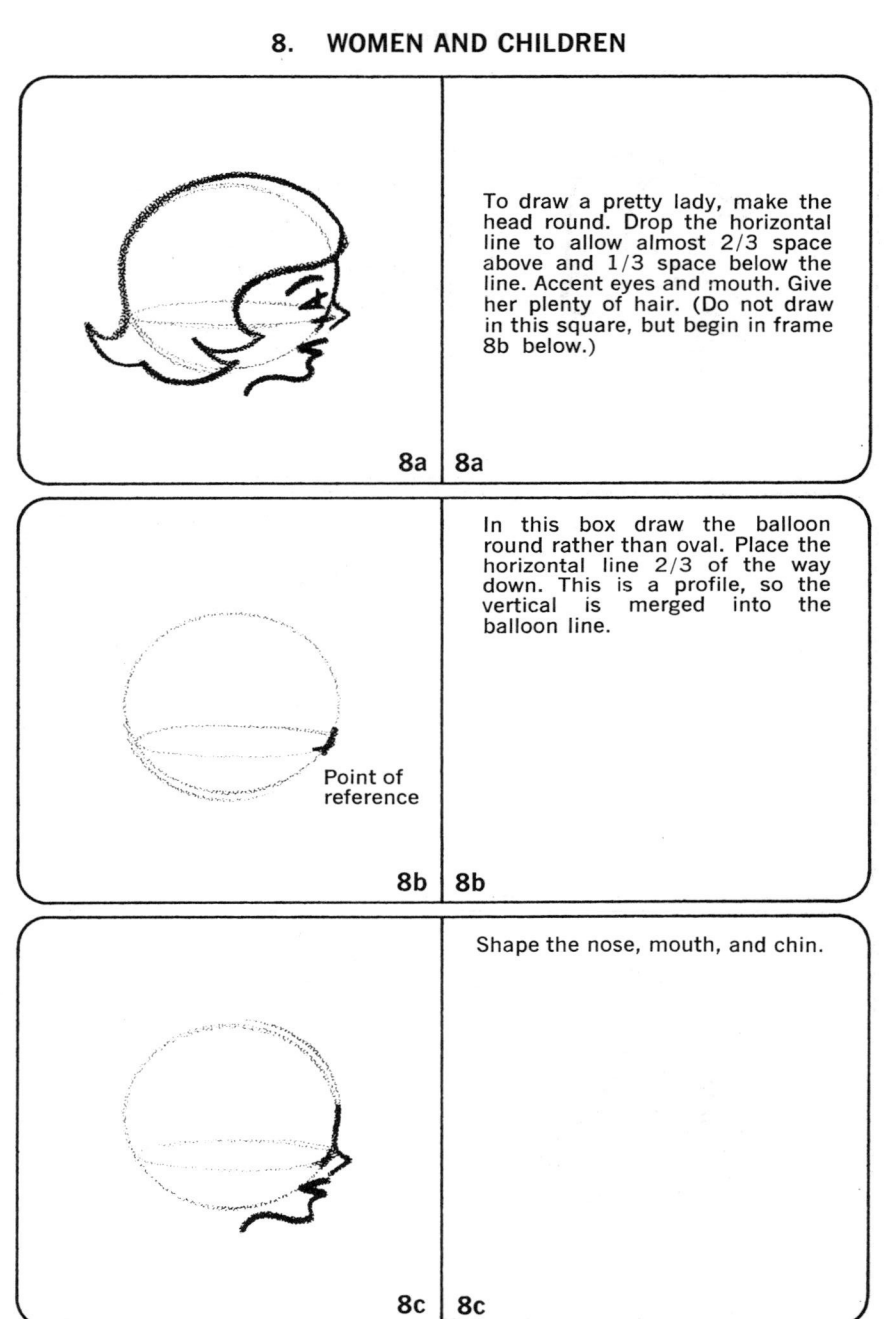

8a | **8a**

To draw a pretty lady, make the head round. Drop the horizontal line to allow almost 2/3 space above and 1/3 space below the line. Accent eyes and mouth. Give her plenty of hair. (Do not draw in this square, but begin in frame 8b below.)

Point of reference

8b | **8b**

In this box draw the balloon round rather than oval. Place the horizontal line 2/3 of the way down. This is a profile, so the vertical is merged into the balloon line.

8c | **8c**

Shape the nose, mouth, and chin.

Add eyes and hair. Give plenty of hair around the outside of the balloon.

8d | 8d

In this box draw the entire head of the lady. If you are having difficulty, go through the above steps again.

8e | 8e

A child's head is also round rather than oval. Make large eyes and place them wider apart than an adult's. Hairstyle also helps identify the person as a child. (Do not draw in this square, but begin in frame 8g on following page.)

8f | 8f

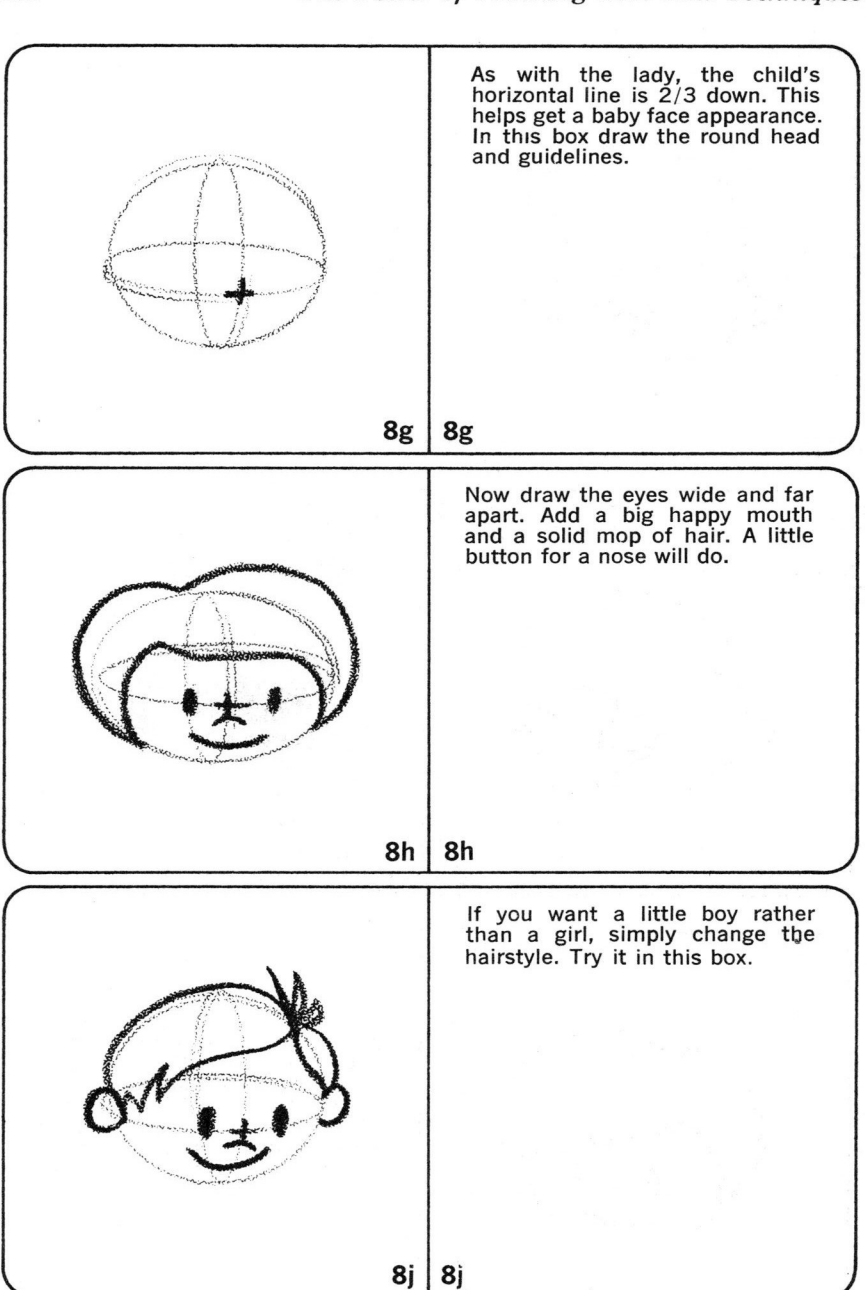

As with the lady, the child's horizontal line is 2/3 down. This helps get a baby face appearance. In this box draw the round head and guidelines.

8g | 8g

Now draw the eyes wide and far apart. Add a big happy mouth and a solid mop of hair. A little button for a nose will do.

8h | 8h

If you want a little boy rather than a girl, simply change the hairstyle. Try it in this box.

8j | 8j

Practice the above techniques on the chalkboard.

How to Make 49 Different Expressions

As was pointed out earlier, facial expression is found mainly in the eyes and mouth. For practice, try combining each different eye expression with each of the various mouth expressions below. Do this by placing a see-through scratch paper over this page. Trace the heads with eye expressions (1-7); then place one of the heads with eyes over one of the heads with mouths (8-14) and trace. If you try out all the possibilities, you should come up with 49 different expressions. Practice these on the chalkboard.

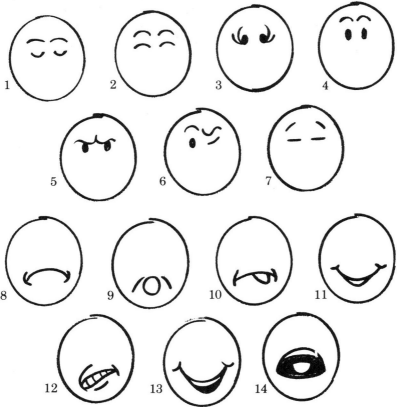

Depending on how far you want to go in developing your chalkboard skills, you could spend many hours practicing cartoon heads. It is useful to carry a small pad of paper and a pencil. Whenever you are waiting for a friend, or otherwise have time on your hands, take out the pad and pencil and practice. With the manipulation of a few simple lines, you can make almost any type of facial expression one might see in a busy shopping center on a Saturday afternoon.

In your daily activities, become more observant of people's heads and faces. You will begin to see more vividly beaming smiles, Roman noses, Dumbo ears, ratted hair, and sleepy eyes.

When using your head in preparing a lesson or practicing on the chalkboard, magnify the toothless grin, the crooked nose, and the double chin. Try sketching various expressions using varied combinations of the eyes, ears, noses, and mouths below.

Give special emphasis to that part of the face that tells your story.

Observation of the characters in the newspaper comics will assist greatly in developing imaginative little people for classroom use.

In preparing to present your own chalkboard illustrated lessons, we will now turn to chapter 17 for props to go with your stick figures and heads.

Chapter 16
NOTES AND REFERENCES

[1]Adapted from Charles R. Hobbs, "You Too Can Illustrate on the Chalkboard," *Instructor*, April 1963, p. 144. Some of the ideas in this chapter I have gleaned from my experience as a student with the Famous Artists School. The Famous Artists' Cartooning Correspondence Course in which I was enrolled is available from the school at Westport, Connecticut. This is a course I heartily recommend for those who want to go all the way.

Simple Symbols Make Chalk Talk

A study conducted by the United States Navy disclosed that people absorb up to 35% more when an appeal is made to the eye as well as to the ear, and that they retain what they thus learn 55% longer.[1] There can be considerable instructional value in the use of visuals. What is difficult for most teachers is finding the visual that concretely symbolizes specific ideas to be taught. Even with the great numbers of visuals now being produced for use in our Church teaching programs, teachers often find themselves groping for helps. With the needed media not at their fingertips, they often resort to a less effective technique.

A teacher who is qualified with the chalkboard seldom catches himself empty-handed as he walks into the classroom. While preparing lessons, he finds himself on fewer dead-end streets. He is the teacher who naturally undergoes longer and more intensive preparation, but who reaps tenfold results from his efforts. He is the teacher who is a master of detail in his preparation. He is ready to illustrate a representative symbol for many of the ideas he wishes his students to perceive.

This chapter will place at your fingertips twenty-eight simple symbols that, in my observation, are most commonly used in teaching the gospel with chalk.

Make your sketches simple and large. Encourage students to copy them in their notes, using their own creative touch.

The twenty-eight symbols by general categories are:

Books and Records

1. *Closed book*
2. *Open book*
3. *Plates*
4. *Papyrus roll*
5. *Papyrus scroll*
6. *Paper and quill pen*

Buildings

7. *Temple or church*
8. *Home*
9. *Ancient city*

Means of Transportation

10. *Car*
11. *Boat*
12. *Covered wagon*

Objects

13. *Mountain*
14. *Cloud*
15. *Tree*
16. *Grave*
17. *Light bulb*
18. *Stairs*
19. *Money*
20. *Strong drink or Indian pottery*
21. *Sword*
22. *Altar*
23. *Scale*

Animals, Whale, and Bird

24. *Sheep*
25. *Camel*
26. *Horse*
27. *Whale*
28. *Bird*

As in the two previous chapters, on the righthand side in each frame completely redraw everything that appears in the adjoining lefthand frame.

Books and Records

1. *Closed book*

Draw a rectangle tipped on one corner as illustrated in the left-hand box.

1a | 1a

Draw the same size box offset beneath the original rectangle.

1b | 1b

Connect the two boxes with three curved lines, all parallel to each other.

1c | 1c

This symbol could be representative of scriptures, knowledge.

2.   *Open book*

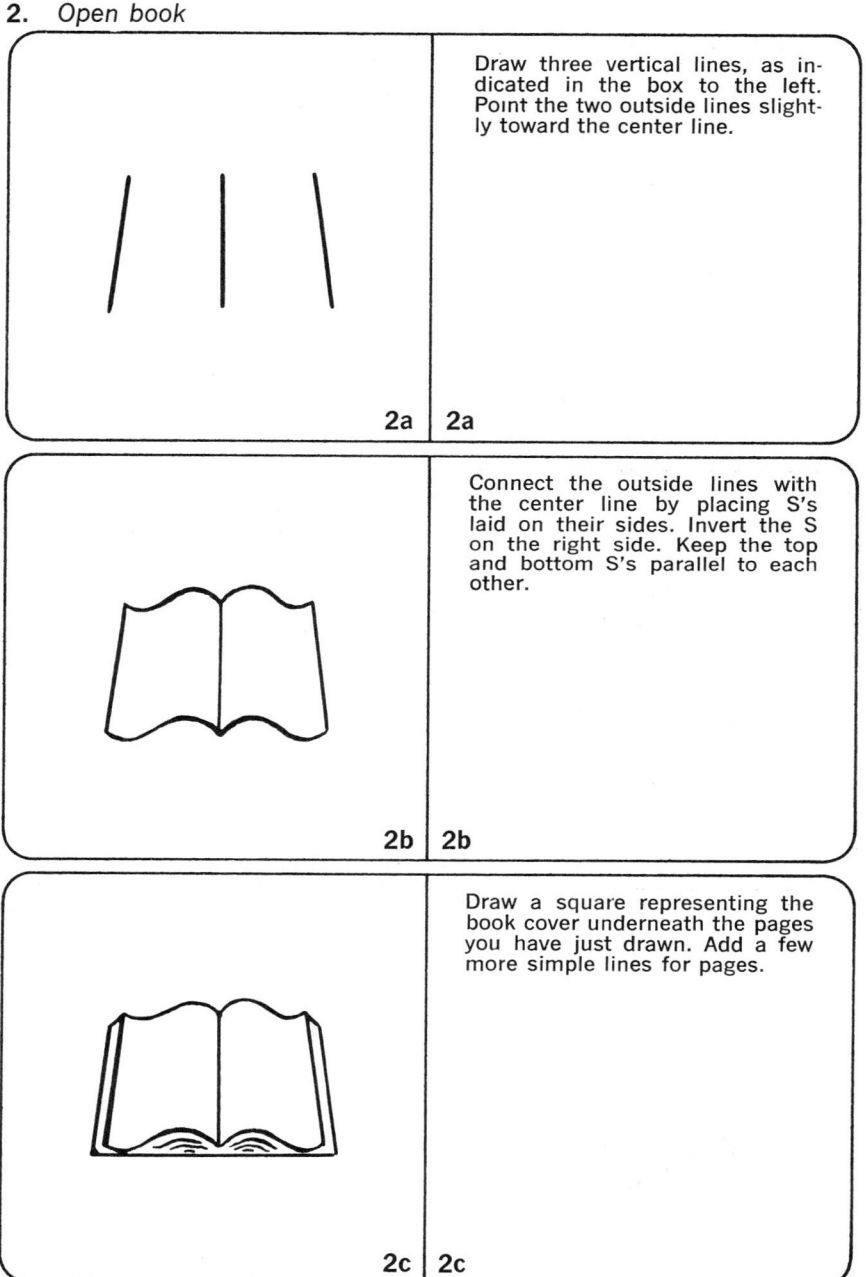

Draw three vertical lines, as indicated in the box to the left. Point the two outside lines slightly toward the center line.

2a | 2a

Connect the outside lines with the center line by placing S's laid on their sides. Invert the S on the right side. Keep the top and bottom S's parallel to each other.

2b | 2b

Draw a square representing the book cover underneath the pages you have just drawn. Add a few more simple lines for pages.

2c | 2c

This symbol could be representative of reading, studying, understanding.

3. Plates

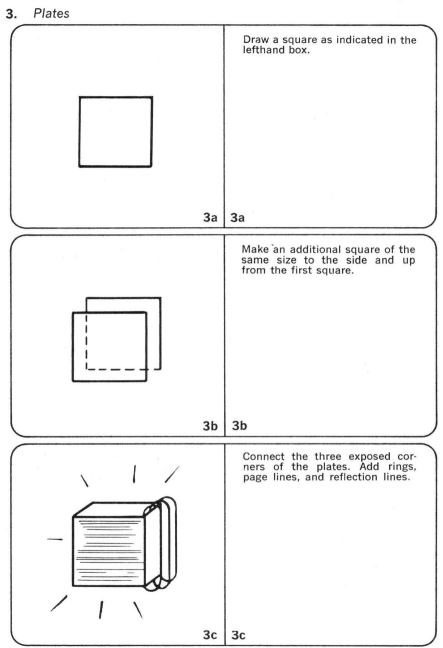

Draw a square as indicated in the lefthand box.

3a | 3a

Make an additional square of the same size to the side and up from the first square.

3b | 3b

Connect the three exposed corners of the plates. Add rings, page lines, and reflection lines.

3c | 3c

This symbol could be representative of golden plates, brass plates of Laban, plates of Ether, Book of Mormon.

4. *Papyrus roll*

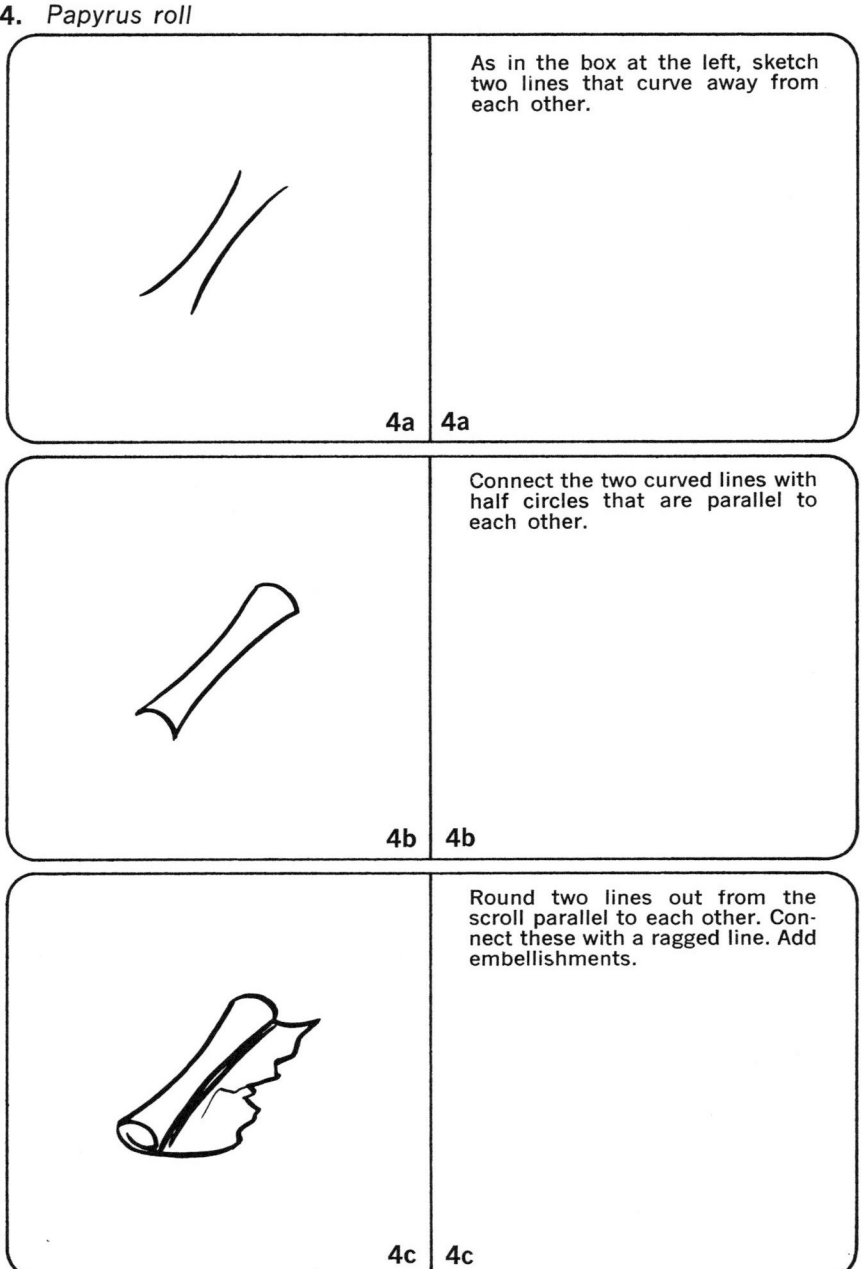

As in the box at the left, sketch two lines that curve away from each other.

4a | 4a

Connect the two curved lines with half circles that are parallel to each other.

4b | 4b

Round two lines out from the scroll parallel to each other. Connect these with a ragged line. Add embellishments.

4c | 4c

This symbol could be representative of lost scriptures, original **Book of Abraham** manuscript, how ancient records were kept.

5. *Papyrus scroll*

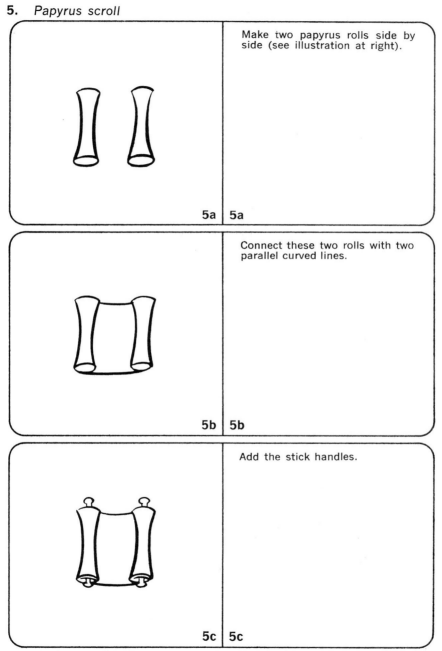

Make two papyrus rolls side by side (see illustration at right).

5a

Connect these two rolls with two parallel curved lines.

5b

Add the stick handles.

5c

This symbol could be representative of the sticks of Judah and Joseph, ancient records, Dead Sea Scrolls, Pentateuch.

6.   *Sheet of paper and quill pen*

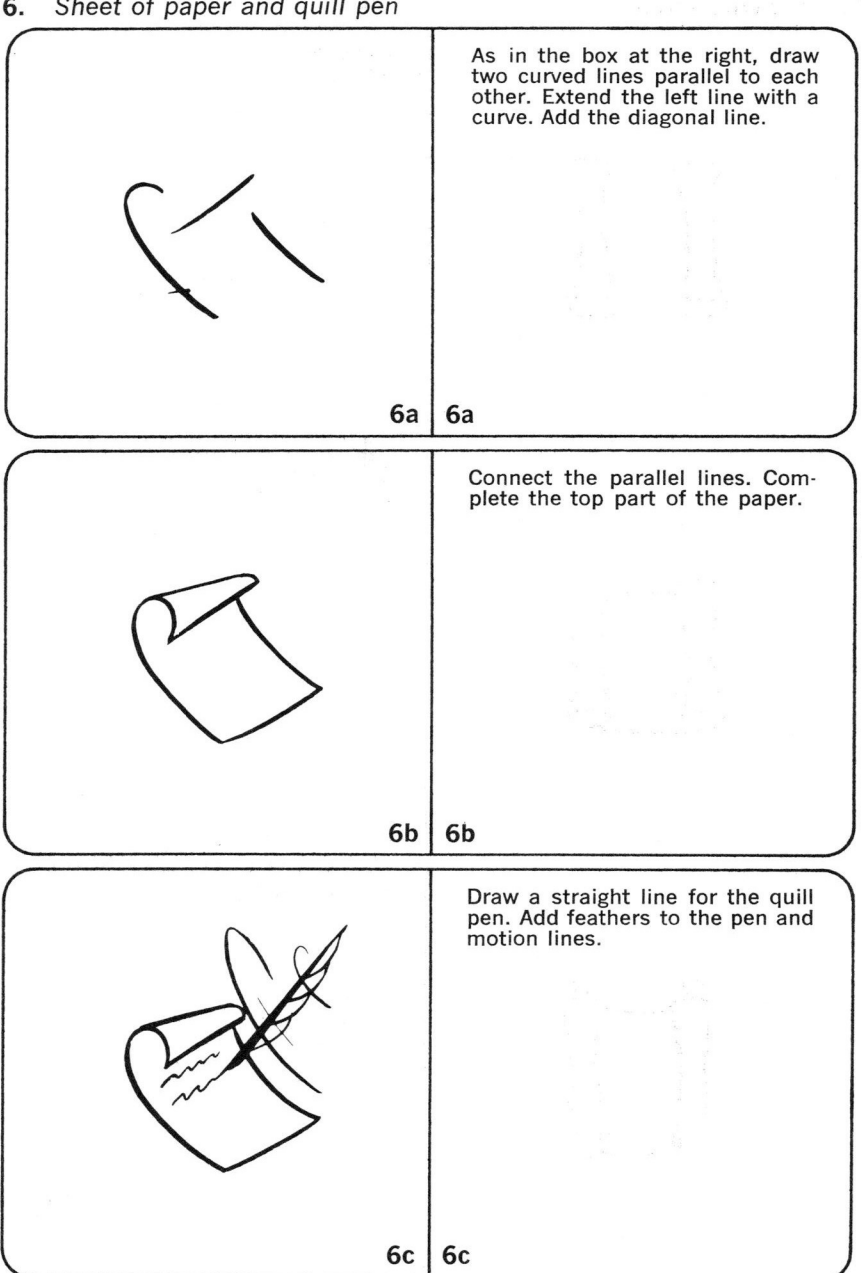

As in the box at the right, draw two curved lines parallel to each other. Extend the left line with a curve. Add the diagonal line.

6a

Connect the parallel lines. Complete the top part of the paper.

6b

Draw a straight line for the quill pen. Add feathers to the pen and motion lines.

6c

This symbol could be representative of writing a letter, writing a life history, a written commitment.

Buildings

7. *Temple or church*

Sketch a flat rectangle.

7a | 7a

Add smaller rectangles at the top.

7b | 7b

Add the spire.

7c | 7c

This symbol could be representative of temple marriage, genealogy work, worship, reverence, Sabbath day.

8. *Home*

Draw a large and small rectangle connecting each other as at the left.

8a | 8a

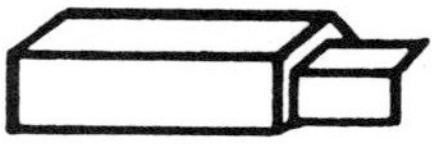

Add a roof to the two parts of the home.

8b | 8b

Finish the sides of the home. Add doors and window.

8c | 8c

This symbol could be representative of family, preparation for marriage, sibling rivalry.

9. *Ancient city*

Draw a section of the ancient city skyline as in the box at the left.

9a | 9a

Try another section of the city skyline as at the left.

9b | 9b

Try putting it all together as at the left.

9c | 9c

This symbol could be representative of Bethlehem, Jerusalem, Nineveh, Jericho, Sodom and Gomorrah (two cities), city of Enoch (add rays of light and cloud beneath), Book of Mormon cities.

Means of Transportation

10. *Car*

	Make a rectangle with rounded ends as illustrated at the left.
10a	10a

	Add the cab to the base of the car.
10b	10b

	Add wheels, window, and embellishments.
10c	10c

This symbol could be representative of travel, reckless driving, dangers of immorality with cars, traveling the road of life, each part of the car may represent a phase of the gospel.

11.   Boat

11a | 11a Make the water and put the hull in it. See picture at left.

11b | 11b Add the mast and sail with a slightly altered triangle.

11c | 11c For Noah's ark, replace the sail with a roof over the hull.

This symbol could be representative of being fishers of men, apostles on Sea of Galilee, Paul sailing for Rome, Lehi coming to America, Columbus coming to America, Noah and the ark.

12. Covered wagon

Make a rectangular box as at the left.

12a | 12a

Place the hoops on the box.

12b | 12b

Add wheels and embellishments.

12c | 12c

This symbol could be representative of pioneers, colonization.

Objects

13. *Mountain*

Draw an outline of a mountain peak as illustrated.

13a | 13a

Add the shading and snow.

13b | 13b

For depth, sketch two declining smaller distant peaks.

13c | 13c

This symbol could be representative of Mount Sinai (Moses), Mount Moriah (Abraham), Enos receiving a witness, faith can move mountains, climbing the mountain of life, the mountain of stern justice.

14. *Cloud*

Try drawing curved and wavy lines.

14a | 14a

Put the curved and wavy lines together in a fluffy shape.

14b | 14b

Add shading and rays of light.

14c | 14c

This symbol could be representative of revelation, exaltation (happy man on a cloud), rain, storm cloud of discouragement, dream (place the cloud around a picture).

15. *Tree*

Turn the cloud sideways (see illustration at left).

15a | 15a

Add the stump and ground.

15b | 15b

For a row of trees, make two light lines pointing toward each other. Use these as guidelines for perspective.

15c | 15c

This symbol could be representative of fall of man (tree of life, tree of knowledge), family tree (genealogy), tree of life (Lehi's dream), allegory of the olive tree (Jacob 5-6), Christ cursing the fig tree.

16.   Grave

	As at the left, make a mound of dirt with an oval above it.
16a	16a

	For humor, give the remains a pair of shoes and a daisy.
16b	16b

HERE LIES SAM	Add the tombstone inscription and embellishments.
16c	16c

This symbol could be representative of death, resurrection, careless driving, smoking, sin.

17. Light bulb

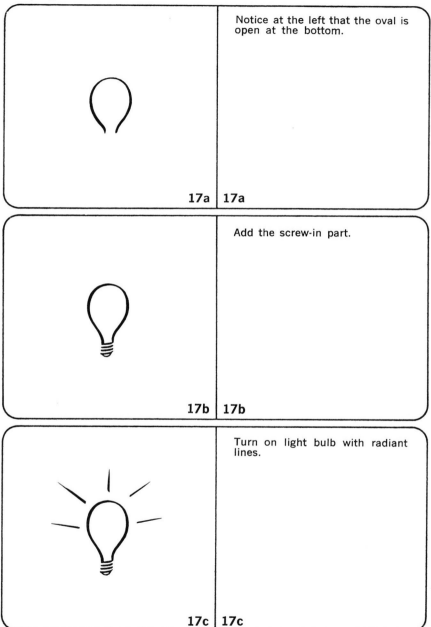

Notice at the left that the oval is open at the bottom.

17a | 17a

Add the screw-in part.

17b | 17b

Turn on light bulb with radiant lines.

17c | 17c

This symbol could **be representative of** intelligence, truth, understanding.

18.   *Stairs*

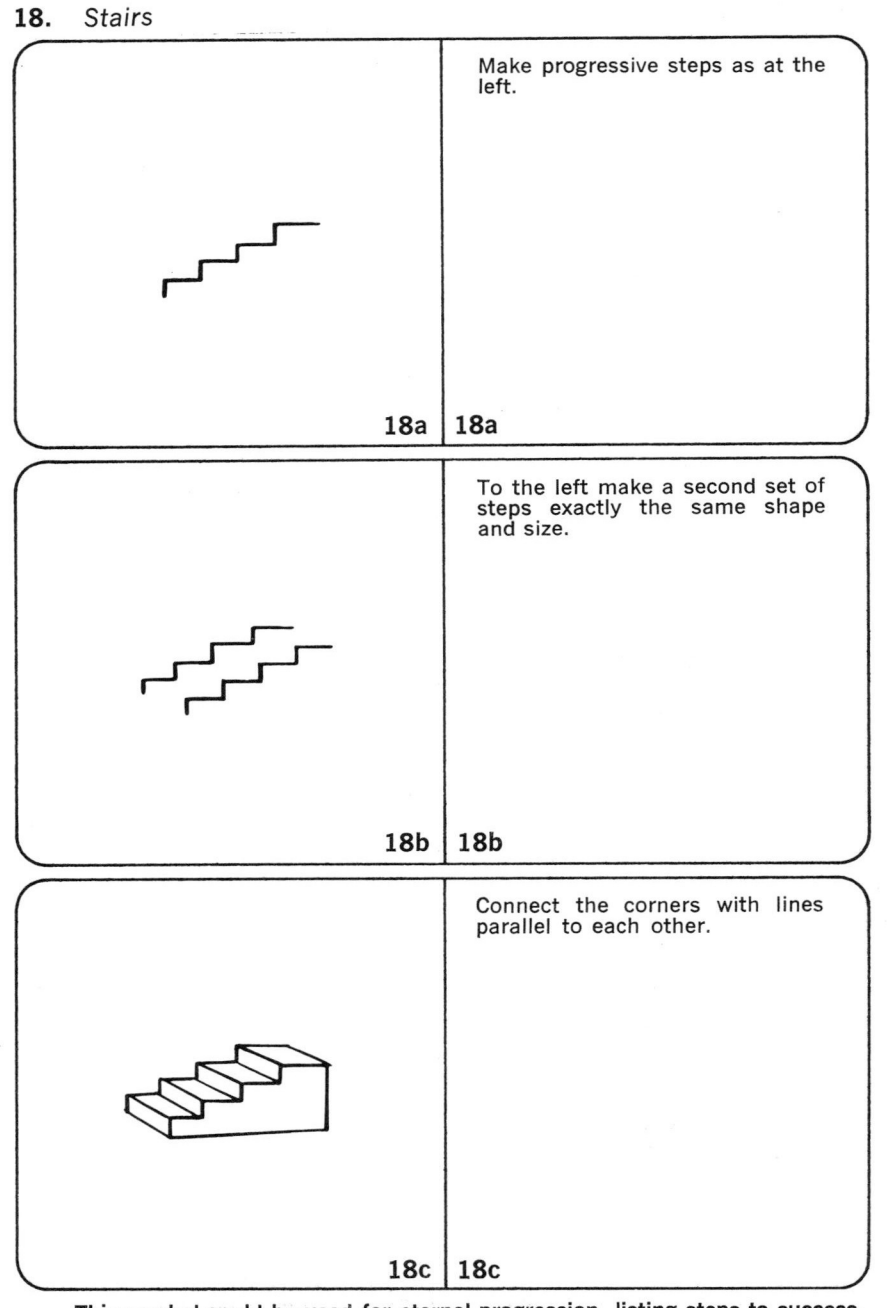

Make progressive steps as at the left.

18a | 18a

To the left make a second set of steps exactly the same shape and size.

18b | 18b

Connect the corners with lines parallel to each other.

18c | 18c

This symbol could be used for eternal progression, listing steps to success, gaining a testimony, repentance.

19. Money

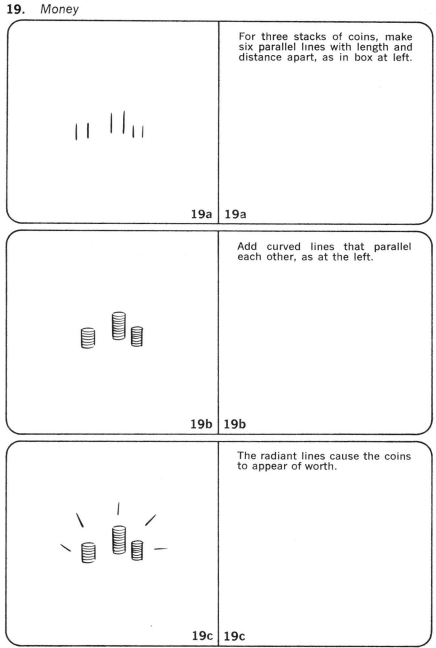

For three stacks of coins, make six parallel lines with length and distance apart, as in box at left.

19a | 19a

Add curved lines that parallel each other, as at the left.

19b | 19b

The radiant lines cause the coins to appear of worth.

19c | 19c

This symbol could be representative of tithing, donations, serving mammon, honesty, Christ betrayed for 30 pieces of silver, choosing proper values (parable of the rich young ruler).

20. *Strong drink or Indian pottery*

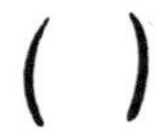

( )

20a | 20a

Make a set of parentheses. See box at left.

20b | 20b

Draw three horizontal curved lines parallel to each other.

20c | 20c

Put on the neck of the bottle and accessories. Add cigarette if teaching Word of Wisdom.

This symbol could be used in teaching the Word of Wisdom. Without the cigarette, the whiskey bottle is transformed into Indian pottery.

21. *Sword*

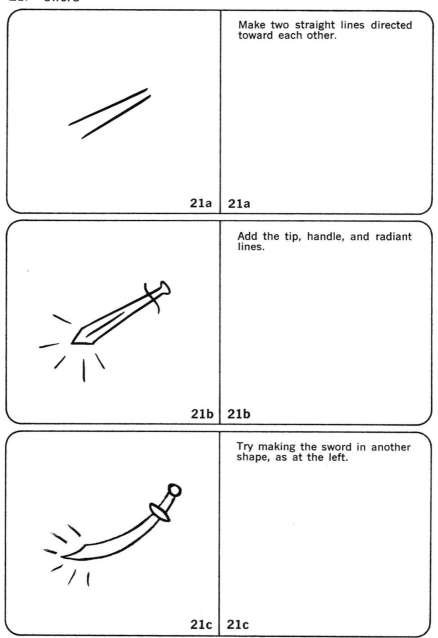

	Make two straight lines directed toward each other.
21a	21a
	Add the tip, handle, and radiant lines.
21b	21b
	Try making the sword in another shape, as at the left.
21c	21c

This symbol could be representative of sword of Laban, sword of truth, war, Book of Mormon battles, commandment not to kill.

22. *Altar*

As at the left, make wavy lines for the sides of the altar. Draw a line for the ground.

22a | 22a

Fill in the altar with rocks.

22b | 22b

Add the sticks and fire.

22c | 22c

This symbol could be representative of law of sacrifice, Adam's sacrifice, sacrifices of Cain and Abel, Abraham's sacrifice, Saul's improper sacrifice.

23. Scale

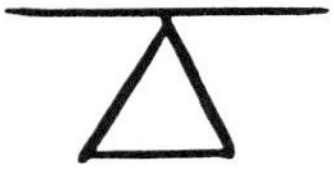

Place a bar on a triangle as illustrated.

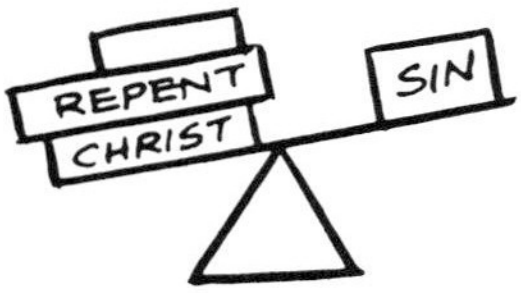

23a | 23a

Now draw the triangle with the bar tilted. Place more or heavier weights on the lower side of the bar.

REPENT
CHRIST
SIN

23b | 23b

Try drawing a different version of the scale as at the left.

23c | 23c

This symbol could be representative of weighing good against evil.

Animals, Whale, and Birds

24. Sheep

24a	Make a fluffy cloud. **24a**
24b	Add eye, ear, and legs. **24b**
24c	Draw a shepherd with sheep. **24c**

This symbol could be representative of story of the good shepherd, the lost sheep, conformity (following the crowd).

25. *Camel*

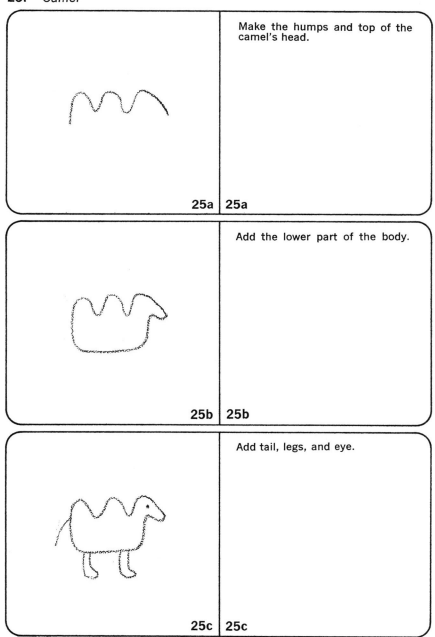

Make the humps and top of the camel's head.

25a | 25a

Add the lower part of the body.

25b | 25b

Add tail, legs, and eye.

25c | 25c

This symbol could be representative of the camel through an eye of the needle, ancient travel, Abraham going from Ur to Canaan, Jacob's travels to and from Haran, the wise men.

26. Horse

As at the left, draw the back and stomach of the horse.

26a | 26a

Add legs and head.

26b | 26b

Add tail, eyes, and nose.

26c | 26c

This symbol could be representative of ancient and modern means of travel.

27. *Whale*

27a	Place a wavy line for water as illustrated. 27a
27b	Place a question mark on its side over the water. 27b
27c	Add tail, eye, mouth, and water spout. 27c

This symbol could be representative of the story of Jonah, the creation, respect for life.

28. *Bird*

Notice the flock of birds at the left. Draw those in this box.

28a | 28a

For a loony bird, make a blob. Add eye, beak, and legs.

28b | 28b

Try drawing the proud and the humble loony bird.

28c | 28c

This symbol could be representative of the story of the gulls and crickets, creation, respect for life or, with the loony bird, pride, humility, or a scapegoat.

Chapter 17
NOTES AND REFERENCES

[1]A. Hamer Reiser, *A Reader for the Teacher,* p. 196; Basil C. Hansen, "Learn to Talk with Chalk," *Instructor,* November 1955, 90:344.

How to Create Your Own Chalkboard Illustrated Lesson

In chapter 15 you studied how to draw the animated stick figure in eight basic positions. Chapter 16 helped you in learning to draw the simple cartoon head with various expressions in dimension. Chapter 17 was intended to assist in drawing simple symbols for chalkboard use, such as books, buildings, means of transportation, objects, and animals. The purpose of the present chapter is to help you apply your newly acquired skills in chalkboard illustrated lessons. In this chapter you will be putting together what was learned in the previous three.

Chalkboard illustrating, when applied to gospel instruction, certainly should not be used as an end in itself. It should be used mainly as a means of stimulating student interest and advancing the students' understanding by concretely symbolizing ideas being taught. Don't overemphasize your illustrations. And a word of caution: *Do not illustrate sacred scenes, such as earthly appearances of the Father and the Son.*

You will find that the subject matter of some lessons does not lend itself to chalk illustrations. Some teachers may not be responsive to this method of teaching. But I have observed that with the right subject matter, the right approach, and the right teacher, almost any type or age group of students is responsive and usually enthusiastically welcomes chalkboard illustrated lessons.

Chalkboard illustrating is but one of many teaching techniques. If this type of lesson gives the desired effect in a given teaching situation, then use it. Otherwise, turn to whatever other method promises to give the greatest effect. You of course should be willing to develop a certain amount of "know-how" if you intend to produce effect with the chalkboard.

There are different degrees to which you might illustrate on the chalkboard when teaching a lesson. In one lesson you might use no more than one simple stick figure. In another lesson you might fill up a large chalkboard with illustrations and notes of clarification.

The first question you should ask in preparation is, "Are there ideas in this lesson that are illustratable?" Make a careful examination of key ideas in scriptures to be used in the lesson or in specific parts of the subject matter. For example, here are two scriptures and a small excerpt from a story. I have underlined those words that might most easily be illustrated. You will notice that nouns are usually the easiest to get hold of.

> *Example 1: Therefore, whosoever heareth these sayings of mine, and doeth them, I will liken him unto a <u>wise man</u>, which build his <u>house</u> upon a <u>rock</u>." (Matthew 7:24.)*

If you have done your homework in the previous chapters, you should be able to draw a wise man and a house resting on a rock. The rest of this story about the house on the rock and sand would probably call for a stupid-looking man with a rickety old house (tilt the sides of the house) on a horizontal line for sand.

> *Example 2: "But when ye <u>pray</u>, use not vain repetitions, as the <u>heathen</u> do: for they think that they shall be heard for their much speaking." (Matthew 6:7.)*

Would it not be a rather simple matter, as you have learned in chapter 15, to draw a stick figure with head bowed in humble prayer while the heathen kneels with head held high?

Example 3: That evening Dad asked me to carry the large box into the house. I was a little fellow only four years old at the time (and small for my age at that!), but I did what he asked. Now can you imagine what was in the box?"

When you draw this idea, remember to give the little boy a big head and a king-sized box.

In your next lesson preparation, look for ideas in the lesson that might be illustratable. It may help to underline them as we have done in the above three examples.

Always remember to illustrate key ideas that are at the heart of the subject matter. The illustrations are justified insofar as they help put over the message you hope to transmit. The illustrations must be directly relevant to your predefined subject matter. Consider the following three examples.

Teacher A prepared a lesson on love, building it around the objective "The students will express greater love to friends."

At the beginning of the class period, Teacher A walked from the back to the front of the classroom, reaching energetically for the chalk. Without saying a word, he sketched two circles on the chalkboard. Within each circle appeared a nose, a mouth, eyes, ears, and a mop of hair. Above the angry face, he wrote *hate*. The pleasant face received the caption *love*.

Teacher A turned to the students and said, "Which of these two people are you?"

The question led into a discussion on what specific acts and thoughts have gone into making up the hateful or the loving faces. The pupils sketched the two illustrations in their notes and received instructions to use their own creative imagination. Each student responded to the respective questions below the illustrated heads, "What causes one to become hateful?" and "What specifically can I do to spread love among my friends?" Later the students left the lesson with specific plans for loving their friends and a commitment to carry out the plans.

Teacher B launched into a lesson about Samson by sketching a head covered with so much hair that only the eyes and nose were visible to the observer. Turning to the class, he said, "While you are drawing this man on the sheet of paper I have given you, let's see if anyone can guess who he is."

With the proper answer revealed, the class discussed the story of Samson and the meaning of his hair. It was brought out that his hair was symbolic of strength. Each student sketched his version of Samson on a plain sheet of paper while the story of the fallen strong man of Israel was related.

Teacher B concluded the class with a discussion about the relationship between the life of Samson and the lives of the students.

A group of sixteen-year-olds were stimulated and determined as they left teacher C's classroom.

"Can't you see me sparkling already?" said Bob to his pal Fred.

"You look happy for a change."

"I got Brother C's message today, Fred. I found a hidden talent—it's smiling! From now on I'm going to smile at every human being I ever see, just to make them happy."

"That's wonderful! I learned I could do something too," mused Fred.

"What did you find, pal?"

"That I can draw!"

Teacher C had presented the lesson "Let your light so shine before men that they might see your good works and glorify your father which is in heaven." Before class he had sketched a burning candle on the chalkboard. A smiling face was sketched in the flame, with radiant lines extending in all directions. With the other students, Bob and Fred had the fun of sketching glowing candles of their own. An outstanding lesson had followed wherein Teacher C taught how the students could find hidden talents within themselves and then use these to make others happy.

On one of the radiant lines extending from this candle, each student had been assigned to indicate a talent he now had determined to develop. On the other radiant lines he listed how he planned to go about developing this talent. This led to a linking assignment that Bob and other students enthusiastically carried out.

Teacher D summarized a lesson about King Noah by sketching a large balloon on the chalkboard. Each student then drew a part of the wicked king's head.

Let's look in on the lesson Will B. Handy is teaching. We will be observing only enough of the lesson to see how symbols can be combined on the chalkboard to give students a visual image of an idea and guide the students toward practicing that idea.

Here is the main idea of the lesson, "We have a responsibility to fulfill moral obligations."

Brother Handy is speaking. "Students, Jonah was commanded by the Lord to preach repentance to the wicked city of Nineveh. Jonah could not bring himself to fulfill this obligation because he unwisely felt that the pagan city of Nineveh should not receive the word of the Lord."

By this time Brother Handy has sketched the city of Nineveh on the left side of the chalkboard, as in the top panel on page 244.

Brother Handy continues. "Jonah therefore ran from his responsibility by sailing for the city of Joppa. What happened next in the story, students?"

George is called on and tells of the ship's being threatened by a great storm, of Jonah's being cast into the sea, and of Jonah's experience with the whale. Brother Handy illustrates with chalk. The students listen, observe, and sketch what they see in their notes.

At the bottom of the board Brother Handy writes, "Jonah, you can't run away from the Lord!" and asks the students to write in their notes their own names followed by "you can't run away from the Lord!"

The city of Nineveh becomes one's moral obligations. The stick figure Jonah becomes the student, representing an urge he might sometimes have of running from a distasteful responsibility. The whale represents the law of justice, who always makes his demands of punishment or blessings, depending on whether an obligation is carried out.

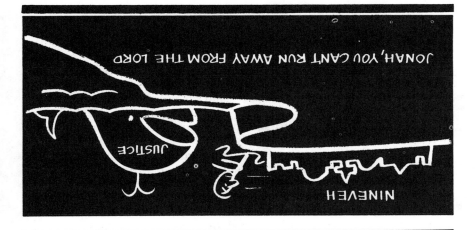

Draw the city of Nineveh and landscape in this box as illustrated above.

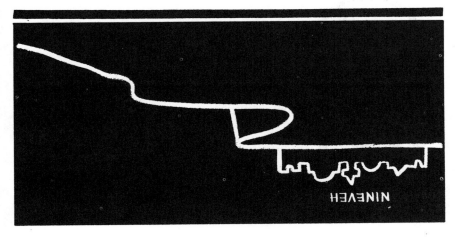

> **Draw Johah and the whale in this box as illustrated on preceding page.**

Brother Handy points out, "Punishment always eventually follows when an obligation is not fulfilled. Blessings follow the fulfillment of responsibility. Justice never fails—no matter how large or small the act may be. Through his ordeal, Jonah repented and was thus spared to fulfill his obligation at Nineveh."

A discussion now follows on why it is necessary to fulfill one's moral obligations.

Concluding the lesson, Brother Handy says, "Students, will you list in your notes under the city of Nineveh your personal obligations? After making the list, go over each item and evaluate how well you are carrying out each obligation. Find your weak area. Set a goal and determine a plan on how to meet this obligation more effectively. I will check with you in three days to see how you are doing."

Brother Handy clarifies the assignment by writing it on the chalkboard and assisting individuals during the study period.

The lesson is now over. Fifteen thoughtful students leave the class with renewed determination to fulfill a specific personal responsibility.

Here is an example of one student's notes:

You might consider using classroom funnies for emphasizing a list of ideas for overview, review, or simply enumeration. For example, let's assume that you are preparing a group of adolescent male students for qualified missionary service. You have prepared a behavioral objective that reads, "At the end of this lesson the students will be able to list six procedures that will help them prepare for qualified missionary service."

The six procedures are:

1. *Pray*
2. *Don't become emotionally involved with girls.*
3. *Choose good friends who do not drink or smoke.*
4. *Study the scriptures.*
5. *Attend all church meetings.*
6. *Pay on honest tithing and save.*

Give each student a plain letter-size sheet of paper. Instruct the students to divide their papers into six sections and number the sections as below:

1	2
3	4
5	6

As you present each idea on the chalkboard in sequence from one to six, the students copy the illustration in their notes. While drawing the illustration in each square, clarify through discussion the implications of the idea to be practiced. The completed chalkboard illustrations might appear something like this:

What you probably need now is practice in preparing your own chalkboard illustrated lessons. Below is a lesson objective, two scripture verses *supporting* the objective, and a statement of ideas that further expands the subject matter of the lesson. See what you can do in working out illustrations on the chalkboard for the lesson objective and supporting ideas. You may want to expand on the ideas presented here.

Objective (non-behavioral)

The students will gain insights as to how they can come closer to Christ through trials in life.

Scripture

"I am the good shepherd, and know my sheep, and am known of mine." (John 10:14.)

"And when . . . the good shepherd . . . putteth forth his own sheep, he goeth before them, and the sheep follow him: for they know his voice." (John 10:4-5.)

Additional Ideas for the Lesson

In Christ's day shepherds in Palestine had small flocks of sheep. Along the narrow trails the shepherd would lead the way by going first. Each sheep would have his own place in line and would follow along behind the master. Each sheep had a personal name given at birth by the shepherd. The master would train the sheep to come to him simply by the call of its name. Often the shepherd would learn to love his sheep.

On one occasion a shepherd was carrying a lamb in his arms. The lamb had a splint on its left hind leg. The leg was broken. When asked how the leg got broken, the shepherd admitted that he had broken it intentionally with his staff to teach the lamb obedience. The shepherd said, "I was teaching the lamb, whom I had named Jonathan, that he was to hold his place in line while we traversed narrow trails. With many remindings Jonathan persisted in breaking from the flock and running away. The last time he ran away and I finally caught up with him, I broke his leg. Then I took him in my arms and loved him. I set the bone, placed the splint on his leg, and will carry him until the leg is healed. This way he will learn the will of his master. When I call "Jonathan," he will come."

The Good Shepherd, Christ, allows trials to come into our lives in order that we may be humbled and learn to know His voice.

The challenge to you as a teacher is to begin using chalkboard illustrations in helping to put over lessons you teach more effectively. Here are some points to remember in preparing and presenting chalkboard illustrated lessons.

1. Define the lesson objective, or main idea, and identify the ideas to be taught.
2. Underline key words that are important in getting over the message. The words you underline must be illustratable. Often an illustrated object can be used to symbolize an abstract idea, such as a ring representing the endlessness of eternity.
3. Select from the words that you have underlined those that can be simply illustrated and are most relevant to the ideas you hope to teach.
4. Practice sketching out these ideas on a pad of paper. Simplify and refine your sketches.
5. Practice drawing the final illustration(s) on the chalkboard.

6. When presenting the illustrated lesson, it is usually a good practice to involve the students by having them copy the illustrations in their notes.

Remember, anyone can illustrate on the chalkboard who has the "I want to" and the "I am going to" attitude.

CHAPTER 19

Other Uses of Chalk in Teaching

Years ago when I was beginning to study cartooning, I decided to try out my very limited knowledge on an Old Testament class. The lesson to be taught was entitled "Joshua, the Conqueror." I wanted to emphasize Joshua's courage and relate this principle to the students' lives. Many of the pupils were boys with an eye for football. To start the lesson I therefore fumbled for a piece of chalk and made a feeble effort to sketch Joshua's determined face framed in a football helmet as battle gear. I had to label my masterpiece *Joshua* and *football helmet* and explain where his eyes were before convincing students it was not a rabbit sleeping under a rug. Yet in this lesson I made a marvelous discovery. All eyes were glued to the chalkboard. The students were intensely interested to learn of Joshua's courage in playing the game of life. As a result of chalkboard illustrating, the students were *motivated*. Now that you have completed chapters 15-18, you may have even better success stories to tell about the usefulness of illustrating lessons on the chalkboard. But there is more to be said about uses of chalk. This chapter is intended to help you use the chalkboard effectively in other ways than freehand illustrations.

Directing Discussions: Organizing with Steps and Lists

A very common and useful technique of teaching is the discussion method, which is considered in chapters 9 and 21. Organization and control of course help to make effective discussions. And appropriate use of the chalkboard can help you organize and control this method with students.

Many teachers seem to have difficulty keeping their discussion problem in mind during a lesson. There is often even greater difficulty for students to keep sight of the discussion problem and refrain from bringing up unrelated issues. For this reason, when presenting a question for discussion, *write the question on the chalkboard.* Then recognize and honor student answers by listing the responses under the question. For example:

WHAT ARE THE FRUITS OF GAMBLING?   (*Discussion question presented by teacher*)

1. LOSS OF MONEY

2. YOU BECOME A SLAVE TO HABIT   (*Student responses*)

3. YOUR FAMILY WILL DISRESPECT YOU

4. YOU WILL LOSE RESPECTABLE FRIENDS

Figure 1

With this approach, the students' eyes are directed toward the discussion problem and they can see the relationship of one response to another. Repetition of responses is also minimized because students can see the ideas that have been contributed.

Show the relationship of controversial issues by dividing them into contrasting lists. After the pros and cons or do's and don'ts have been voiced by the students and listed on the board by the teacher, the contrasting issues can be weighed against each other and a decision made as to which position is most acceptable. For example, in a class of seventeen-year-olds some of the students feel that it is all right to go steady in high school while others disagree. Rather than the teacher saying, "You shouldn't go steady in high school," he writes the questions in figure 2 at the top of the chalkboard, and as students express pros and cons, he writes them down.

When everyone has had an opportunity to voice an opinion, the teacher gives his pupils the responsibility of being objective in evaluating the two lists. It is obvious that the objective thinker will see weaker premises in the lefthand column. Students thus bring themselves to the proper conclusions. As you can see, the teacher must be skillful in directing the discussion and evaluation so the students reach the right conclusion.

All students should write these chalkboard lists in their notes to involve pupils more fully in the important learning process of *doing.*

Should We Go Steady in High School?

Yes!
Why?
1. You can always depend on a date.
2. It gives you a sense of security.
3. You have someone to talk over problems with.
4. It makes you feel important.

No!
Why?
1. It ties you down.
2. Might break up and get feelings hurt.
3. Parents don't want you to.
4. The Church discourages it.
5. Danger of getting serious too early.
6. Danger of close relationships that lead to necking and petting.

Figure 2

When discussing steps one must take to achieve a given goal, always list these steps on the chalkboard under a main heading—for example, "How can I gain a testimony of the Book of Mormon?" (Figure 3.)

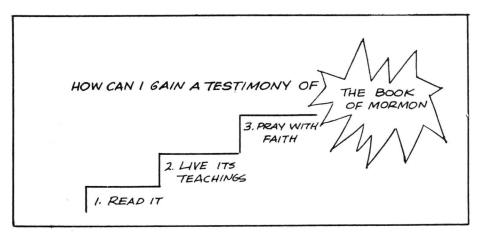

Figure 3

Making Charts and Maps

The chart in figure 4 is an authentic reproduction that was created by a Sunday School teacher in a ward in central Utah as he was explaining to us the law of eternal progression.

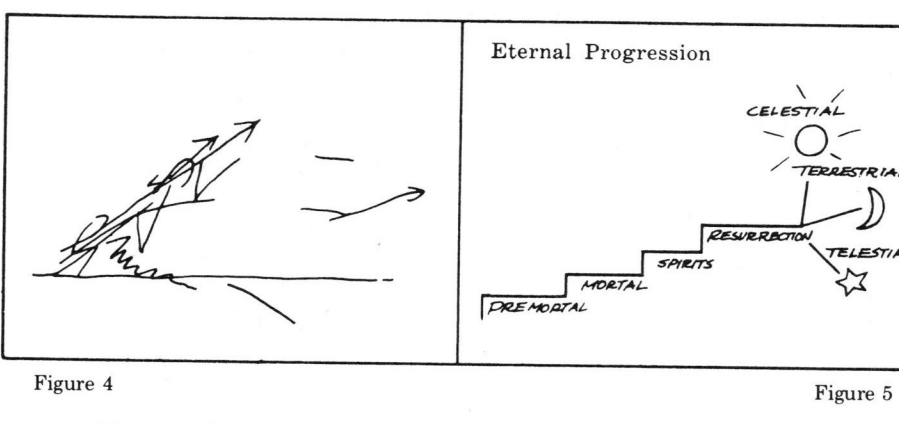

Figure 4

Figure 5

This teacher had undoubtedly failed to draw out the chart be-fore presenting his ideas to the class. He had not previously thought out the details of his lesson, and so he cluttered our minds as well as the board.

Don't you agree that the chart in figure 5 on eternal progression, although simple, is more instructive?

When planning a lesson, visualize the entire chalkboard, including how it will look at various stages of the lesson presentation as well as at the end of the presentation. It is often useful to draw out the schemes on paper beforehand. If you are going to put much on the board during the lesson, it is usually a good idea to start at the upper lefthand corner and work down and to the right.

Here are a few other helps in making effective chalk charts and maps.

1. A yardstick and chalk compass are helpful tools when accuracy is needed.

2. Make charts comparative in effect, distance, time, weight, cost, distribution, and proportion. Maps should be comparative in size. Students learn a new concept most effectively when they can see it or are able to relate it to something they already know. On a distance chart, rather than indicating that "one cubit equals eighteen inches," indicate that "one cubit equals eighteen inches, which is from the tip of the elbow to the tip of the finger." Then if the student looks at his forearm, he has a pretty good idea of how long a cubit is. Rather than indicating on a cost chart that "one silver New Testament talent equals $1,146," put "one silver New Testament talent equals $1,146, which would buy a nice used car or fifty-seven dresses." Rather than just draw-ing a map of Palestine on the board and saying, "This country is 120 miles long," draw the map of Palestine over the state in whch you are living, along with the number of miles wide and long.

Students who have traveled within their state can readily perceive the size of Palestine when they see the comparison.

The following bar graph on *effect* helps students see themselves in relation to the greatness of Christ and other magnanimous people. It can also serve as a motivating item in teaching students their unlimited potential. Place the outline of the chart on the board, and then ask students who they feel are the five greatest people who have ever lived. As names are given, write them at the bottom of the chart. Have them write their own name under the last vertical column in their notes.

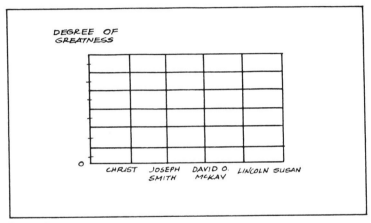

Figure 6

Holding a one-half inch piece of chalk sideways in your fingers, start drawing a bar graph upward above Christ's name. Let the students evaluate by telling you when to stop. Do this with each of the other names. Above the student's own name, have him mark with a heavy bar the distance toward greatness in comparison to the other names on the chart that he feels he has now achieved. With a lighter line, have him indicate his potential in his life. Discuss the potential of individuals in the classroom.

3. When a needed wall map is not available, sketch your own on the chalkboard. This is greatly simplified by using the dot system and can be sketched during a lesson as students observe. From a Bible or atlas find the map that is desired to be sketched on the chalkboard. Trace the basic outline of this map onto a plain sheet of paper. Place dots on the main points of the outline you have drawn and study the relationship of the dots to each other. For practice, take another plain sheet of paper and

place the dots in the same areas as on the outline map (figure 7). Now draw a line from the dot to the next to complete the outline map (see figure 8). Try copying the outline map by placing dots on the chalkboard, the same distances apart but on a larger scale. Draw lines from one dot to the next as you did on the paper outline map, and the chalkboard outline map is completed. Cities, lakes, rivers, and mountains can be added (as in figures 11 and 14).

Colored chalk can be very effective on chalkboard map drawing. Bright orange might be used to emphasize a city, river, or route. In presenting a map-o-graph (history explained graphically on a map), the ocean could be in blue; fertile land, green; cities, white; written historical explanations, bright yellow. Color is eye-catching and thus useful in chalkboard work.

Figure 7

Figure 8

Figure 9

Figure 10

Figure 11

Figure 12

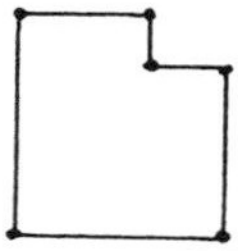

Figure 13

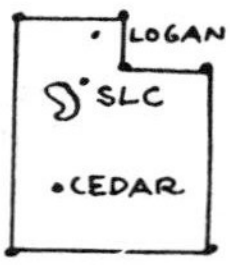

Figure 14

To make a permanent outline map, place the ready available small map in an opaque projector. Shine this map on the chalkboard, trace the outline, and then paint over the lines with white enamel paint. An advantage to this type of map is that the eraser removes temporary chalkwork but not the outline map.

A semi-permanent map can be done in beautiful color with chalk paste. Chalk paste is easily made by pulverizing the chalk and adding enough water to make the powder into a paste. Tint to the desired hue and value with water colors. Paint the chalk paste on the outline of a map or picture with a brush. The chalk paste is easily washed off the chalkboard with water when the illustration has served its purpose.

Emphasizing the Lesson Objective and Thought-Provoking Statements

An idea in a lesson stated in the form of a question tends to put the students' minds immediately in motion looking for an answer. Abraham Lincoln said, "I like the question mark because it has a hook on it." The key idea you are talking about is no secret and should not necessarily be hidden from the learners. It is a good idea to let people know where they are going. Therefore, place the simple question on the chalkboard and then shoot for the bull's-eye, which is an answer to the question raised. Any one of the following questions could lead to effective lessons.

1. How can I know God lives?
2. What is a covenant people?
3. What if I make a mistake? (Repentance.)
4. Where have I been? (Premortal life.)
5. What in the world are you doing for heaven's sake? (Genealogy.)
6. Too much too soon? (Dating and early marriages.)

Remember to let the chalkboard help you put over the ideas to be taught.

If you have a point you would like to emphasize, dramatize it by writing it on the chalkboard. For example:

1. Start out a lesson with a large question mark on the chalkboard. Use this to lead the students into the objective.

2. When you are discussing a principle of the gospel and you want the students to be more energetic in defending the point, write on the board, "So what?" or "Are you sure?"

3. At the conclusion of a lesson on Christ's crucifixion, write on the board, "Christ died for you; would you willingly live for Him?"

Outlining Units or Blocks of Study

As an overview of the unit or block of material to be covered, the outline helps the students to see where they are going. Assignments can be included in the outline so that students who desire to work ahead will know what is expected of them. It is generally a poor practice to start out each lesson with an outline. This can be monotonous and, if of any length, consumes valuable class time.

Using the outline to review a block of work can be effective. It helps to re-establish relationships that have been studied earlier in one's thinking.

Making Assignments

One way to present an assignment is to *write it on the chalkboard* so that students can see it, ask questions for clarifications, and copy it in their notes.

Directing and Scoring Instructional Games

The chalkboard is probably the best scoreboard for instructional games, because it is readily available and its marks can be easily added or erased. Instructions of any length might be written on the board previous to class time. Chapter 11 presents instructional games.

Making Summaries and Conclusions

A teacher should ordinarily end a lesson with a summary where conclusions are drawn on the ideas considered. Summaries are naturally more conclusive when the students can see as well as hear what has been decided. Written summaries assist the student in carrying from the class a unified message. What is written on the chalkboard could well be statements of action that the students might take in practicing the principles considered in class.

Presenting Detailed Illustrations, Charts, Maps, and Guide Lines

1. The *grid* is useful in transferring maps, illustrations, or charts to or from the chalkboard on a larger or smaller scale. It can be done quickly and accurately by teacher or students. It is a process of drawing vertical and horizontal lines over the original illustration. Similar lines are drawn on a larger or smaller scale on the chalkboard or plain paper. The grid lines are then used as a guide in redrawing the illustration.

When transferring from a small illustration to the chalkboard, draw one-inch squares on the smaller picture (see figure 15). Make squares on the chalkboard according to the size desired, and then copy the picture on the chalkboard (see figure 16) and erase the guidelines.

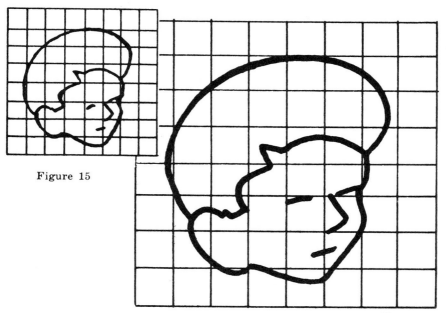

Figure 15

Figure 16

When transferring from a chalkboard illustration to a letter-size sheet, reverse the process.

2. The *stencil* is useful in copying pictures directly on the chalkboard. Trace or draw the desired picture freehand on paper, oilcloth, or an inexpensive window shade. If an enlargement is desired, use the grid method. Punch an outline of small holes on the paper at $\frac{3}{4}$-inch intervals with a $\frac{1}{4}$-inch punch. Holes can be punched with a ballpoint pen. The broken edges must face away from the chalkboard when the transfer is made, however. Hold the stencil against the chalkboard and pat it with a chalk-dusted eraser. Remove the pattern and connect the dots.

3. To obtain long *guide lines,* powder a string by running it over a piece of chalk. A person at each end of the board holds the ends of the string tightly against the board. Flip the string, and the chalk line transfers to the chalkboard. These lines can be used in dividing the chalkboard into sections and for guide lines in detailed lettering.

4. The *templet* is useful for tracing outlines of objects such as trees, human silhouettes, and maps. The value of a templet is ac-

curacy and being able repeatedly to sketch an identical object. Draw an outline of the desired object on a piece of plywood or other hard material. Cut it out with a coping saw or jig saw. Screw a handle on the back for easy manipulation. Place the templet on the chalkboard and trace the outline with chalk (see figure 17).

Figure 17.

5. The *opaque projector* is one of the most effective methods for enlarging detailed pictures, charts, and maps. It is done simply by placing the picture in the projector, adjusting and focusing the picture on the chalkboard to the larger size desired, and then tracing the picture. With an opaque projector, the room should be darkened. The picture can then be colored in with colored chalk or chalk paste.

Some Helpful Hints

1. Unless what you have to put on the chalkboard is detailed, complicated, or elaborate, sketch it while the students observe. This adds interest to the illustration. It also makes it possible for students to respond in their notes along with you in simplified steps.

2. When illustrating or writing, sketch rapidly only when the students are not copying the symbols. When students are copying, do the illustration or written work methodically in steps.

3. Talk while you sketch. For example: "Here is the door. It is the way to eternal life. What must you do to open it?" or "This stick man represents the Good Shepherd who is ever thoughtful of his flock. This sheep is Bill. The little one is Beverly."

4. As was stated earlier, start on the upper lefthand side of the chalkboard, progressing down and to the right. This is important for neatness and organization.

5. Unless you are an excellent penman with longhand, you might print your words on the chalkboard. Make each letter large and wide. While writing phrases, read them to the class to assure understanding of what has been written.

6. Do not spend long periods of time writing on the chalkboard.

7. While writing, stretch out your writing arm and stand away from the chalk so the pupils can see what has been written. Write as rapidly as you can write neatly.

8. Remove written work from the chalkboard immediately after it has served its purpose.

9. Keep the chalkboard, erasers, and chalk tray clean.

10. It is generally better not to place permanent pictures or posters on or over the chalkboard. This lessens the usability of the chalkboard. Further, the permanent illustration may not relate to the lesson objective after a given lesson or unit has been taught.

11. Do not have a thought for the day or other material on the board unless it supports the lesson objective. Every concept written or spoken in a lesson should support the objective—otherwise, the mind becomes cluttered and confused with the complexity of unrelated concepts.

12. Squeaking chalk is annoying. Change the angle or break the chalk and use the broken end.

13. As a reminder, train your students to be chalkboard users by giving them every possible opportunity to write and sketch on the chalkboard.

Summary Outline

There are several chalkboard uses and techniques other than freehand illustrating. Some of these are:

1. Directing discussions—organizing steps and lists.
2. Making charts and maps.
3. Emphasizing the lesson objective and thought-provoking statements.
4. Outlining units or blocks of study.
5. Making assignments.
6. Directing and scoring instructional games.
7. Making summaries and conclusions.
8. Presenting detailed illustrations, charts, maps, and guidelines, using:

    a. Grid method.
    b. Chalkboard stencil.
    c. Guidelines for dividing the chalkboard into sections or for detailed lettering.
    d. Templet.

e.   Opaque and overhead projectors.

A good quality chalkboard should be made available in every classroom and home in the Church, because it has so many potentially effective uses while being inexpensive and easy to maintain.

CLASSIFIED METHODS OF TEACHING

PART

4

Producing Effect by Using a Variety of Teaching Methods

The following three chapters (21, 22, and 23) are intended for use by the teacher in preparing lessons. A chart has been provided on pages 269-71 for referral to the fifty-six methods explained in these chapters.

The chart serves to help you, the teacher, try new procedures, expanding your repertoire of methods. The chart can also be helpful partly to evaluate the extent to which you are inventive or stereotyped in the use of various teaching methods.

The fifty-six teaching methods are presented in a classified manner to help you find them quickly and organize your plan for teaching a lesson with dispatch. However, you should use a good deal of adaptation to what is offered on these printed pages. Any method you use should be intrinsically a part of *you*. Use the suggested methods simply as a help to enlarge upon your own techniques and teaching style. Try to use a variety of teaching methods.

Avoid the pitfall of pigeonholing your teaching procedures by saying, "In this lesson I will use the general discussion method and in that lesson I will use the chalkboard." Rather, think and plan in terms of how you might combine methods to strengthen instructional power. Your task is to help make the excellencies of the gospel secure in your students' experiences.

Whatever gives the greatest power to influence in each teaching moment should be acted upon by you. Don't let your mechanics show while teaching. Remember that a key source of power is the Spirit of God in man. Maintain a firm grasp on the message in chapter 1 of generating power through spiritual excellence. I also suggest that you once again refer to chapter 6, "Organizing for Instruction," as well as the teaching methods chart as you set forth to plan your next lesson.

In considering the fifty-six teaching methods that follow, it would be well to take into account the interrelationships among the teaching components presented in the introductory chapter. As was suggested in the Introduction, these components, which exist in all teaching situations, are *teacher, student, subject matter,* and *materials.* How these components and their many parts are organized in process is what we call teaching methods. The fifty-six teaching methods represent fifty-six basic ways of organizing for instruction. A method should never be prepared without carefully considering the qualities of *all four* components and their interrelationships as they are to be dealt with in class.

As you plan your procedures for instruction, try to maintain a balance among the four teaching components of teacher, student, subject matter and materials.[1] By balance I do not mean to give them equal emphasis. Rather, give appropriate distribution of focus to each component and its relevant parts. For example, materials might be de-emphasized on some occasions to attain balance. Mark Hopkins' best moment in teaching might have been in the use of only a log for materials. On another occasion the entire lesson might consist of an instructional movie, thus giving considerable emphasis to the use of materials.

Unfortunately imbalance often occurs in the use of teacher, student, subject matter, and materials in teaching situations.

One teacher of young adults over-emphasized the subject matter by means of rigid theological exposition. With excessive attention to the ideas being taught, the teacher was almost unaware that students were sitting before him. He appeared to give no thought to the students' needs, interests, feelings and understandings. Some of the students could not even understand what he was talking about. He used no materials nor variety of method that might have strengthened his presentation. He simply talked to his subject matter, pleasing himself abundantly.

Another teacher was so wrapped up with gimmicks to entertain his students that the purposeful use of the subject matter was hardly definable. This teacher, along with many less gimmick-oriented teachers, would likely be quick to puppet a commonly expressed cliche, "I don't teach subject matter; I teach students," as if subject matter were simply not a part of his teaching. This teacher used a variety of techniques but provided little meaningful substance to his subject matter.

Still another teacher found that pictures held the attention of her five-year-old students. So lesson after lesson she limited her instructional materials to pictures, disavowing the chalkboard, filmstrips, overhead projector, and many other materials that might have given the children a less stereotyped experience.

Yet another teacher of an adult class insisted on having an overhead projector to use in every lesson he taught.

I have seen teachers get on pet subject hobby horses, such as the Word of Wisdom, dating, tithing, or spirituality, and run the particular subject matter into the ground.

All of these improprieties suggest imbalance that can limit instructional power.

Your challenge as you prepare lessons and teach is to have a firm grasp on the key elements of your *subject matter*, which is defined by the lesson objective; to understand and be sensitive to the needs, interests, feelings and understandings of your *students;* to draw upon whatever *materials* might best be used to initiate the students into the subject matter; and to organize all of these into methods best suited to your personality that will give students blended meaningful learning experiences.

May the Lord bless you as you proceed with such a magnificent challenge.

Chapter 20
NOTES AND REFERENCES

[1]For a more detailed description on Balance, see Charles R. Hobbs, "Balance in Teaching," *BYU Studies,* Winter 1972, 12:209-222.

Teaching Methods Chart

Instructions

Skim over chapters 21, 22, and 23; then return to the Teaching Methods Chart.

Place a check mark on the chart to the right of each method you can possibly use. This will help orient you to the methods at your disposal and will also alleviate reading fifty-six methods each time you use the chart. Note that the methods are categorized by *Student, Teacher,* and *Materials Centered* methods and listed in alphabetical order.

When preparing a lesson, write the lesson title in the space at the top of the first column of the chart, under *Name of Lesson.* In this same column, color in the square adjacent to each method you plan to use in the lesson. At least three to five methods would ordinarily be used in each lesson presentation. For example, the chalkboard might be used in a discussion period, the flipboard could be used to enhance a lecture.

Some teachers may choose to fill in the chart after the lesson as a procedure of evaluation. In this event, examination of the chart and study of reference sources should still be used during lesson planning.

When preparing the second lesson, write the lesson title in the second space at the top of the second column of the chart, following the same procedure as indicated above. Continue this procedure throughout the course. In time the chart should indicate that you are using a variety of methods, not only in each lesson, but from lesson to lesson, and that you are continually trying new methods. The chart will also bring out certain stereotypes in your teaching.

Naturally, some methods are justifiably used more frequently than others. Discussion, note-taking, chalkboard, and storytelling are examples of methods that might be used frequently.

As you discover and develop methods that are not listed, write them in the blank spaces provided so they will not be forgotten (see chapters 6 and 20 for further instruction in planning teaching methods).

TEACHING METHODS CHART		CHECK EACH METHOD YOU CAN POSSIBLY USE	TEXT REFERENCE								
METHOD											
STUDENT CENTERED	1. Assignments, Linking		273, 145								
	2. Brainstorming		273								
	3. Buzz Sessions		274								
	4. Case Study		276								
	5. Debates, Student		279								
	6. Discussion, General		279, 118								
	7. Discussion, Panel		280								
	8. Discussion, Problem-solving		281, 111								
	9. Discussion, Question Box		281								
	10. Examinations		282								
	11. Field Trips		285								
	12. Games, Instructional		286, 131								
	13. Home, Class Coordinated Methods		287, 55								
	14. Inquiry Techniques		287, 59								
	15. Inventories		290								
	16. Memorizing		291								
	17. Note Taking		292								
	18. Programed Instruction		293								
	19. Questioning Techniques		294								
	20. Questioning, Rapid Fire		295								
	21. Reading Orally		296								
	22. Reports and talks		297								
	23. Role Playing, Pre-structured		299								
	24. Role Playing, Spontaneous		300								
	25. Singing, Instructional		301, 121								
	26. Study Periods		302								
	27. Testimonies		303								
	28. Tutorial		303								
	29. Worksheets		304, 155								
TEACHER CENTERED	30. Demonstration		307								
	31. Jokes and Puns		308, 27								
	32. Lecture		308								
	33. Preassessment and Evaluation		309								
	34. Reading Orally		310, 296								
	35. Storytelling		310, 91								
	36. Summarizing		312								
	37. Visiting Authority		313								
MATERIALS CENTERED	38. Bulletin Boards		317								
	39. Chalkboard, General Uses		319, 251								
	40. Chalkboard Illustrations		319, 171-250								
	41. Charts and Maps		320, 253								
	42. Displays, Table and Mobiles		325								
	43. Filmstrips and Sound Filmstrips		327								
	44. Flannelboard		328								
	45. Flash Cards		329								
	46. Flip Board and Groove Board		330								
	47. Motion Pictures		331								
	48. Object Lessons		332								
	49. Opaque Projections		333								
	50. Overhead Transparency Projections		333								
	51. Pictures		335								
	52. Posters		336								
	53. Puppet Shows		337								
	54. Records, Dramatized and Music		337								
	55. Tape Recordings		338								
	56. Television-Video Tape Recordings		339								

CHAPTER 21

Student-Centered Methods

(During instruction the student develops the ideas to be taught with guidance from the teacher.)

1. **Assignments, Linking**

This is a well-thought out and clearly defined task suggested by the students, or teacher, wherein the pupils are to practice the truths they have come to understand and accept through instruction. For the student, this type of assignment links the classroom with the outside world of reality. It brings students to perform, usually out of class, the principles studied in class. The students are led into becoming *doers* of the ideas taught them. Helps are presented in Chapter 12.

    a. Examples of how to use linking assignments, pages 145-46.

    b. Techniques that might be used as bases for linking assignments, pages 147-50.

2. **Brainstorming**

When brainstorming, students join together informally in a group with the purpose of solving a problem through uninhibited informal discussion.

This technique is effective in arriving at linking assignments, creating new ideas for lessons, planning special class projects, and solving specific student problems.

There are five steps a leader should follow to insure effective results in a brainstorming session. They are:

    a. *Instruct students how to brainstorm.* Do this as an introduction to the brainstorming session.

b. *State the problem.* Then write it on the chalkboard. Present only one problem, and see that it is specific and clearly defined. Instruct students that ideas are to be given on this problem, and none other, throughout the brainstorming session.

c. *Carry out free thought expression.* When the problem is understood, students should be instructed to contribute any idea as a solution that comes to mind, no matter how foolish or far-fetched it may seem to be. An odd idea may suggest a better contribution to someone else. Every suggestion should be written on the chalkboard. Fill the chalkboard with ideas. During the free thought expression, ideas are absolutely not to be criticized. No evaluations are to be made. A congenial, relaxed atmosphere is necessary to accomplish this purpose.

d. *Evaluate.* Restate the problem so that all agree on the goal. The evaluation is to be objective. No one is to be given blame or credit for the ideas appearing on the chalkboard. Use the process of elimination, and combine ideas. Erase an idea when it is rejected by the group. No ideas should be eliminated without a justifiable reason. Bring ideas together. Narrow the topics on the board to the more useful solutions. It may be helpful to have the evaluation period extend into or take place another day to allow incubation of the ideas brought out in the free thought expression period.

e. *Summarize.* State the original problem. Then state the solution to it. Have members of the group re-state the action they are going to take in solving the problem.

You are encouraged to use the problem-solving techniques presented in chapter 8 as you conduct brainstorming sessions.

There is often merit in dividing a class into small groups and conducting brainstorming buzz sessions (see method 3, "Buzz Sessions").

3. Buzz Sessions

The class is divided into subordinate or small groups. The purpose is to give direct responsibility of interactive problem-solving to a larger number of students than would have the opportunity in regular class discussion.

The classroom sounds like an active beehive as the groups interact on the given problem(s). Thus this method is referred to as a "buzz session."

Particularly with large classes a major problem with buzz sessions is that pupils may discuss items of personal interest and ignore the problem of discussion. When a buzz session is properly structured, however, this problem usually does not occur. Structure a buzz session as follows:

a. Prestructure a problem through such methods as general, case study, or question box discussion; a film; a recording; or story. Write the problem on the chalkboard so the small groups can refer to it when in their discussion sessions. Take care to assure that the problem is relevant to student need, interest, understanding, and feeling.

b. When the problem is understood and students are motivated to find its solution, divide the class into small groups. Three to five students should be assigned to each group. Depending on the problem to be considered, the groups can be divided by the students choosing their own groups or by the teacher assigning students to groups. When assigning individuals to groups, you might use such criteria as sex, intellectual ability of individuals, spiritual qualities of pupils, or problems common to particular class members. For example, how would you divide a group of sixteen-year-olds when teaching that steady dating is unwise? Some of the pupils are steady daters. Others have no steadies.

After presenting the problem "What are the advantages or disadvantages of going steady in high school?" you may have different choices such as the following: (1) Let individuals choose their own group. (2) Place the boys and girls into separate groups. (3) Group students according to individual aggressiveness, and social problems.

As you can see, student placement can have definite bearing on the outcome of the problem-solving discussion groups.

c. A chairman and secretary-reporter should be assigned in each group. The chairman directs the discussion. The secretary-reporter records the decisions of the group and gives oral report to the class after the sub-group session.

d. Separate the students into smaller groups. It is generally best to allow three to eight minutes for a buzz session. If none of the groups is finished in the allotted time, an extension can be added. The short session gives pupils the feeling that time cannot be wasted. This alleviates the problem of small group discussions wandering away from the objective.

Announce when one or two minutes remain so the groups will have time to pull their ideas together and summarize.

Throughout the buzz session, the teacher should walk from group to group assisting with the activity.

e. Call the class together even though some groups are not finished.

f. Have each of the secretary-reporters sit in the front of the classroom facing the group. As each reporter presents the decisions of his group, these are written on the chalkboard by the teacher.

g.   After all reports have been given, reporters return to their chairs and the teacher opens the session to general discussion.

h.   The teacher summarizes and conclusions are made.

Use the problem-solving techniques in chapter 8 as you conduct buzz sessions.

4.   Case Study

A case is a story or situation that is used in class for study and problem solving. The story is credible and is usually directly related to types of conditions that are relevant to the students' own experiences. A case is usually a real-life occurrence. When a case is used in teaching, the characters should be kept anonymous.

Four approaches in the use of a case for study in class are suggested here: (a) to structure for discussion, (b) as a written assignment, (c) as cases prepared by students, and (d) as pictorial case studies.

a.   *To structure for discussion.* Use the case as an open-end story. When the story reaches its climax, the individual telling the story says to the students, "What would you do?" The students, who have identified with one or more characters in the story, seek to find solutions to the problem through discussion. At the end of the discussion, a summary is usually made where students conclude what action they plan to take when confronted with similar problems. The teacher should be cautious not to reveal the solution to the problem while telling the story. Also it is usually a good idea to tell the students the outcome of the story after they have arrived at the solution to the problem being considered. (See chapter 7, pages 95-97, for sample open-end story.)

b.   *As a written assignment.* Provide each student with a written copy of a case that is in the form of an open-end story. Instructions are written beneath the case. An example of a student sheet appears at the top of the following page.

c.   *As cases prepared by students.* Have students think of a problem that is troubling them. On a sheet of paper, students are to write out their problems in story form. When the case is completed, they are to find a solution to the problem, using the instructions under the *written assignment* above. Students should be cautioned not to select problems of a highly personal nature.

d.   *As pictorial case studies.* In a pictorial case study, the story is presented in the picture. On the back of the picture are written questions that are asked the group by the moderator. Classes with more than ten students should be divided into buzz sessions with four or five students in a group. A picture should be available for each group.

PRAYER[1]

Name of Student _____ Date _____ Class _____

George was reared in the Church. He is now fifteen. One day after sitting through what he called "a boring lesson," George told his friend Pete, "I don't believe what Brother Smith taught us today in our priesthood class. God never answers any of my prayers."

Pete responded with surprise, "Don't you say your prayers, George?"

"No! I haven't prayed for over two years. Anyway my folks don't seem to care. They never ask me if I pray. Why bother praying? It's a waste of time."

What would you do if you were Pete?

1. After reading the story above, think it through carefully.
2. Use the following scriptures to assist in solving the problem: Mosiah 4:11-12, Alma 37:36-37, Luke 18:1-8.
3. Discuss the story with parents and friends.
4. On a sheet of paper state the problem presented in the story.
5. List all possible solutions to, the problem.
6. Analyze the solutions. Place a check mark next to that solution you feel should be carried out.
7. Predict the short-term and long-range results of your decision. Do this in writing.
8. Be prepared to defend the decision you have made.

The moderator holds up the picture and reads the questions on the back of the sheet. The students discuss the questions, seeking to arrive at a solution to the problem.

You can prepare your own pictorial case studies by mounting large colored pictures from magazines that tell the story you want to put over. On the back of the mounting, write questions that may be used by the moderator.

Here are questions to accompany the picture used as an example on page 278.

(1) What kind of student is cheating?

(2) Do you think he is an "A" student?

(3) Did he prepare for the test?

(4) What should the other boy do?

(5) Does he have any obligation to stop his friend from cheating?

(6) What are you going to do the next time you see someone cheat on a test?

(7) What would Christ have done?

The pictorial case study should be summarized by the teacher. In buzz sessions, this can be done bringing the class together into one group and having a reporter from each smaller group report the decisions of the group. At the end of the reports, the class arrives at conclusions.

You are encouraged to adapt the problem-solving techniques presented in chapter 8 to your case study procedures.

PICTORIAL CASE STUDY

5. Debates, Student

Debate is a type of formal problem-solving discussion method. It develops ability in carefully planned and spontaneous organization of ideas.

The British-style debate, based on House of Commons procedures, brings the audience into the debate. A problem is formulated and a speaker for the affirmative and one for the negative make a five to eight minute formal presentation. A second member from each side then gives a shorter talk; these two speakers may yield to a question or a contribution from the floor or audience. This is followed by an open period in which the floor may speak or ask questions of a debater or of someone in the audience who has already spoken. These speeches however must be in affirmative-negative sequence so that an equal number of people speak on each side of the question. A speaker from each side then makes a summary presentation, after which members of the audience may speak again.

For eliciting audience interest, participation, and identification with the problem, the British type of debate is far superior to the more formal style. An interesting way to adapt this type of debate to classroom use is to limit debate to half the period and use the remaining time for whole-class or small-group discussion of what has been said.[2]

There is a tendency for debaters to seek weaknesses in their opponents' logic. Desire to win may also become of more importance to the participants than defending what is right. Debate suggests that there are two sides to a question, one of which might be proved incorrect. Do not present a principle of truth to question its validity. The strongest debater may create doubt if defending a falsehood. Therefore, do not debate such issues as "revelation is necessary" or "the sacrament should be passed only to members of the Church," or "the Manifesto in the Doctrine and Covenants is of divine origin." The Lord has already decided such matters.

To debate, one must gather data to substantiate his case. Choose topics for debate that are controversial and offer information through research. *Do not debate anything that is purely religious in nature.* Such topics might be used as, "home television inhibits one's creativity" or "queen contests are harmful to contestants" or "the United States should intercede in the colonization of other countries threatened by Communist powers."

6. Discussion, General

In the simplest form of general discussion, the teacher presents an idea that elicits student response. Through verbal expression, students reason, sift, and examine the idea presented with collective effort to find the truth to the question.

General discussion is a popular method of teaching in Church classes. It is also one of the most abused methods. To conduct an effective discussion calls for careful planning and considerable skill. Here are a few suggestions that should give strength to your discussion procedures.

a.   Give much thought to the preparation of a discussion question. The question should be accurate and concise. It should be relevant to the interests, needs, feelings, and understandings of the students. It should be thought provoking and directly related to the lesson objective.

b.   When starting a discussion in class, a better effect is usually attained if the teacher prestructures with a story, a case, a film, a record, or the like.

c.   It helps to maintain focus on the key discussion question by writing the question on the chalkboard and asking students to focus on this key idea.

d.   Do not answer your own question. Give students a chance to think through the issue and respond.

e.   Try to involve all students in the discussion, but do not embarrass students.

f.   Do not allow talkative students to monopolize.

g.   Now and then encourage the participants to evaluate the progress of the discussion.

h.   Listen carefully to what students have to say, and be flexible, adapting to their responses. It is often helpful to list appropriate responses on the chalkboard.

i.   Summarize the discussion. Pull the loose ends together. Determine with students what action might be taken on the useful ideas brought out in the discussion.

For further help, see chapter 9, "How Effective Are Your Discussion Techniques?" (particularly p. 118).

7.   Discussion, Panel

Panel discussion is a formal discussion technique. From two to six participants sit or stand in the front of the classroom facing the group. The teacher or a student moderator directs and controls the discussion.

The topic for discussion must contain a problem. Each panel member makes a two- to five-minute presentation on a specific area of the discussion topic or problem. If the moderator deems it beneficial to the discussion, panel members are instructed that they may make comments or ask questions as each panel member is speaking. Another approach is for panel members to hold comments and questions until after a report is given or until all presentations have been made. Class members should have opportunity to ask questions and discuss the problem either at the end of each report or at the end of the panel discussion. The moderator is to steer the discussion toward the topic for discussion, pull loose ends together, and summarize the ideas that have been presented.

With the informal panel discussion, the moderator directs questions to the panel. Panel members respond informally to the questions.

This latter approach is usually more interesting because it eliminates memorized or orally read essays.

Panel members should be given several days to prepare on the topic for discussion. One technique is to assign all class members to prepare for the panel discussion, with the instructions that on the day of the discussion five or six class members will be selected extemporaneously to participate on the panel.

8. Discussion, Problem-Solving

A problem is an unsettled question raised for consideration and solution.

A problem exists when the student's previously acquired knowledge is insufficient, or inappropriate, to enable him to arrive at an acceptable solution.

As outlined in chapter 8, page 105, a problem should be built upon knowledge the students now have, and the students should be provided with ideas or materials that will be necessary in arriving at a solution to the problem. The basic classroom procedures in problem-solving discussion are:

    a.   Prestructure the problem (p. 105).
    b.   Define the problem (p. 106).
    c.   See that the students clearly understand the problem (p. 106).
    d.   Guide the students toward arriving at a solution to the problem through carefully controlled discussion procedures (p. 106).
        (1) Help students understand new relationships without solving the problem for them.
        (2) Act spontaneously to uneven advances made by students.
        (3) Reinforce student responses.
        (4) Summarize.

Further helps in conducting problem-solving discussion are located in chapter 9 as follows:

    a.   How to prepare a problem statement for discussion (p. 112).
    b.   How to conduct a problem-solving discussion session (p. 114).

9. Discussion, Question Box

This is an extemporaneous technique, allowing the group to discuss anything they wish in relation to their social or personal problems.

Give each student a small slip of paper on which he is to write any problem he may have that he would like to have discussed by the group. If he has no problems, he is to hand in the paper blank. Each paper is to be kept anonymous. If the teacher or a student recognizes who wrote a problem when it is read to the class, he is not to reveal this person. Instruct students to each fold the paper uniformly, adding to the anonymity. When the papers are folded, the teacher takes the question box around the room to gather the questions. After mixing the papers in the box, he draws one from the box and reads it silently. If the question is appropriate for discussion, he reads it aloud. If inappropriate, he returns it to the question box and draws again. The teacher should not read problems of a highly personal nature.

Students must be instructed to be supportive of each other when the questions are discussed. Each student must take upon himself the responsibility of helping solve his anonymous classmates' problems. Keep in mind that the students, not the teacher, are to solve the problems. The responsibility of the instructor is basically to help the class focus on and extend into a common problem. Then he is to help the group recognize the solution to that problem by summarizing the ideas presented.

If a student violates the discussion rules, you should discontinue the discussion immediately. This will place social pressure on the violator, because students usually enjoy this type of discussion. The next question box discussion period will undoubtedly progress with proper student support.

10. Examinations

An examination is a process of testing a student's progress, knowledge, understanding, and capabilities on a given subject. The major purpose of an examination is to assist the student in learning and in self-evaluation. Examinations also provide the teacher with evaluations of student work.

Outside of weekday religious education, examinations could be used more frequently in the gospel classroom. Many teachers in priesthood and auxiliary organizations do not use examinations because of lack of knowledge as to how to prepare an examination and because of the emotional upset a test frequently brings to students. Pupils often feel that a gospel class is a time to rest from learning activities that require student effort. If the teacher understands the cause of pupil emotional upset with tests, it will assist when instituting testing in a class.

Emotional upset, relative to examinations, might be caused by the following:

a. Pressure of a grade. A low test score may cause intense emotional upset within a student. (In priesthood and auxiliary classes and family home evenings, a grade is not necessary, although it is well to have students correct and score their own papers.)

b. Test questions too difficult.

c. Insufficient time for students to complete an examination.

d. Students with the feeling that examinations should be reserved for regular school. (This problem can be partially alleviated in priesthood and auxiliary classes by giving examinations unannounced and by not calling them examinations or tests. Refer to them rather as games or simple evaluations in helping students learn.)

e. Lack of student preparation. (Student preparation should be a constant process and not a cramming experience for a pre-planned test.)

Following are some of the various types of examinations:

a. *Essay.* The essay examination calls for a composition extemporaneously organized and written by the student with the intention of solving a problem or proving or illustrating a point.

When you correct an essay examination, items for consideration are length, organization, legibility, neatness, spelling, grammar, factual detail, reason, utilization of graphs and diagrams, and style.

An essay examination can include from one to any number of questions or statements that solicit student response. The question must call for more than a yes, no, or other one-word response. The problem-solving essay, using a short written case study to introduce the problem, makes excellent essay questions.

b. *Comparison Examination.*[3] This is a type of problem-solving examination in short essay form. Each item of the examination is given in statement form, such as, *The Book of Mormon is the word of God.* Next to the statement, the student is to write *agree, disagree,* or *uncertain.* Below the statement, the pupil is then to write in short essay form why he disagrees, agrees, or is uncertain.

Later in the test another statement is presented that is comparative to statement number 1. This item, which is comparative to item 1, might appear as item 9, *The golden plates were preserved by the power of God.* Both items 1 and 9 test the students' testimony of the Book of Mormon, although each is stated in a different way.

When correcting the examination, item 1 is compared with item 9. If the answers on both items are consistent, the student receives credit on these items. If the responses vary, the pupil loses credit on them. Although scores can be arrived at in this manner, grades should ordinarily not be given on this examination because of its subjectivity.

If there are twenty items on a comparative examination, ten of these should be comparative with the other ten items, as illustrated in items 1 and 9 above. The comparative items should be scattered throughout the test and not presented in a particular order.

c. *Completion Sentences.* These are thought-provoking sentences with one or more words deleted. The student is to complete the sentences by filling in the blanks. Here are two examples of completion sentences:

1. *The four standard works of the LDS Church are the Bible, _____ _____ _____, Doctrine and Covenants, and _____ _____.*
2. *We believe that man must be _____ for his own _____, and not for _____ _____.*

d. *Multiple Choice.* In this type of examination question, the right answer appears along with wrong ones. The student is to select the proper answer, circle it, underline it, or write it in a provided blank. For example: *When the physical and spiritual bodies are reunited, it is called (a) reincarnation, (b) resurrection, (c) judgment, (d) death. (circle the correct answer).*

e. *Matching.* The matching examination consists of a list of statements. Each statement has a companion word listed in a second column. The student has the task of arranging the companion words to match each statement. For example: (*Place the correct prefix letter in the following blanks*):

1. _____ Jerusalem   a. Home town of Rebecca, wife of Isaac.
2. _____ Haran   b. First city in which Abraham lived.
3. _____ Ur   c. City of David.

f. *True or False.* This type of examination item presents a statement that is either correct or incorrect. The student is to judge whether the statement is true or false and write *true* or *false* in a blank at the left of the statement, such as:

1. *True   Jesus Christ is God of the Old Testament.*
2. *False   The Relief Society was an outgrowth of the Kirtland Safety Society.*

g. *Open Book Problem-Solving.* Students are allowed to use their scriptures or other textbooks for reference while taking this examination. The student is to arrive at solutions to problems that relate to his life and tie into textual content. Here is an example of an open book problem-solving question (notice that a case is used):

An old man is sitting on your front lawn. Your mother tells you to give the stranger something to eat. While fulfilling your errand, a friend stops you and says, "That old tramp ought to suffer. He brought this sorrow on himself. Besides, you'll never get rid of him once you feed him." (Use Mosiah 4:16-19 to explain what you would do.)

Following are suggestions for preparing and administering examinations:

a. Whenever possible, present test questions that are of a problem-solving nature.

b. Avoid including trick questions in an examination.

c. Every question in an examination must have a justifiable

reason for being there. When presenting factual questions, see that they are of significant value to the student. *What day, month, and year was the first miracle performed in the Church?* is extraneous. *Give the day, month, and year the Church was organized* is an important date on which a student can build his understanding of the history of the Church.

    d. Arrange test items in ascending order of difficulty. The easiest question in a test should be item 1.

    e. An examination should be planned according to a student's ability to do the work, and not just according to what the teacher thinks the student ought to know.

    f. Increasing the number of questions in a test increases the accuracy of the test in measuring student knowledge and ability. Therefore, plan as many questions as classtime will allow.

    g. Use two or three different types of test questions in each examination. For example, you might include in a test essay, multiple choice, and true or false questions. A test is limited if it comprises only one type of question, such as true or false.

    h. Use pictures, maps, and graphs in examinations.

    i. Duplicate examinations, providing a copy for each student. Next best is to write the examination on the chalkboard and cover it until time for the test. Least desirable is to read the questions to students as they write the responses, or to write the questions on the chalkboard while the students are taking the test.

    j. All books should be removed from student's desks while a test is being administered.

    k. Give all instructions at the beginning of an examination. Do not interrupt once students have started.

    l. The teacher should not sit down during a test. When a student has a question, have him raise his hand. Then go to him. Do not have him come to you.

    m. When a student has completed an examination, he should turn over his test paper and wait quietly until the rest of the class has finished. Once a student has handed in a paper, this seems to give him a release to start talking. Therefore, do not call in papers until all have finished.

    n. Always go over a completed test with students. This provides an additional learning experience. In many cases it is well for students to correct their own papers. Students should always learn the correct answers to questions missed.

11. Field Trips

When teacher and students leave the classroom as an organized group with a particular objective in mind, they are participating in a field trip. A field trip should grow out of class interest in a particular problem or place being studied. Such places might be visited as:

    a.   A Church school.

    b.   A Church history landmark.

    c.   A temple to do baptismal work for the dead.

    d.   A field or canyon when studying the creation or application for God's creation. (this does not include holding a class on the lawn on a warm spring day—such a practice should be discouraged among teachers).

    e.   An old folks' home to present gifts or a program.

    f.   A home or public building to help someone in need.

In planning a field trip, the group should consider:

    a.   The educational value of the trip.

    b.   How the trip will be helpful to others.

    c.   Expenses involved.

    d.   Insuring all participants.

    e.   Obtaining a note from parents granting permission for the trip (for young students living at home).

    f.   Obtaining approval from the administration in charge (such as Sunday School president, MIA president, bishop, seminary coordinator, and stake presidents). Permission should be obtained *before* the trip is planned with students.

    g.   Orienting students properly for the trip. Do this by letting the students help plan the trip. Make definite arrangements as to time, date, number of students going, eating facilities, restroom facilities (investigated by teacher), guides, providing sufficient adult supervision, and proper conduct.

    h.   Having group prayer before disembarking on the trip.

    i.   Evaluating the trip and summarizing what was learned.

12. Games, Instructional

An instructional game is a contest or mental competition wherein the knowledge and ability of students is tested. Instructional games are most frequently used in lesson or unit reviews or overviews as a method of motivation and diversion. The subject matter of instructional games should relate to material being studied. Learning, rather than fun, is the prime motive and justification for using instructional games. Therefore, only those games that have educational value should be used in class. After playing an instructional game, it is a good practice occasionally to test its instructional value with an examination.

Chapter 11 contains further suggestions in conducting instructional games and presents ideas for the following games:

    a.   Football

    b.   Clue

    c.   Tic-tac-toe

    d. Picture Identification
    e. I Have It!
    f. Word Recall
    g. Know Your Bible
    h. Know Your Scriptures
    i. Association
    j. Charades
    k. Seven-Up
    l. Getting Acquainted

13. Home and Class Coordinated Methods

Here are four ideas for coordinating your class with the student's home:

    a. Have the students team up as companions. Present a lesson to the class as though they were investigators and you were a missionary. Have the students study this lesson and practice presenting it in class to each other. When they are prepared, send a letter to their parents in the letter to play the role of golden contacts. Have parents fill out an assignment sheet as follow-up to see that the assignment has been carried out effectively. (Chapter 5, pages 64-65, gives detailed suggestions on how to carry out this project.)

    b. Encourage students to teach lessons that they have studied in class to their families in weekly family home evenings. Encourage parents to hold family home evenings so their sons or daughters will have opportunity to teach the lessons.

    c. Prepare a list of lesson titles and objectives that will be studied in class during the following several weeks. Each student is to take this list home and discuss it with parents. The list may be posted in the dining room by the dinner table. The parent is to use the list as a guide in asking the student questions about lessons studied in class. This is to be done at mealtime.

    d. Make it a practice to visit the home of each student at least once a year. In this visit with parents and student, express appreciation for the student and for parental support. Ask for suggestions on how you might help the student become even a better Latter-day Saint.

14. Inquiry Techniques

Inquiry techniques in teaching, in the broad sense, are processes wherein the students probe for answers to thought-provoking problems and questions. A key purpose in using inquiry techniques is to stimulate students to think. During inquiry, every effort should be made to guide students in controlled investigation. Students should be encouraged to investigate thoroughly the subject being studied and to probe the question deeply.

The type of inquiry suggested here is cognitive (intellectual), and at times may call for questioning, doubting, or challenging. Therefore, caution should be taken by the teacher on the type of subject matter used and the way it is used. Under no circumstances should a Latter-day Saint teacher raise doubt in the students' mind concerning the authenticity of revealed truth as interpreted by the prophets.

Agassiz Technique. One of the techniques used by Agassiz in guiding students into inquiry was to identify a common element in the student's environment, such as a glazed brick, a dead fish, or pile of bones. Agassiz would then pose a question to the student that would lead the student into inquiry: "Write me a paper on the nature of glazed brick" or "Tell me everything you can find out about the dead fish or pile of bones." Agassiz would then become a hard taskmaster, requiring that the student make a thorough and complete systematic investigation.

A gospel teacher might adapt this approach to such questions as, "Write a paper on all you can find about the relationship between light and truth in the scriptures" or "Give all scripturally documented evidence you can find that the Bible prophesies of the coming forth of the Book of Mormon." (For further information concerning the Agassiz technique see chapter 5, pp. 59-61.)

Here is another inquiry approach that calls for more direct guidance from the teacher:[4] The teacher presents a situation, object, or word that is unfamiliar to the student. The student then attempts to resolve the issue by asking questions. From each response to his question, the student formulates in his thinking ideas that might lead him to the answers. (The answers have, of course, been predetermined by the teacher.)

With this technique, the student should ask questions that can be answered with a yes or no. The teacher might give clues beyond a yes or no response to a question, but he must induce the student to discover the answers out of his own powers of reason. The student should attempt to discover answers in as few questions and little time as possible. Here are two examples:

Example 1

Teacher: Students, Moses built a tabernacle for his people to use in the wilderness. I want you to learn as much about that tabernacle and its uses as you can through the process of inquiry learning.

Student: Was it intended to be moved from one place to another?

Teacher: Yes.

Student: Would the design of its construction help us to understand its purpose or have much relevance to its purpose?

Teacher: It doesn't have much relevance to its purpose, but it is important to our discussion.

Student: Is it important to our discussion because of the circumstances the Israelites were under at the time—that is, because of necessity of travel?

Teacher: Yes.

Student: Did the nature of its construction contribute to its mobility?

Teacher: Yes.

Student: Is the reason its nature is important that it was mobile?

Teacher: Yes, and that tells you something about the Israelite people.

Student: Was its purpose centered around worship?

Teacher: In a way.

Student: We think of a tabernacle today as a place to hold conferences. Was it more than a gathering place for worship?

Teacher: Well, it was different from that.

Student: Did it serve any of the same functions that the temple serves?

Teacher: Similar functions.

Student: Did they offer sacrifice in the tabernacle?

Teacher: Yes.

Student: Did they perform sacred priesthood activities and ordinances other than sacrifice?

Teacher: Yes.

Student: Were revelations received in the tabernacle?

Teacher: Yes.

Example 2

Teacher: While Enos was out hunting, what did he do?

Student: Prayed.

Teacher: What else did he do?

Student: It says he "supplicated."

Teacher: What's that?

Student: I don't know.

Teacher: All right, let's learn it through inquiry.

Student: Okay, is it something like praying?

Teacher: Yes.

Student: Not identical with prayer apparently?

Teacher: Not quite.

Student: *Supplication*—is that a form of pleading?

Teacher: Yes, in a way.

Student: More than that?

Teacher: A little. That would be the major factor.

Student: Pleading with faith?
Teacher: Yes.
Student: Promising? Does it involve promising things?
Teacher: Not necessarily.
Student: Does it involve praying fervently?
Teacher: Yes.
Student: I don't know what else to ask.
Teacher: All right then, how would a prayer with supplication differ from a prayer that didn't have supplication?
Student: A prayer with supplication would involve asking, and a a prayer without might not entail asking.
Teacher: All right, that would be part of it.
Student: Perhaps the earnestness with which you do it—a supplication would be more earnest asking than the other.
Teacher: You're suggesting then that it has something to do with a person's attitude.
Student: Yes. He's more intent, more humble, in supplication.
Teacher: Good. All right, that's what supplication means. Let's go on with our lesson. Now what happened to Enos next?

Problem solving as a method of inquiry (see pp. 103-109).

15. Inventories

An inventory, as we will use the term, is a questionnaire administered by the teacher and completed by the student. The purpose of the inventory is to assist the teacher in becoming better acquainted with each student and gaining insight into individual needs through preassessment. The questionnaire is only for teacher use and should be kept strictly confidential. For this reason, it is wise to keep the completed forms anonymous. Do this by giving each student a number on a sheet of paper. Write this number on the back of each sheet. Rather than having a student sign his name to the inventory, use the number for identification. He should be given to understand that you will know the paper is his, but that you will keep the information confidential. You might find such questions as the following helpful for inclusion in the inventory:

a. Give your age.
b. What is your hobby or special interest?
c. What are your plans for future education?
d. What is your future occupational choice?
e. Name your brothers and sisters, from oldest to youngest.
f. Do you have private prayer often, usually, seldom, never (circle one)?
g. Do you have family prayer often, usually, seldom, never (circle one)?
h. List three of your main goals in life.

    i. Give your (if a child or youth, give father's)
      (1) Occupation
      (2) Church affiliation
      (3) Priesthood (if LDS)
      (4) Church responsibilities (if active)
    j. Does your wife (or mother) work? Part time? Full time?
      (1) Mother's church affiliation
      (2) Mother's church responsibilities (if LDS)
    k. If you had the opportunity to meet the Prophet Joseph Smith, what questions would you ask him?
    l. Write any problems you feel your teacher might be able to help you with.

If you are a professional teacher, you might record the above data on each student in a personal roll book. This roll book might also be used for student grades. Because of its confidential nature, this book should never fall into the hands of students. During study periods the teacher can stand at the back of the room studying personal data and observing students. Another attendance roll book can be used by the class secretary.

16. Memorizing

Memorizing is the retaining of knowledge of past events, ideas, or impressions. It is recalling to memory specific areas of study. Memorizing scriptures and scriptural locations is and should be a popular form of memory work in the gospel classroom.

Before deciding on a scripture for student memorization, ask yourself, "How useful will this passage be to my students in future years?"

When a scripture is introduced to a class for memorization, the teacher should discuss the background of the scripture, answering such questions as the following. "What prophet wrote it? When was the scripture written? Why was it written? Where was it written? What value is it in our lives today?" After reading the scripture to students, one approach is to have the students go through the following steps:

    a. Write the scripture and scripture reference on a 4" x 6" or 3" x 5" card. (Carry this card wherever you go. Whenever there is a free moment, take the card out and study it.)

    b. After writing the scripture on a card, underline key words. Associate these words with something familiar. For instance, in Revelation 14:6, we read: "And I saw another *angel fly in the midst of heaven, having the everlasting gospel* to preach unto them that dwell on the earth, and to every *nation,* and *kindred,* and *tongue,* and *people.*"

Now build a visual image of an angel flying through the heavens carrying in his hands a book that contains the everlasting gospel.

Picture in your mind's eye nations of people speaking different tongues and reaching up with outstretched arms to receive the message.

c.   When you have the visual image, write and rewrite the passage word perfect. Now and then close your eyes and recite the words to yourself. Open your eyes and check yourself.

d.   After the scripture is memorized, review it every day for five days. Then review it once a week for five weeks. Every few months review again the scriptures you have memorized. (See p. 137 for the game Know Your Scriptures.)

17. Note-Taking

Students should often take notes in classes where a subject is being studied that is so vital as the gospel of Jesus Christ. Note-taking places the student in the process of doing—of interpreting on paper into his own language what is presented in class. If he takes good notes, they are often useful to him for future reference and study. We should teach students to form the habit of writing excellent ideas as they are communicated and become meaningful. There is no better place than your classroom to teach this practice.

To take notes, one should have a hard surface on which to write. If tablet arm chairs are not provided in your classroom, obtain masonite lapboards or have students bring looseleaf binders.

Many students have difficulty organizing thoughts and putting them on paper. Therefore, instruct students on how to take notes. Here are a few ideas that might help them:

a.   When taking notes, listen for the idea and then write. Don't try to write everything you hear. Just take down the key ideas.

b.   Itemize your notes or use the outline form. To itemize, simply make a list of major points brought out in the discussion, such as:

> *What is the Bible?*
>
> *1. Divine library of many books.*
> *2. The word of God.*
> *3. Written by the Jews.*
> *4. Written in the Near East.*

The outline form is superior when it is necessary to organize in detail. It requires more practice to gain proficiency than does itemizing. Outlined notes would appear as follows:

> What is the Bible?
>
> I.   Divine library of many books. (Main heading. The next idea is written as roman numeral II, unless it relates to item I as below.)
>
>   A. Are 39 books in Old Testament. (Minor heading that relates to the main heading, and thus falls under it as indented capital

A. If other ideas are given in this same capital letter hierarchy, they would be listed B, C, D, E, etc.)

1. Pentateuch. (Minor idea that relates to heading A, and thus falls under it as indented arabic numeral 1. If other ideas are given in this same hierarchy, they would continue as 2, 3, 4, 5, etc. If necessary, the hierarchy breakdown continues as follows:

a. Genesis

(1) Creation

(a) First period of,

Technically, if an A appears in an outline, it should be followed by a B. If there is no B, A should become part of its main heading I. This principle follows through each level.

Listen for cues given by the teacher, such as voice inflection, repetition, and points emphasized on chalkboard. (As the teacher, you should assist students in selecting important areas to note by giving emphasis to the important ideas.)

18. Programed Instruction

Programed instruction is a sequence of items such as questions or statements to which the student makes responses. Each item, which is sometimes called a frame, begins with knowledge already possessed by the student. Each frame adds a small increment of new knowledge to what the student understands. As the student progresses through the frame, he is in process of achieving predetermined performances that are built into the program. Before the student commences with the sequence of frames, he is usually given an understanding of what he will be able to do or know when he has completed the sequence.

Most programs are housed in programed booklets and teaching machines. It is getting more common to see programed instruction principles of predefined student behaviors, small step increments providing reinforced rewards of new knowledge, and carefully controlled learning sequences in filmstrips and records and other instructional media.

Programed instruction is used in the seminary home study curriculum. It is used to a limited extent in a few other teaching programs of the Church. It could be used much more extensively as an individualized instruction technique.

Programed instruction will not replace the teacher or the vital social experiences so necessary for pupil growth in the gospel classroom. It gives considerable control over the learning process in comparison to most other teaching methods, and it provides students with an opportunity to progress at their own speed.

See chapters 15 and 16, pages 173-202, on chalkboard illustrating for an example of one type of programing.

19. Questioning Techniques[5]

Teachers can lead students through many kinds of thinking by the way their questions are formed. Some teachers ask questions of quality, but many teachers usually ask questions that require students only to remember. The approaches that follow will lead students into *using* ideas rather than simply *remembering* them.

Norris Sanders[6] has applied Bloom's taxonomy of educational objectives[7] to types of questions that might be asked in the classroom. The taxonomy provides a way of classifying knowledge in formulating objectives. There are seven major categories and thus seven basic ways of forming questions. Each category is presented below, along with the definition and a sample of how it might be used in questioning.

a. *Memory*
Definition: The student recalls or recognizes information.
Sample question: What is meant by truth? (The student is asked to recall the definition presented to him earlier.)

b. *Translation*
Definition: The student changes information into a different form of language.
Sample Question: The Prophet Joseph Smith said that "truth is a knowledge of things as they are, as they were, and as they are to come." Restate this definition in your own words.

c. *Interpretation*
Definition: The student discovers relationships among facts, generalizations, definitions, values and skills.
Sample question: Doctrine and Covenants 93 teaches that "the glory of God is . . . truth." How does knowledge of things then relate to the glory of God?

d. *Application*
Definition: The student solves a lifelike problem that requires the identification of the issue and the selection and use of appropriate generalizations and skills.
Sample question: We can grow into becoming worthy of the glory of God by gaining knowledge of truth and then by practicing this knowledge. Identify a single practicable truth that will give you some claim on God's glory. What truth have you identified?

e. *Analysis*
Definition: The student solves a problem in the light of conscious knowledge of the parts and forms of thinking.

Sample question: Drawing from other scriptural verses, analyze the reasoning in this quotation, "The glory of God is intelligence, or in other words light and truth." What is the relationship of intelligence, light, and truth?

f. *Synthesis*

Definition: The student solves a problem that requires original creative thinking.

Sample question: (This question should follow the application question given above.) Suggest how this truth that you have identified can be practiced under the following circumstances. (Here a case might be given that leads students into probing for solution.)

g. *Evaluation*

Definition: The student makes a judgment of good or bad, right or wrong, according to designated standards.

Sample question: (Taken from a specific student response from the application question.) Do you think it is right to go steady before age sixteen?

These various forms of questioning often elicit discussion or lead to other types of teaching methods. Questions should be stated briefly and concisely and should be adapted to the experiences and abilities of the students. A series of questions should be carefully sequenced and directed toward the achievement of an objective or goal. Avoid digressions and ambiguities.

20. Questioning, Rapid-Fire

Rapid-fire questioning is a recitation procedure whereby the teacher asks students questions in rapid succession on material previously studied. Students recite back to the teacher answers to the questions. The type of questions is usually factual and students recall from memory. This technique is representative of "Memory" in the seven classifications of questioning techniques (method 19). In contrast to general discussion procedures, one word from a student may answer a question sufficiently. Ordinarily questions are fired at students with such rapidity that time is not allowed for volunteer response through hand-raising.

In preparing for rapid-fire questioning, you should adjust the difficulty of questions to each student's ability to answer. There is little learning value in asking a student a question he cannot answer. This only deflates his ego and causes emotional upset. Students should, however, be expected to prepare to answer questions on past lessons. Because students have limited time to recall answers, questions should be short and simple. Do not ask, "What might you have done had you been a prisoner in Egypt as was Joseph?" This is a problem-solving question (it is a good question in the context of discussion). Simple response would come from such questions as, "Name the previous occupation of one of Joseph's prisoner friends" or "What was the previous occupation of the other friend in prison?" or "What did Joseph do to help these two men?" or "How did they agree to help him?" or "Did they help him when they were released from prison?"

When preparing to use this method, write thirty or forty questions you plan to use. Study them, get them in mind, and decide which questions will be directed to specific students. Do not read the questions to students, but have them on the tip of your tongue so you can fire them at a rapid pace.

Rapid-fire questioning alleviates monopolizing the discussion by one or two students. It causes pupils to be alert, because they do not know when they will be asked a question. This also does not allow time for one to thumb through his notes for an answer he cannot recall. Enthusiasm is stimulated. When the method is handled skillfully, students have an enjoyable experience.

As a caution, this method may make of the teacher an inquisitor rather than a helper.

21. Reading Orally

Reading orally reproduces written words in sound so that the reader and listeners are fully able to gather the meaning and intent of what is presented. Students should be motivated to want to read. They should be instructed on what to watch for in this reading.

It is usually more effective to tell or dramatize a story than to read it. A serious limitation with reading is that eye contact with the listeners is often lost. Reading an idea usually does not transmit it as effectively as telling an idea.

Some stories, prolific statements, and pertinent scriptures are justifiably read orally in class. It is up to you as the teacher to make proper selection of materials for oral reading. Never should a full class period be used in oral reading.

Where any amount of oral reading takes place in class, variety should be employed.

Here are some ways of conducting oral reading in class:

a.   Go down the row, having each student read a part of the article. (This technique should be used only when all students read fairly well.)

b.   Choose one outstanding student reader to read the article.

c.   When an article is to be read, ask for volunteer readers.

d.   You, as the teacher, read the article.

e.   You, as the teacher, read the difficult parts of the article, having students read the other parts.

f.   For short articles, have students read them together in concert recitation. If each student does not have the article, write it on the chalkboard so all can see it.

g. Read a part of the article orally. Then have pupils continue reading silently.

h. Have pupils read the entire article silently.

i. Use an opaque projector and project the printed page on a screen so all can read orally or silently.

j. When different character parts are portrayed in the reading, assign students to read these parts as though they were reading a play.

Here are a few suggestions that you might study and then pass on to your students in assisting them to make their oral reading meaningful:

a. While reading, watch for punctuation marks. Commas, dashes, parentheses, periods, exclamation and question marks, and paragraphs are all signposts on how to make reading expressive. Breathe only at a comma or end of a sentence. Pause between periods. Pause longer between paragraphs. And pause only at punctuation marks.

b. Think about what you are reading. If you do not understand what you're reading neither will your audience. After all, reading is nothing more than "enlarged conversation." Put meaning into *What? Oh! Now, Well* and the like.

c. Read ahead. This helps in giving proper expression. It also makes it possible for you to look at your students and establish eye contact periodically.

d. Speak audibly. Pronounce every syllable. Practice opening the mouth widely and articulating sharply.

e. Practice variety by reading fast with clear articulation; then go slowly with meaning and emphasis. Using the piano, read in different pitches as you play the notes.

f. Have students stand while reading.

22. Reports and Talks

An oral report or talk is when a student verbally gives an account of information that specifically relates to material being studied in the lesson.

All too often when a report or talk is being prepared, the student thinks only of imparting information to his classmates. In the presentation, he thus stands and reads a uninteresting treatise. The only person who benefits, to any degree, is the reporter.

An oral report should be presented in the same manner that an effective talk is presented. It should stimulate listener interest, give authoritative information made understandable through illustrations, examples, and visuals, and it should lead the listeners into doing something about what has been said. Usually the report or talk should not be over ten minutes. It is supplementary to the lesson, not the lesson itself.

Teach your students to use the following techniques of effective speaking when class reports or talks are assigned.

When preparing a talk, don't jump on six horses and ride in twelve different directions all at the same time. Choose one main idea and go only in the direction of that idea. When choosing a talk topic, try this: Think of the most thrilling experience you have ever had. Let this spiritual experience be the body of your talk. Build your main idea around it. If you can't think of such an experience, then think of that in which you are most interested. Use this as the objective of your talk.

After taking the matter to the Lord, prepare a brief outline of your talk as follows:

a. *Think of a simple project that ties in with your main idea that will set the audience on fire.* For example, you might write a question mark on the chalkboard, hold up a visual aid, make an unexpected statement, tell a funny story, or relate a spiritual experience. Item 1 of your outline will then be a brief statement of what you are going to do to get the attention and interest of the entire class.

b. *Present your case by answering the question "So What?"* In writing, state exactly the main idea you wish to put over; then back it up with facts and statistics. Quote well-known authorities. These procedures will make your talk convincing. All statistics and quotes should be written in your outline so they can be easily referred to while presenting the talk.

c. *Back up your case with an illustration or example.* Tell a story or personal experience so the listeners see vividly what you mean in the main idea you are trying to put over. To make your illustration live with the listeners, don't say, "A dog came running toward me," but rather, "A monstrous St. Bernard came at me in great leaps and bounds!" Tell the story as though you were relating an exciting experience to your best friend. In this part of your outline, make only a note of the story you are going to relate. Do not write out the story. In the delivery, it should come out in thought patterns from the heart, not words from a paper.

Use charts, maps, pictures, flannelboard, or the chalkboard to illustrate your case.

d. *Answer the question "What are you going to do about it?"* At this point the main idea has been presented and illustrated to the listeners. Step four is to show the listeners how this idea is to become part of them. Tell the class specifically how they can put your idea into effect. Don't say, "Everyone should pray," but say, "Before climbing in bed tonight, fall on your knees and thank the Lord for your blessings. Then let this be your practice every evening the rest of your life."

e. *Bear testimony.* If you have been talking about prayer, say,

"I know that God lives and answers prayers. Jesus is the Christ, and I know that this is His true Church." In expressing your convictions, be sincere by stating exactly how you feel. Everything expressed in a testimony should be positive rather than negative in nature. If you have negative feelings about something or someone, do not let it be a part of your talk.

Your talk will tend to be as effective as the amount of time you spend in qualified preparation. It has been said that many great orators prepare at least one hour for every minute they spend before an audience. Sincere prayer should be a part of this intensive preparation.

As a final step in your preparation, think through every thought and word you are going to say. Do this while glancing over your notes. Go completely through the talk at least two times in this manner. Do not memorize or read a talk.

Remember to draw your listeners into your talk by expressing appreciation or by telling of an outstanding character trait of a classmate. Talk in terms of their interests.

Be yourself. Be natural in your presentation. Vary your voice inflection, smile, get the group to laugh. Be enthusiastic. Never tell them you are scared or unprepared. Analyze strong and weak points in talks as you hear them. Act confident, and you will become confident. Radiate spirituality.

23. Role Playing, Prestructured

In pre-structured role playing, students perform parts or character roles which were previously assigned and practised by the actors.

When properly handled, almost all age groups enjoy and learn from this activity. Generally, this method of teaching is used to act out a story in a lesson, and thus give greater insight into its meaning. At least one day before the production is to take place, students are assigned the various character parts in the story. They are to study the story carefully and then practise once or twice together. Ordinarily the parts should not be memorized. The dramatization is often enhanced by using simple props such as a hat, blanket, or mask. Interest is created by using students for animals, rocks, and trees.

One teacher introduced the commandment "Thou shalt not kill" with pre-structured role playing.

Bill and Jim were asked by Brother Overs to assist him in introducing the next day's lesson. The boys were given the general information of what was expected. It was left up to their own creative imagination to put in the details. This is what happened the next day in class.

Students were sitting quietly waiting for Brother Overs to start the lesson when Bill shouted across the classroom at Jim, "Who do you think you are, taking Alice out last night! She's my girl!"

Jim responded, "It's none of your business!"

The group was shocked as a hot argument ensued. Finally Bill jumped from his desk, grabbed Jim by the collar, and shoved him against the chalkboard. Jim shoved Bill back. Angrily Bill drew a water pistol from his pocket and shot Jim. Jim slumped forward with a groan —a dead man.

Two other boys marched forward. One lifted Jim by the head. The other picked up the feet, and Jim, stiff as a board, was carried out of the room.

Brother Overs stood before the group and said, "This brings us to our lesson for today. It is 'Thou shalt not kill.'" The role players returned to the room, and Brother Overs thanked them. The role play was then used for case study discussion in giving students an understanding of the relationship between anger and killing.

24. Role Playing, Spontaneous

In spontaneous role playing, students perform parts or character roles in unrehearsed informal dramatizations that grow out of lessons or student problems. Almost any age group enjoys role playing.

Role playing must be carefully planned and skillfully conducted to be productive. Pre-structuring in class of a dramatization is vital to its success.

Spontaneous role playing often works effectively as an outgrowth of class discussion. When students are at the point of seeking a solution to a problem, suggest that they act out the problem. If their response is favorable, write the parts to be played on the chalkboard. Then assign these parts, writing the name of the actor next to the part he will be playing, Parts should be given to students who might gain personal development through playing the role or who will enhance the quality of the production. Define the roles to the players. Orient the class as to the purpose and function of the play so each student will be able to make an intelligent observation. Have the players come to the front and begin acting. After the production is over resume the discussion. Ask pupils, "What new insights did you receive? How might the participants have acted differently?" At this point, it may be desirable to replay the drama, switching the roles or soliciting new actors. Role playing should always be followed by a summary.

The following student dramatization took place in a Provo seminary classroom some time ago:

The class was discussing parents' not allowing children to stay out at night later than an appointed hour. Many students felt that parents were too strict and unfair. During the energetic discussion, it was decided to role play the problem. Roles were assigned and written on the chalkboard.

The opening scene of the dramatization was an anxious father and mother pacing the floor late at night, with the daughter and her date walking slowly up to the house thirty minutes late. The boy said good-night to the girl, and she stepped into the house to face her parents. From this point, the extemporaneous actors were on their own.

As the girl entered the house, a family argument ensued with the parent actors playing their own parents' roles and the young girl playing her own role. The scene was then replayed reversing the roles of the actors, thus giving them opportunity to experience both points of view.

During the plays, an observer would now and then voluntarily speak out, exclaiming, "That's my dad!" or "That's the very thing I go through!"

Later the role players ventilated their feelings and reactions, usually stating that they were much too harsh and misunderstanding in the play. In summary, it was concluded that the students' responsibility was to endeavor better to understand their parents' viewpoint, and where misunderstanding existed, the child should discuss the matter with his parents.

You are encouraged to adapt the problem-solving discussion technique in chapter 8 to your role playing.

25. Singing, Instructional

Music in the classroom is a way of expressing ideas clothed with feeling. This can be done by—

a. Having the class sing an inspirational hymn during a lesson (see p. 121).

b. Requesting a talented student to sing a vocal solo, the words of which give students further insight into the lesson objective (p. 121).

c. Teaching students to conduct Church hymns, thus preparing them for future opportunity to conduct in class and in other Church organizations (see p. 124).

d. Singing an assignment to be memorized, such as the books of the Old Testament, New Testament, or Book of Mormon (p. 122).

e. Using the record player or tape recorder.
   (1) In presenting soft background music in study periods (see p. 128).
   (2) In teaching appreciation for the classics (see p. 128).
   (3) In strengthening the lesson with spiritual music (see p. 129).

The teacher should be highly selective in his choice of records to be used in the gospel classroom, keeping in mind that only that which is upbuilding is of God.

26. Study Periods

A study period is an allotment of time wherein students individually or collectively apply their thinking to a given subject or problem.

The length of time spent in study periods in class should be determined by the concentration span of the students, by the amount of student motivation relative to the material to be studied, and by the nature of the material to be studied.

Generally the younger the students the shorter the study period should be. Only in exceptional cases with students in their late teens and beyond should an entire period be utilized in study. Ordinarily not more than one-third or one-half of the period should be used for study in child and adolescent classes. From lesson to lesson, it is best to vary the length of study periods to provide variety. Often the class might be conducted without any study period.

It is usually better for a study period to follow other class activities that prepare the student for study.

One of the most frequent causes of unruly students in study periods is improper motivation on the material to be studied. To create motivation, the teacher should give complete explanation and examples relative to the assignment. He should also show students how the material to be studied will be useful and interesting to them.

Usually greater learning takes place during class study periods than out-of-class study. The reason for this is that the teacher is available to answer questions and give explanations. Out-of-class study is advantageous, however, in that it does not involve precious classtime. Linking assignments are usually completed outside of class.

During a study period, keep the following in mind:

a. Be available to assist students. If they need help, they should remain seated and raise their hands. The teacher is then to go to the student. Ordinarily it is best for the teacher to stand during a study session, periodically walking quietly among students, observing and assisting.

b. The teacher should whisper when giving help so as not to disturb others. This also encourages others to whisper when problems are discussed.

c. You may find that soft melodic orchestrations or choir selections played on a phonograph create an atmosphere for study. However, background music should not be used if it is disturbing to even one student.

d. Ordinarily do not start a study period five or ten minutes before the end of the period. This is a student's most restless time. It is hard for him to settle down to study, thinking the bell is going to ring any minute.

e. Once a study period commences, do not continually interrupt to give further instructions. Take care of this before study begins.

f. Be sure that students have necessary supplies. Make at least one dictionary available to students.

g. Provide proper lighting, heat, and ventilation. Eliminate annoying noises.

h. If students are studying a textbook or scriptures, provide bookmarks on which they can write questions. After writing a question on the marker, the student leaves it in the book on the page he is reading. He then continues reading, using a new marker for the next question.

27. Testimonies

A testimony is a solemn affirmation of what is felt to be right. It is bearing witness of the divinity of truth. Expressions of appreciation and gratitude are also considered a part of testimony bearing.

As students study and learn a truth, they ought to be given opportunity to express their convictions relative to the truth. The Lord has provided a monthly fast and testimony meeting for this purpose. Students should therefore be encouraged by their instructor to participate in these meetings.

Opportunities for students to bear testimony in class should be provided. After teaching a truth, the instructor may ask individuals to express conviction of what they have learned. Occasionally a testimony meeting might be held in class. Such a meeting should grow out of a lesson on testimony bearing or out of a spiritual experience the class has enjoyed together. Students should never be compelled to bear testimony. For this reason it is improper to have participants bear testimony in a particular order. They should voluntarily express themselves as they feel impressed to respond.

As teachers, our major purpose is to assist pupils in attaining strong conviction. Our first responsibility is to build undeviating conviction within ourselves, and then we must impart these testimonies in word and deed to our students. With every lesson, the teacher should directly or indirectly express a sincere affirmation and conviction of the divinity of that principle. When an instructor is unable to do this sincerely, he ought not to teach that principle.

28. Tutorial

The tutorial method is represented with the idea of a teacher sitting on one end of a log and a student on the other end. It is characterized by a teacher and student in a face-to-face relationship interacting meaningfully on given subject matter.

Socrates is usually given credit for inventing the tutorial approach. This Greek philosopher made a departure from the age-old notion of pouring new ideas into an empty brain, with an emphasis upon drawing out universal truths from the mind in which they already lie concealed. His teaching was done by conversation. He would often disarm strangers with a cheerful kindly demeanor and an attitude of humility, expressing his ignorance and the need for a little instruction. He would have a positive end in view that he concealed from the student until near the end of the conversation. He would proceed by asking questions, guiding the student skilfully to his pre-planned purpose. Through questioning, he would cause the student to search hard and long within himself for answers. Socrates would often refrain from turning on his full power by playing down his own originality. At the end of the conversation the student would, however, have new insights and be quite aware that he had been under the tutelage of a master of the art.

The tutorial approach is a powerful method because of the student's immediate and ongoing accessibility to the teacher and thus to the teacher's knowledge. But it is costly in professional instruction time. One teacher must spend many hours week after week with his protege. Ann Mansfield Sullivan literally spent years in tutoring Helen Keller.

In higher education the tutorial system is perhaps most evident when a faculty adviser spends many hours and days working with a student who is preparing a dissertation. The pupil prepares a body of work by himself. He then takes it for criticism and correction to to the tutor. The tutor goes over it with the greatest possible thoroughness, criticizing everything to the tiniest detail. Observing his mistakes, the student then returns to private study and revision. Each experience of the student with his mentor builds on former experiences together, thus giving continuity to the student's educational experience.

Classroom teachers can use various forms of the tutorial method by working with individual students outside of class. The tutorial method can be used on a more limited basis in class through individualized instruction. A natural setting for the tutorial method is in the home between parent and child. To be effective with the tutorial approach, the parent or teacher must carefully plan objectives, subject matter, materials, and learning activities that are meaningful to the child. He should meet on a regularly planned basis with the child and see that his ongoing instruction is systematic.

For further information on the tutorial method see Gilbert Highet, *The Art of Teaching.*[8]

29. Worksheets

A paper with duplicated instructions, questions, and problems is presented to each student in class. The sheets are usually completed by pupils on an individual basis during a study period. During the study period the teacher moves about the classroom assisting those in need of help.

Chapter 13, page 155, presents techniques in developing the highly-effective graphic art worksheet. Beginning with page 156 is a presentation on how to make good questions for student worksheets. Page 157 explains in simple form how to illustrate a graphic art worksheet.

In case you do not have a duplicator or mimeograph machine, instructions on how to use the inexpensive hectograph duplicating process are provided on page 163 of chapter 13.

Chapter 21
NOTES AND REFERENCES

[1]Adapted from materials used by the LDS Department of Education.

[2]Herbert J. Klausmeier, *Teaching in the Secondary School* (New York: Harper & Row, 1958).

[3]The comparison examination was developed by Donald B. Jessee.

[4]Presented with the approval of the Department of Seminaries and Institutes, The Church of Jesus Christ of Latter-day Saints.

[5]Adapted from Norris M. Sanders, *Classroom Questions: What Kinds?* (New York: Harper and Row, 1966); see particularly pp. 1-5.

[6]Ibid.

[7]Benjamin S. Bloom, ed., *Taxonomy of Educational Objectives* (New York: Longmans, Green, 1956).

[8]This section on the tutorial method was largely adapted from Gilbert Highet, *The Art of Teaching* (New York: Vintage Books, 1955), pp. 107-116.

CHAPTER 22

Teacher-Centered Methods

(During instruction the teacher develops the ideas to be taught.)

30. Demonstration

Demonstration is a process of showing, illustrating, or explaining an idea, object, or skill. Role playing and dramatization are among the many techniques for demonstrating an idea or skill. The presentations of a map or physical model are examples of demonstrating objects. Giving an object lesson is a demonstration process.

The possibilities of what might be demonstrated when teaching gospel lessons is almost unlimited. For example, leadership skills or teaching skills might be demonstrated by role playing what to do and what not to do. How to baptize might be demonstrated in a priests class. How to be an effective homemaker might be demonstrated in Relief Society. How to present a stimulating talk or throw a basketball might be demonstrated in MIA. In a formal class of gospel instruction or in family home evening, the crucifixion might be brought to life by demonstrating a crown of thorns, a real cross, and a large spike. The degrees of glory might be demonstrated by using a mobile hanging from the ceiling of the classroom.

When presenting a demonstration—

a. See that all necessary materials are on hand before the lesson starts.

b. Have each step of the demonstration clearly in mind as well as the lesson objective. It is often a good idea to practice the demonstration before class.

c. During the demonstration, be sure that what you are showing is in view of all class members.

d. Ordinarily tell the students in advance what to look for during the demonstration.

    e. Keep the presentation simple.

    f. Keep the demonstration moving and use varied approaches.

    g. Involve students as much as possible.

    h. At the end, review key points of the demonstration.

31. Jokes and Puns

Jokes and puns are used to excite or elicit a laugh. This is accomplished by saying the unexpected, by creating an illusion, or by a play on words. Jokes and puns have no equal as escape mechanisms for strained classroom relationships, and no class is immune or free from such relationships. Students want to laugh, and they appreciate a teacher who will laugh with them.

Prepared jokes that tie in with the lesson objective may be good; yet spontaneous humor is often most effective. Both are skills that can be developed.

Suggestions on how to develop spontaneous humor are presented in chapter 3, page 27. People often encounter pitfalls when making an effort to be funny. Cautions are therefore given beginning on page 28 of the text.

32. Lecture

A lecture is a formal verbal discourse intended for instruction. It is usually presented by the teacher.

Some people have the false concept that lecture is the least desirable teaching method used in the gospel classroom. It would be more realistic to say that Lecture is among the most abused teaching methods.

Lecture can be productive when properly presented. With this method the student must have the ability to interpret word images into what he already understands. Young minds are often unable to relate the verbal message into their inexperienced lives, particularly if the message is received in vague wordology and a monotone voice. Many adult minds are also inexperienced with the concepts they hear. Therefore, to bridge this gap and make the lecture, productive the lecturer to any age group should employ every possible aid at his disposal. Here are a few suggestions to enhance your lectures:

    a. Be effective in what you say and how you say it (see chapter 3, pp. 33-37 for specific helps).

    b. Use stories, examples, and comparisons to illustrate a point. Let objects help you tell your story (see chapter 14, p. 166, for instructions on how to develop an effective object lesson).

    c. Dramatize your presentations (see pp. 92-93, 100).

d. Bring enthusiasm and spontaneous humor into the lecture. (see pp. 25-28).

e. Use chalkboard illustrations, charts, and maps to help you talk (see chapters 15-18, pp. 171-263, on how to use the chalkboard effectively).

f. Use the flannelboard (see method 44, "Flannelboard").

g. Bring in colorful pictures (see method 51, "Pictures").

h. Present your lecture, using a flipboard demonstration (see method 46, "Flipboard,").

Lecture is almost always over-used in gospel classes to the exclusion of many more desirable student-centered methods. The student tends to learn best when he is seeing and doing, rather than merely hearing. Therefore, lecture should not be used exclusively, nor as a major instructional technique. It does have the advantage of covering a large amount of material in a short amount of time.

When lecture is used in presenting a lesson, it should generally be limited to less than one-half or one-third of the classtime. Research on language in the classroom points out that teachers usually talk from 65% to 75% of classtime, which of course is excessive. When presented properly, lecture can be useful in the following types of presentations:

a. Overviewing a lesson or unit.

b. Presenting information not available in a student text.

c. Explaining a process.

d. Expressing a point of view.

e. Presenting a large amount of material in a limited amount of time.

f. Summarizing a lesson or unit.

33. Preassessment and Evaluation

When a teacher preassesses a student, he makes an appraisal of the student's needs, feelings, interests, or understandings. This he does by observing the behavior of the student from other sources such as friends, parents, other teachers, pretests, and inventories. A good deal of preassessment can and should take place during the lesson as the student acts and reacts to his instructional environment. For example, the teacher might preassess as the student responds or fails to respond in a class discussion; when the student participates in an instructional game, debate, buzz session, or test; or when the student supports or violates class rules.

How a student thinks and feels is often not easily discernible. For effective preassessment, the teacher must be alert and sensitive to students in interpreting their performances. A teacher who is worthy and sensitive to the promptings of the Holy Spirit may receive spiritual discernment in appraising his students' needs.

Preassessment provides a basis for the teacher to establish relevancies between the student and himself as teacher, the subject matter, materials, and methods. This technique can therefore help to make the students' learning experiences more meaningful. Preassessment is then a means of appraising students before and during any given teaching moment with the purpose of making what is to be taught more meaningful.

The term *student evaluation* is generally used as an appraisal in or out of class of what the student *has learned as a result of instruction.* It differs from preassessment in that it is a measurement of what students have learned from what they have been taught.

Because a lesson objective is a definition of what is to be taught and a statement of intended change that will be made in students, the lesson objective is the key criterion for evaluating what students have learned as a result of instruction. An effective way to evaluate is to compare student behavior during or at completion of a lesson or unit of lessons with the preplanned objective.

Evaluation takes place by means of observation of student performances as students participate in learning activities, such as linking assignments, discussion, written assignments, problem solving, question-answer, summarizing, and instructional games. The most common means of evaluating is the administering of examinations and tests (see method 10, p. 282). Whether preparing an examination or using other methods to evaluate, use the lesson objective as the primary basis to make the evaluation.

34. Reading Orally

One of the most serious errors a teacher can make is to read a lesson from the manual. Extensive scriptural passages and long articles should not be read orally in class unless the material is of exceptional interest to students, and it is read skillfully.

(See method 21, "Reading Orally, p. 296).

35. Storytelling

Storytelling is the portrayal of an incident in which the students visualize the action of a narrative unfold before them. The students associate themselves directly with what is taking place in the story.

Someone once said, "A definition is a prison, but a story is a sunrise." Christ acknowledged the sunrise, because storytelling in the form of parables was among the most common teaching methods with Him.

Preparation is indispensable to effective storytelling. While preparing, as you read the story, visualize each character and event as though your were actually there. Let every episode become a visual picture in your mind. Think through the story over and over again until it is a living part of you. When telling the story, establish these visual images in the minds of your listeners. You will do this if you relive the visual images as you tell of them. Let the listeners become imbued with your spirit. Be specific and colorful in your expressions. This will give the story action and help create visual images. Rather than saying, "It was a rough ride on the boat," say, "The boat tossed and rocked and pitched." Bring actual conversation into your story.

Here is the climax to the thrilling story of Magnus written by Lorin F. Wheelwright and presented in chapter 1 (p. 00). Notice the detail, the colorful descriptions, the action, and the conversation.

> In the dim light he could not see his little boy, but he could hear little feet running toward him; and in a moment he reached out into the darkness and clasped his son to his heart. Then Angelo spoke, "Daddy, Daddy, how did you find me?" And Magnus, with tears running down his cheeks, sobbed, half-answering and half praying a thanksgiving, "Son," he said, "I fould you by becoming a child again."

The story you choose is justified in a lesson when its message is aimed directly at the lesson objective. The story is also enhanced if it is real to the students—if there are visual images and people with whom pupils can identify. A science fiction story of a Martian flying to the moon may be exciting to hear, but such a story may have little relationship to a fifteen-year-old's real-life experiences. The Old Testament story of the boy Joseph's being sold into slavery by his brothers may have particular value if the student listeners have brothers with whom they are sometimes incompatible. Because this part of the story relates to the listeners' lives, it is the part of the story that should be emphasized. A story will live with the listeners if it is actually a part of the listeners—if it envelops their feelings, needs, interests and understandings.

Often visuals will help tell your story. If listeners are fully enrapt with you in a story, however, a visual might distract.

You might dramatize your story. In practice, picture your listeners as "seated beyond a glass wall in a soundproof room. Every good effect you achieve must result from how you look at those watching you from that glassed-in room, how you impress them initially, how you behave throughout each moment that your story lasts."[1] The "eye-appeal score" your make-believe audience gives you will help determine your success as a story-dramatizer. After the practice presentation, ask yourself, "Could the audience read the story in my actions, or did I stand almost lifeless with only my mouth moving?" Your face and hands can do a lot of talking. You might try putting physical action into your stories, but be sure that this action appears natural and complements the mood of the story. Don't let your mechanics show!

Build a story file. Collect stories of great men and women, old-time tales, bedtime stories, and fables. Add to this file the most valuable of all storytelling resources—your personal experiences. No one knows these stories as you do. No one can relate them as vividly as you can. Why? Because you have actually lived the experiences. The visual images are already before you. They are your very own. Make use of your file by telling the stories frequently.

Chapter 7 gives more extensive coverage on the art of telling a story with dramatization (p. 100), selection (p. 93), and preparation and delivery (p. 97).

36. Summarizing

When a teacher summarizes a lesson, he is in process of reviewing key ideas made in the lesson and expressing conclusions. The period of summary is a time to refocus on the lesson objective in cumulating effort to give students direction. Effective summaries in gospel lessons frequently call for action by the students.

Some of the purposes in summarizing are to—

    a. Illuminate important ideas.
    b. Formulate meaningful conclusions.
    c. Refocus on the lesson objective.
    d. Correct inaccurate ideas of class members.
    e. Give direction for future action.

Here are a few ways to summarize a lesson:[2]

    a. Preassign one or two students to summarize the lesson objective for the class.

    b. Prepare and use a worksheet that helps class members summarize the main idea of the lesson as they fill it out.

    c. Have each student write or tell what he thinks the objective is in his own words.

    d. Have each student tell one thing he learned from this lesson.

    e. During the summary say, "If someone asks you today what you learned in class, what will you tell them?"

    f. As the lesson proceeds, make a list of ideas discussed on the chalkboard to be used at the end of the lesson to summarize.

    g. (For young children.) After the lesson, have children *draw* a *picture* of something significant that happened in the lesson. Then call on each child to tell about his picture.

    h. Have students summarize a series of lessons, especially those in which there has been a continuing story (like Joseph Smith's receiving the plates for the Book of Mormon or the crucifixion and resurrection of Jesus Christ), by taking a whole class period and drawing a mural or acting out a play.

    i. For unit summaries or review, play the game of Charades. The class divides into small groups, and each group in turn acts out some part of a lesson or story. The other groups try to guess what is being depicted (see p. 137).

37. Visiting Authority

A visiting authority is one invited into the classroom to make a special presentation. He is well qualified and commands respect in his topic of presentation. This person is called in not to give the teacher a rest, but to answer a classroom need of specialized instruction relative to a lesson.

Visiting authorities in a gospel classroom might include, for example, an LDS medical doctor to discuss the Word of Wisdom, a police officer to give instruction in obeying the laws of the land, a returned missionary to stimulate enthusiasm within students relative to going on a mission, a scientist to lecture on scientific evidences that there is a God, a stake president to explain a principle of church organization, or a bishop to discuss his relationship with youth. Parents might consider occasionally inviting an authority to participate in family home evenings.

Much caution should be taken by the teacher in selecting the visitor he brings into the classroom to make special presentation. The visiting authority should have a strong testimony of the gospel and be well grounded in Church teachings. He should be qualified in his field, have personality appeal, and show evidence of teaching ability. When asked to participate, he should be given a thorough understanding of what the class is studying and of what is expected of him in his presentation.

Only occasionally should a visiting authority be invited into the classroom. The teacher is the classroom authority. Ordinarily if he feels unqualified to teach a given subject. he should study, research, and pray until he becomes qualified. The teacher should be competent and confident in the principles he teaches from the course outline.

It has frequently been a practice in Church classrooms to assign class members to take turns teaching the lesson. Although student participation is highly desirable, this practice is educationally unsound. Here is why:

Lessons from day to day or from week to week should be related. This is done through reviews (repetition of major points is essential for learning to take place) and through the teacher's comparing and relating the present presentation with principles studied in previous lessons. Having a different teacher give each lesson weakens this continuity and follow-up.

Each time a new teacher takes over a lesson, students must readjust to his personality, philosophy, and methods of teaching. Thus, time is lost and frustration increased. Teachers can be most effective when they teach every lesson consistently over a period of months and years, with a visiting authority presenting a lesson only occasionally.

Chapter 22
NOTES AND REFERENCES

[1]A. Hamer Reiser, *A Reader for the Teacher,* p. 164; Thatcher Allred, "Test Your Storytelling," *Instructor*, Aug 1953, 88:249.

[2]Adapted from *Teacher Development Inservice Administrator-Instructor Materials,* Series 3, 1972-73, lesson 6, "Challenge at Conclusion."

Materials-Centered Methods

(During instruction, materials are used as a primary means of transmitting subject matter to students.)

38. Bulletin Boards

A bulletin board is an area of such surfaces as cork sheet, celotex, peg board, rope, or fabric on which instructional materials are attached to demonstrate ideas.

Gospel classrooms could be enhanced if each were outfitted with a large bulletin board, and if the board display were utilized and changed periodically.

A bulletin board should be placed on the back or a side wall of the classroom so it can be seen by students as they enter and leave the room. If placed on the front wall and the concept displayed on the board does not relate to the lesson objective (which often is the case), the board will lead student thinking away from the lesson rather than toward it. With the board placed at the side or back of the room, the teacher would do well at times to relate it to a lesson or series of lessons being taught. Ideally, a bulletin board would cover at least one-third of the wall space on which it is displayed in a classroom.

A bulletin board in the dining area or family room of a home, as in the classroom, can be used to provide children with creative experiences as they plan and prepare interesting and colorful charts and scenes using various materials. In the home or classroom, the bulletin board can be used to post family home evening or class assignments, reminder cards, and special announcements.

Here are a few ideas for making an effective and appealing bulletin board:

Plan the entire layout before going to work on the actual display. With a pencil, sketch different layouts. With each layout, plan color combinations, letter sizes and styles, shapes, and materials to be used. Plan the bulletin board display from an idea, rather than from a picture or illustration that is already available.

Keep it simple. Try to put over only one major idea, rather than several. Don't let your bulletin board become a conceptual junk yard. For example, if the display is on the Sermon on the Mount, don't clutter the board with several colors, a large amount of writing, several different sizes and styles of letters, or several pictures depicting a different idea in the sermon. Rather, confine yourself to two or three solid colors; limit the number of words, using not more than three sizes; use simple bold or block lettering; and use few pictures, which are uncluttered, large, and vivid in color. Silhouettes, outline drawing, and cartoons help attain simplicity. There may be value in keeping the key idea specific. For example, rather than labeling a display "Sermon on the Mount," boil it down to a more specific idea such as prayer, anger, or the Beatitudes.

Make the lettering large and readable. Use letter stencils on colored construction paper or cut out block letters. When cutting out letters, place a contrasting color of construction paper beneath the original and cut the two sheets at once. When tacking the letters on the board, place one color of the letter above the other. Then slide the outer letter up and to the left. This makes a shaded letter, giving a third dimension to the lettering.

To obtain other three-dimensional effects, use such materials as cork, balls, pipe cleaner, cotton, crumpled cellophane or tissue, fish net, angel hair, folded cardboard, folded construction paper, yarn, styrofoam, and wire. Children's plastic toys can easily be attached to a bulletin board with wire or tacks representing large objects in miniature.

Good adhering materials are masking tape, bulletin board wax, map pins, straight pins, thumbtacks, and wire.

To attach objects to rope-type bulletin boards, glue or tape a clothespin on the back side of the object. Pin the object on the rope.

The eye should be able to sweep in a definite path over the board, and the parts of the composition should ordinarily lead into a focal point. All parts should thus appear to harmonize or belong to each other. Watch magazines for layout ideas.

A bulletin board is to complement lessons being studied and enhance the classroom or home environment. It should serve as a learning experience to students. Teach pupils how to create neat impressive displays and then give them the responsibility of keeping the board up-to-date. To stimulate interest, hold competition between classes or individuals to see which group or individual can produce the best bulletin board display. Special judges might be chosen outside of the class or home. They should judge the compositions on such items as purpose, simplicity, neatness, balance, interest, and style.

39. Chalkboard (General Uses)

The chalkboard is a functional instructional material for gospel teaching. Every classroom should be equipped with a large slate board placed in front of the room. At least a portable chalkboard should be available in every home for use in family home evenings and for other family educational activities. The value of a chalkboard lies in the fact that it is usually accessible. Printing, writing, sketches, graphs, maps, and other markings can be produced quickly and erased immediately. Chalk is inexpensive, and there is little cost of time and money for chalkboard upkeep.

Suggestions are given in chapter 19 on general uses of the chalkboard other than chalkboard illustrations as follows:

a. Directing discussions and organizing lessons in steps and lists (p. 251).

b. Making charts and maps (p. 253).

c. Emphasizing the lesson objective and thought-provoking statements (p. 257).

d. Outlining units or blocks of study (p. 258).

e. Making assignments (p. 258).

f. Directing and scoring instructional games (p. 258).

g. Making summaries and conclusions (p. 258).

h. Chalkboard grid (p. 258).

i. Chalkboard stencil (p. 259).

j. Chalk and guidelines (p. 259).

k. Chalkboard templet (p. 259).

l. Using opaque projections and overhead transparencies on the chalkboard (p. 260). (see also method 50, "Overhead Transparency Projections," p. 333, and method 49, "Opaque Projections," p. 333).

m. Chalkboard hints—thirteen suggestions on improving chalkboard techniques (p. 260).

40. Chalkboard Illustrations

Freehand illustrating on the chalkboard can be used effectively even by teachers who feel they do not have artistic ability. Chapters 15-18 present chalkboard illustrating techniques on such a simplified basis that anyone can learn. The following list will help you locate specific study areas on chalkboard illustrating:

    a. How to sketch the eight basic positions of the *stick figure* (pp. 171-87).

    b. How to sketch eight different facial expressions in balanced dimensional form (pp. 189-202).

    c. Practice sheet for learning 49 different facial expressions (p. 203).

    d. How to sketch the following *symbols* (pp. 207-36):

Books and Records

    (1) Closed book
    (2) Open book
    (3) Plates
    (4) Papyrus roll
    (5) Papyrus scroll
    (6) Paper and quill pen

Buildings

    (7) Temple or church
    (8) Home
    (9) Ancient city

Means of Transportation

    (10) Car
    (11) Boat
    (12) Covered wagon

Objects

    (13) Mountain
    (14) Cloud

    (15) Tree
    (16) Grave
    (17) Light bulb
    (18) Stairs
    (19) Money
    (20) Strong drink
    (21) Sword
    (22) Altar
    (23) Scale

Animals, Whale, Bird

    (24) Sheep
    (25) Camel
    (26) Horse
    (27) Whale
    (28) Bird

    e. How to create your own chalkboard illustrated lessons (pp. 239-50).

41. Charts and Maps

A chart provides information in such forms as a graph, diagram, map, or map-o-graph. A key purpose of a chart is to help pupils visualize an idea that would be more difficult to understand if taught only in words.

A chart can be duplicated on letter-size paper for student use or presented on a large classroom poster, flipboard, roll-up, folded cardboard of plywood, or long strip of paper (butcher paper and newsprint are inexpensive and practical).

When developing a chart, ask yourself:

    a. What main idea is to be presented?

    b. What supporting ideas should I use in conveying the main idea?

c. Is a chart the best means of putting over the idea?

d. Which type of chart will best put over the idea?

The following types of charts will help in giving you an idea of what to use and how to develop it:

(1) *Bar Graph.* The bar graph is particularly useful in showing comparisons and in representing mass. The bars can be made to run vertically or horizontally. By cross-hatching or making part of the bar darker, it can be subdivided to give more facts.

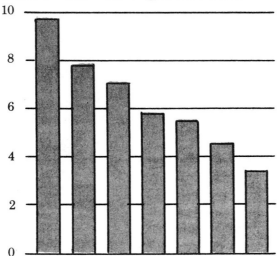

(2) *Line Graph.* Line graphs are useful when you want to tell a statistical history. The lines are used to indicate a specific quantity, amount, or degree—one scale, for example, showing the date, and another scale showing fluctuation. The graph line can be arranged either vertically or horizontally. Comparisons can be shown by using solid, broken, darkened, colored, or dotted lines.

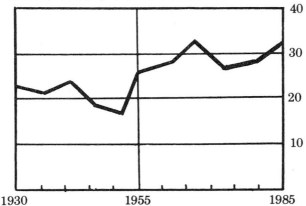

(3) *Pie Graph.* Use the pie graph to compare parts of a whole, such as the population of the Christian religions in relation to world population.

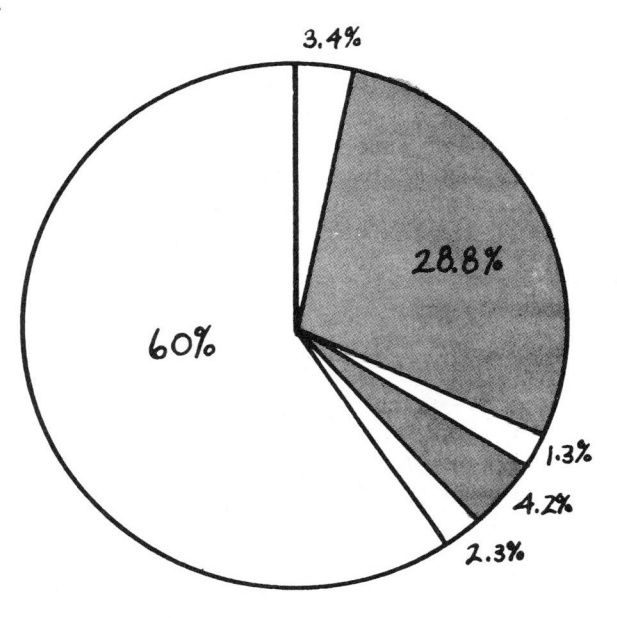

(4) *Pictorial Graph.* A graph can often be made more readable and eye-catching by using pictures to tell the story. When using repetitive pictures, as with men and buildings, a stencil or templet might be made so all figures are uniform.

(5) *Map-o-graph.* A map-o-graph is a combination map and line graph. An arrowed chronological line is drawn to different points on the map, indicating both where and when the events took place. Brief explanations usually accompany the line to assist in giving further clarification and explanation to the geographical history (for example, see page 323.)[1]

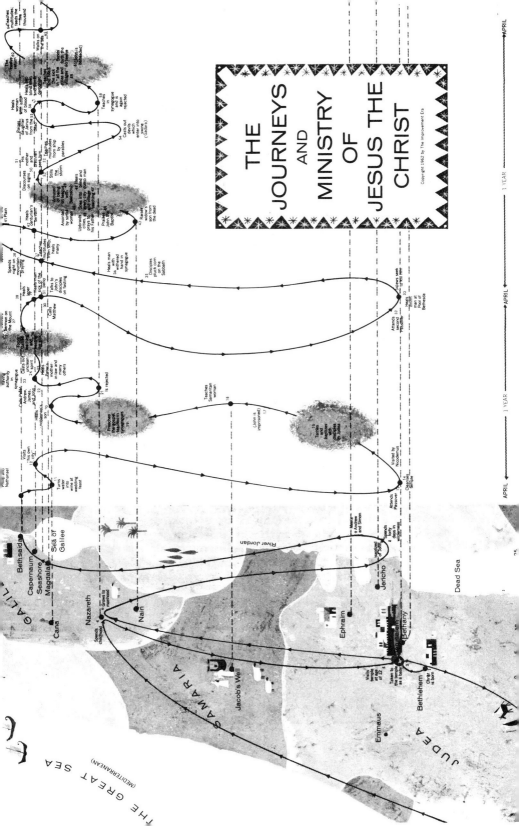

THE JOURNEYS AND MINISTRY OF JESUS THE CHRIST

Copyright 1962 by The Improvement Era

(6) *Map.* Individual student outline maps and larger maps for group use can be very useful in teaching a number of gospel subjects, particularly those pertaining to history and geography. Some of the useful maps in the gospel classroom are the Old Testament world; different periods and divisions of Palestine for study of Old and New Testament; the United States for Church history study; the world for study of missions, Church expansion, and for establishing relationships of countries to each other.

Here are some of the types of maps available in bookstores:

Outline maps are simple line drawings showing boundaries, major cities, and rivers. These are very useful as fill-ins for assignments or tests.

Topographical maps show land surface, indicating elevation, desert land, mountains, and bodies of water.

Relief maps appear almost as miniature models of parts of the earth's surface prepared with three-dimensional effect.

Picture maps illustrate animals, buildings, people, and vegetation as they are located in a given geographical location. The picture map usually covers a small geographical area.

Globes are useful in gospel teaching. They should be large in size if used in group instruction.

(7) *Tree chart.* This chart is used for establishing genealogical relationships. It also can be used to illustrate an idea or organization that has evolved out of a parent idea or organization, such as Protestant churches.

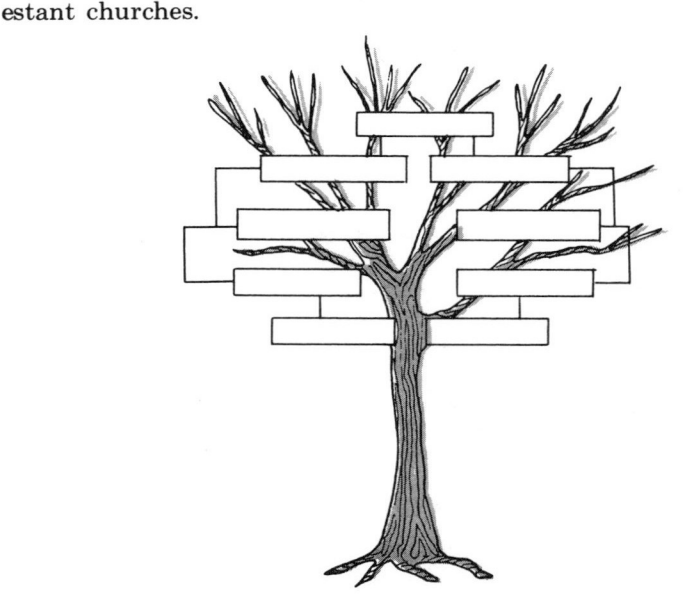

(8) *Step chart.* The step chart is useful in teaching principles of progression or regression, such as repentance or apostasy.

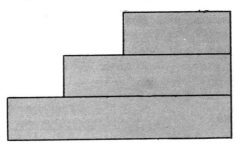

Flat charts and maps are effective when covered with acetate or plastic. Colored or black grease pencils can be used to mark and give emphasis to points of interest. These marks are easily erased with cloth.

Young groups enjoy experience charts on which record is kept of student reading or other individualized class activities.

For further helps on making charts and graphs with chalk, see chapter 19, pages 253-57.

42. Displays, Table and Mobiles

Table displays and mobiles are objects developed and organized into three-dimensional scenes. Their purpose is to provide students with creative construction projects and to furnish the classroom with stimulating instructional objects. Mobiles are displays hung from the ceiling with thin wire or string. They move with the slightest breeze—hence the name mobile.

In assigning display projects to students, complete displays should not be already planned for them. Rather, students should be provided with suggested ideas and materials and then be allowed to use their own creative imaginations in developing the displays. When undertaking special class projects, students who have no interest in model construction should be given alternate assignments such as writing a story, painting a picture, or preparing a book report. Individualized projects stimulate creativity.

Displays can be developed on the hundreds of stories and teachings found in the scriptures. The Creation could be presented as a mobile with the earth displayed in its six creative stages. Six plastic or styrofoam balls could be used for the earths, with colored papier-mache, and tiny objects applied to give necessary effects.

The story of Joseph in the Old Testament could be depicted in a sandbox. Joseph and his brothers could be made by using pipe cleaner for the arms, legs, and torsos. Bubble gum, pecan nuts, or marshmallows could be used for the heads of the sons of Israel. Tiny rocks, moss, a glass underlaid with blue paper, and weeds could be used for scenery. Little tufts of cotton with toothpicks for legs would account for the sheep.

As a project for classroom reverence, students could draw and color a cartoon elephant on poster paper. After the elephant is cut out, the opposite side could be drawn and colored, representing the back of the elephant. It could be holding a sign with its trunk that would read, "Remember where you are!" This mobile could be hung from the ceiling just above the classroom door.

Other properties useful in creating displays are:

Clay (Can be molded into almost any form)
Twigs (Fences)
Wood scraps (Buildings)
Cube sugar (blocks in temples and buildings)
Dirt and sand (hills and mountains)
Spray snow (snow)
Colored tape (roads)
Toys (minatures of life-size objects)
Spray paint (color grass and buildings)
Cardboard boxes (houses or wagons)
Angel hair (cloud)
Cotton (cloud)
Pine cones (pine trees)
Dyed popcorn (shrubs)
Stiff wire (to suspend an object out away from other parts of the display)

43. Filmstrips and Sound Filmstrips

The instructional filmstrip consists of a series of still pictures placed in sequential order usually on 35mm film. Ordinarily twenty to eighty frames are on a reel.

Sound filmstrips are filmstrips as described above but accompanied with tape or disc recordings.

The instructional value in the use of a filmstrip can often be enhanced when used along with recordings, discussion techniques, and special student projects.[2] The sound filmstrip is a popular teaching medium in church classes. The reason for this, along with its instructional value, is that the sound filmstrip is inexpensively produced. Filmstrip projectors, filmstrips, and records are relatively inexpensive. Filmstrips can be rented for as low as one dollar and purchased for less than five dollars each.

Many filmstrips and sound filmstrips are available to Church teachers in meetinghouse libraries; at the motion picture production department of Brigham Young University, Provo, Utah and at commercial outlets for instructional materials such as Deseret Book Company in Salt Lake City. A listing of filmstrips is available in the *Instructional Materials Catalogue* available at meetinghouse libraries and distrubuted by Church distribution centers. Deseret Book will send annotated listings of their available films upon request. Religious filmstrips and sound filmstrips are availabe on such topics as:

Baptism
Bible history
Brotherhood
Life and teachings of Christ
Church history
Christian living
Christmas
Faith
New Testament
Old Testament
Parables
Repentance
Stewardship

Let the following criteria serve as a guide in choosing a filmstrip to supplement your lesson:

a. Does it provide the information I want to teach?

b. Will it create student interest in further pursuit of the topic?

c. Will it supplement and reinforce what we are studying in class?

d. Will it provide students with opportunities in problem solving? Does it promote critical thinking rather than "passive absorption"?

e. Is it on the students' level of understanding and feeling?

It is usually a good idea to prepare students to view the film. The teacher might explain how they will benefit from it, pointing out what to watch for and how to analyze certain scenes. You might write these items on the chalkboard for later reference. The students might be asked to make a list of main points brought out in the film that they have observed from the showing.

After the film, discuss with students what was learned. You may have students ask each other questions about the film. The teacher would do well to follow up on principles brought out in the film that can be applied immediately. This particularly applies to the open-end or case-study film that which ends at the climax of a story and leaves class members to solve the problem.

As a special project, the group might take colored slides when on a field trip and produce their own series of a slide film presentation.

As a point of information, the tachistoscope is a shutter-like device that can be attached to any standard filmstrip or slide projector. It is used for controlled flash exposures. The length of the exposure varies from 1/100 of a second to one second. It has been used effectively in classes for speed reading. Although little has been done with it, it may have application in the gospel classroom as a problem-solving technique.

One last suggestion: Wrap the projector cord around the leg of the table on which the projector is resting. This may help prevent broken bones and broken projectors.

44. Flannelboard

A flannelboard is a piece of rigid material covered with cotton flannel, felt suede cloth, or wool. Pictures and signs, backed with similar adhering material, are placed on the flannelboard in an organized order to teach a story or lesson.

Many flannelboard gospel lessons are available in meetinghouse libraries. However, it is an easy matter to create your own flannelboard lessons.

Prepare your pictures and signs on felt (comes in beautiful solid colors and adheres well), suede back paper, Flocktite (has adhesive backing), or klingtite (high grade art paper on which drawings can be made). Strips of medium or fine sandpaper can be glued to the back of flannel characters. Another process is to apply fingernail polish or glue to the back of the picture. Before drying, sprinkle it with sand or salt.

When placing a picture on the flannelboard, apply it with a slight downward movement and firm pressure. Otherwise the picture may slide off. Another safeguard is to tilt the top of the board slightly back so the pictures are not hanging vertically.

Use colored flannel or felt as background to add contrast and interest. Black may be an effective background if the pictures are white or in light pastels.

The first step in planning a flannelboard lesson is to draw up a thumbnail sketch on a sheet of paper. Plan simple shapes with brief significant statements. Use only a few pictures and signs, and plan everything toward a single idea lesson objective. Let color and design help you leave a lasting mental image with your students.

Before the presentation, pile pictures and signs in the order you plan to use them. Nothing is so distracting to a student watching a flannelboard presentation as to hear from the teacher, "I wonder what happened to the next piece?"

There are many advantages to a flannelboard:

a.   A flannelboard is easily made and inexpensive (simply fasten a piece of flannel cloth to a hard surface).

b.   Portable flannelboards are easy to carry and can be set up in any room or location.

c.   Flannel pictures, signs, and backing can be made in solid vivid colors, which stimulate attention and leave lasting impressions.

d.   Of necessity, flannel materials are prepared in advance. This lends to better prepared lessons. The materials can then be filed in manila folders or envelopes for later use.

e.   In a flannelboard presentation, pictures and signs can be moved about in any order.

f.   Teachers can prepare their own flannelboard presentations.

g.   Flannelboard presentations are adaptable to almost any lesson or subject.

h.   The flannelboard is useful in classes of all age groups.

Disadvantages are that time is required in preparing pictures and signs for a presentation, and the pictures and signs cannot be immediately redrawn to meet unplanned-for changes in a lesson.

45.   Flash Cards

A flash card is a strip of poster paper on which a statement, question, or word is written. A series of card strips are prepared for drill or lesson review. In the drill or lesson review, the teacher holds up the card and solicits student response. The response is voluntary, or the teacher designates who is to react. One technique is to flash the card, allowing only split-second viewing. Another approach is to post the flash card on a groove board, allowing more time for students to formulate an answer.

Scriptural references can be flashed on cards, with students identifying them.

A series of pictures can be used as flash cards. The teacher flashes the picture for a split second, having a student identify the scene.

Flash cards can be used as an instructional game by dividing the class into two groups. Fold each card once, and place the cards in a box or pile. Each team takes turns sending a team member to the front of the classroom. Not knowing what is on the cards, the student selects a folded strip. He reads it to the class, places it on a groove board at the front of the room, and then answers the question or discusses the word or statement on the card. A judge (preferably the teacher) determines the number of points to be given for each student response. Pupils on each team take turns participating.

Here are examples of the three types of flash cards:

a. *Statement* (student elaborates on the statement):
    Apostle Paul's first missionary journey.
    The Bible is the word of God.
    Baptism is essential to salvation.

b. *Question* (student answers the question):
    Where did Apostle Paul go on his first missionary journey?
    How do we know the Bible is the word of God?
    Why is baptism essential to salvation?

c. *Word* (student makes a statement to identify the word):
    Paul
    Bible
    Baptism

Flash cards can be made in any size or shape. A felt-tip pen is one of the most practical mediums for printing the letters.

46. Flip Board and Groove Board

A *flip board* is a series of charts, pictures, or plain sheets fastened to an easel with the purpose of giving a progressive lesson demonstration.

The minimum recommended size of a flip board for small group instruction is 18" x 24", while 24" x 30" is preferred. Newsprint pads are available at newspaper offices and are inexpensive.

A newsprint flipboard can be used as a substitute for a chalkboard when the latter is not available. Colored grease pencils or felt-tip pens can serve in place of chalk. These marks cannot be erased; therefore, when a sheet is filled, flip it over the top of the mounting to expose a clean sheet.

The newsprint flipboard is an excellent medium for presenting "chalk talks." The simple illustrations of chalk talks can be drawn on the newsprint sheets with colored chalk, grease pencils, or felt pens before or during the lesson.

The flip board is also effective in presenting a series of previously prepared graphs, maps, or pictorial charts.

Student interest is stimulated with the flip board in that pupils are anxiously waiting to see what is on the next sheet. Sheets can be flipped back for ready reference, and ideas can be presented progressively one at a time.

A *groove board* is a portable hard-back surface, fronted with $1/2''$-deep groves running horizontally across the board. Flash cards, pictures, and charts can be placed in the grooves for classroom demonstrations.

Quarter-inch plywood, masonite, or firm cardboard can be used for backing. For the grooves or pockets, fold a good quality paper, as illustrated, and glue it to the surface of the board. Another way is to sew plastic, oilcloth, or stiff paper pockets on a piece of cotton cloth or oilcloth. The cloth can then be pasted or fastened to the board. The groove board can be placed on a chalk tray, easel, or teacher's desk when in use.

47. Motion Pictures

A motion picture contains a series of many still frames flashed rapidly on a screen. The viewer sees each for a split second after it leaves the screen. When at least 24 frames a second are flashed on the screen in sequential order, the viewer sees smooth action as if he were viewing a limited area of the actual scene. A motion picture thus has the value of still pictures, plus action and cordinated sound. Motion pictures are limited in providing prolonged viewings of a scene, which is possible with filmstrips. The filmstrip also is less expensive. Motion pictures are, however, of considerable value as a teaching medium, particularly when used along with other teaching procedures and when in color.

More than a half billion dollars have been expended on short educational films in the past fifty years in the United States. Many of the thousands of films are in the field of religious education. Sixteen-millimeter motion pictures are available on a large number of religious subjects. Some motion pictures are available in meetinghouse libraries, regional libraries, and film distribution centers such as Educational Media Services at Brigham Young University, Provo, Utah. Many useful films can be purchased or rented at commercial outlets such as Deseret Book Company in Salt Lake City. A complete listing of religious motion pictures of The Church of Jesus Christ of Latter-day Saints is contained in the *Instructional Materials Catalogue* available at meetinghouse libraries and distributed by Church distribution centers. Catalogues of educational motion pictures may be obtained from many universities in the United States.

Students should be given an orientation of a film before viewing it. There should also be a follow-up discussion or work.activity after the viewing. The following procedure is one technique in accomplishing this purpose. It is use of a film study guide, and serves as a teacher-prepared and duplicated road map to effective motion picture viewing experiences.[3] The guides are prepared and handed out a day or two before the film is to be used. Students are instructed to review the guides as part of their homework.

When the time comes for the film to be viewed by the class, the teacher spends part of his film preparation time reviewing the study guide with his students and answering questions concerning it. After the film, the questions in the study guide are completed by the students and discussed. The guide can also be used as an examination. The guide would include such items as the following:

a. Name of student

b. Date

c. Title of lesson or unit

d. Film title

e. Short synopsis of the film (provided by the teacher)

f. A teacher's statement of the objective in using the film

g. A special vocabulary of words used in the film that may not be understood by the students

h. Points to look for in the film

i. References to texts and supplementary reading

More than eighty-five million people attend theatrical motion pictures weekly. Movies are a great medium of learning. Are you using this medium effectively in your classroom or home?

48. Object Lessons

In an object lesson presentation, a material object is used to demonstrate an idea with the purpose of promoting understanding of the idea.

Almost any object can be used in an object lesson presentation, and an object lesson can be prepared on almost any gospel subject. An object lesson, properly presented, can be an excellent method of teaching. Chapter 14, page 165, presents techniques in developing effective object lessons with emphasis on teaching students to create their own object lessons:

a. How Jesus Christ used object lessons (p. 165).

b. How to create an object lesson (p. 166).

c. Assignment sheet in helping students create their own object lesson (p. 169).

d. General suggestions (p. 168).

49. Opaque Projections

The opaque projector is a piece of equipment used to project non-transparent pictures, maps, diagrams, music, printed words, specimens, and objects onto a screen. These can project from black and white or color. The frame can be focused to almost any size by varying the distance of the projector from the screen. The size of the original to be projected can be from a postage stamp to a 10" x 10" picture. Objects and open books of three-inch thickness or less can be placed in the projector.

The picture in an opaque projector is reflected on the screen by means of a powerful lamp, mirrors, and large lens. The room must be dark to see a vivid image.

The opaque projector is an excellent medium for enlarging pictures, charts, or maps and tracing them on poster paper, chalkboards, or windows. The work area must be darkened for tracing. When tracing on a window, place a blind or sheet on the opposite side of the window from which the image is projected. It is usually best to trace first with a pencil (use black grease pencil on windows). Then lighten the room and color in the outline you have drawn.

The opaque projector is useful in showing any number of pictures to emphasize a point or supplement a lesson. It can be used to demonstrate cloth samples, insect specimens, student assignments, and cartoons.

Another technique is the opaque strip which is a series of flat pictures mounted together in sequential order. Presentations can thus be made similar to filmstrip presentations. An advantage of the opaque strip over a filmstrip is that flat pictures are easily accessible from Church periodicals and national color picture magazines, as well as individual pictures obtained in bookstores. Furthermore, flats are easily mounted and connected to produce a sequential presentation. Few materials have been produced commercially for use in opaque projectors, probably because of the availability of single flat pictures.

As a special project, students can prepare an opaque strip for a class presentation. By way of example, in a Church history class the group gathers pictures they feel will help tell a historical incident it wishes to portray. Students then select from this collection pictures for the presentation, mount them on cardboard backing, and connect the mounts with masking tape (or they can mount the pictures on long strips of paper). A narrative can be prepared and read by a student during the presentation, or it can be presented on a tape recorder. Selected recorded music might also be used to set a mood for the presentation.

50. Overhead Transparency Projections

An overhead projector is a piece of equipment that transmits rays of light through a translucent frame and projects the frame images on a screen. The 7″ x 7″ or 10″ x 10″ frame placed on a glass plate over a powerful beam for projection is called a transparency. The transparency is a piece of colorless or tinted plastic on which images have been drawn, painted, or photographed. An opaque line of any color placed on a transparency may appear black or gray on the screen. Translucent color such as water color, magic markers, and special transparency coloring processes, gives a screen image in technicolor.

Probably because many teachers have not been given an understanding of its value, the overhead projector has not yet found its rightful place with a large number of gospel teachers. Here are some reasons why this piece of equipment is of value in the classroom:

a.   The projected image is behind and over the head of the teacher. The instructor is thus facing his class while making the presentation. A large image can be made on the screen with the projector only a few feet away. The projector can thus be placed on the teacher's desk in front of the room.

b.   Projections can be made in a normally lighted room. Thus students can take notes, observe the teacher, and watch the screen during a presentation. If a screen is not available, projections can be made on a blank wall.

c.   When the teacher is making a presentation, the transparency, rather than the screen, is viewed by him. He can use a grease pencil or felt tip pen to write, draw, or paint during the presentation. Notes can also be attached to the side of the transparency for ready reference.

d.   A transparency can be covered with a sheet of white paper and disclosed line by line on the screen. With the bright underlight, the teacher can see the next items to be disclosed—yet these are not projected on the screen until the paper is removed.

e.   Transparency overlays can be used to add to or take away components of a system or process.

f.   Animated devices can be used, such as movable hands on a clock.

g.   An image can be projected on a chalkboard, and a student can draw or write on the image with chalk. This response can be erased, giving opportunity for the next student to respond.

A disadvantage in using the overhead projector is that pictures, charts, and maps have to be produced in translucent form in order to be projected. This involves more time in preparing the slides and slightly more expense than is involved in opaque projections. The overhead projector should not, however, be compared with the opaque projector as to value, because each serves a particular need.

Many of the meetinghouse libraries have a file of transparencies for gospel instruction as well as equipment to prepare transparencies.

For further helps on the overhead projector, see the book *They See What You Mean* (Johnson City, New York: Ozalid Audio-Visual Department, Division of General Anailine and Film Corporation, 1959).

51. Pictures

"A picture is the shortest distance between two minds" (old axiom of the Orient). When used to supplement a lesson, a picture should be relevant to what the students understand. Pictures that include homes, trees, babies, children, dogs, cats, and parents give small children a basis with which to associate parts of a lesson that before may not have been understood. Teenagers respond readily to such pictures as a car, football game, dance, baseball player, dinner table, or a student reading a book. It is obvious that, as the learner matures, the scope and intricate quality of the pictures can be expanded. All age groups respond to bright solid colors and distinct objects. Storytelling action pictures, humanized animals, and simplified cartoons also have eye appeal to all age groups.

A picture should not be a substitute for lesson preparation. In fact, the picture should be studied beforehand by the teacher so that the best possible use can be made of it in class. If it does not firmly support the lesson objective, it should not be used.

Pictures that are suggestive, immodest, cluttered with detail, drab, dirty, small, wrinkled, or not self-explanatory should not be used.

When demonstrating a picture in the classroom, you might keep it hidden until the proper time for showing. Then hold it high so everyone can see it. If it is to remain in view of the students, place it in a picture holder as illustrated in figure 1.

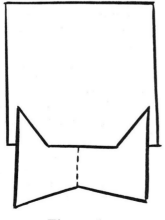

Figure 1

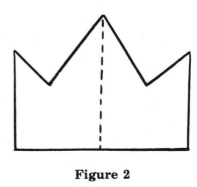

Figure 2

The picture holder is easily made by cutting out the pattern in figure 2 from a piece of cardboard. When the outline is cut out, perforate the cardboard along the dotted line and reinforce the inside with a strip of masking tape. The size of the holder should be determined by the size of the pictures to be displayed.

Church magazines and national picture magazines offer a wealth of pictures for classroom use.

If you cannot find a desired picture to enhance a lesson objective, cut out and combine pictures, letters, or words, thus creating the picture you want. For instance, a picture showing how anger can injure others is desired. In one page of a magazine is a picture of a man pounding his fist angrily. On another page is a man with a painful look on his face. Cut out the two men, discarding the rest of the two pictures. Glue the suffering man beneath the angry man on a plain-colored sheet of construction paper, and the picture is ready for use.

Because of the importance of pictures in teaching, every teacher should keep a picture file. To preserve the pictures, they should be mounted on heavy paper or stiff cardboard. Many meetinghouse libraries have a dry-mount press for mountig pictures so they last. Many pictures are available in meetinghouse libraries.

52. Posters

A poster is a placard posted in a conspicuous place that is large enough for public view. It could be a picture, chart, diagram, map, or part of a bulletin board display.

As a special class project for children or adolescents, students could be assigned to make posters on an individual or small-group basis. Each student or group is handed a large sheet of poster paper with instructions to—

a. Choose a specific idea to be illustrated on the poster.

b. Draw a thumbnail sketch on a letter-size sheet of paper, planning the design, lettering, coloring, and materials to be used.

c. Outline the plan with pencil on the poster paper and color it with crayon, water color, or poster paint. (Students might use the opaque projector to enlarge and trace lettering or "outline pictures" on the poster paper. The teacher should suggest the use of letter stencils, three-dimensional objects, pipe cleaner, glitter, and different types of pictures to encourage creativity.)

As an example of a classroom poster project, one teacher assigned each student to make a poster on one of the Ten Commandments. Pupils were allowed their choice of commandments. When the work was completed, the ten best posters were displayed on the back classroom wall. Names of the artists were signed at the bottom of the posters for identification and to give them recognition.

See Method 38, "Bulletin Boards," page 317, and Method 41, "Charts and Maps," page 320, for further helps.

53. Puppet Shows

A hand puppet is a small image, usually in human form, that is moved by the fingers.

A puppet show can be used with all age groups. It is especially useful in children's classes. Scriptural stories and modern-day experiences provide a vast array of possible puppet dramatizations.

Timid pupils who are reluctant to play a character part in a role-play dramatization are more at ease and willing to participate if they can hide behind a table or in a puppet theater, letting their animated hands represent them. A puppet show can be used as a variation of pre-structured role playing (see Method 23, p. 299).

Hand puppets can be purchased with almost any facial expression at variety stores. They are easily made by using a cloth or paper sack or sock with faces painted on them (see chapter 16, "On Using Your Head," p. 189, for how to make facial expressions). Fill the head of the puppet with rags or crumpled paper and tie at the neck. Use yarn or dyed cotton for hair. Another method is to cut a small round hole in a tennis ball just large enough for the index finger to be inserted. Cut out two patterns with arms and body. Sew these together. Insert the neck of the pattern inside the hole of the tennis ball and fasten with glue.

For a puppet theater, the performers can simply sit on the floor behind the teacher's desk or cut a stage window in a large cardboard box. If desired, curtains can be added to the stage window and the box can be painted.

In planning a puppet show, use few characters. If the script of the story is not written out, at least plan the beginning and ending of the story with the performers. Keep the dramatization short and avoid long speeches. Encourage students to emphasize the message of the story that relates to the lesson objective. Use musical background and sound effects. The dialogue and sound effects might be recorded before the presentation. The participants can then evaluate themselves while acting the parts.

A puppet show should be rehearsed before curtain time.

54. Records (Dramatized and Music)

Commercially produced scriptural readings and recorded stories have utility, particularly for individual study outside of the classroom. However, only occasionally should these records be played in class—only to give variety to teaching methods and to emphasize outstanding scriptures and stories. When scriptural passages are presented, students might read silently while listening. It might be well to provide them with a red pencil to mark important passages when using their own scriptures. Pictures used along with recordings greatly enhance the learning process.

At the present time scriptural readings have been produced on the complete Book of Mormon, Pearl of Great Price, and Doctrine and Covenants. Church history, and Old and New Testament stories are also available on record.

Although scriptural readings and dramatized records are good for deviation, they can be greatly improved when combined with film-strip or opaque strip presentations.

For suggestions on uses of recorded music in the classroom, see page 127, "Letting the Record Player or Tape Recorder Help You Teach."

55. Tape Recordings

Audio tape recorders have many excellent uses in the gospel classroom. Here are a few:

a.   Record radio programs for later replay in class, general con-ference talks, the Sunday morning Tabernacle choir broadcasts, talks of noted leaders, and musical programs for music-appreciation periods.

When taping radio programs, rather than placing the mike in front of the radio speaker (which picks up room sounds), use a patch cord that clips to the radio speaker leads or have a special jack in-stalled. Any radio repairman can assist with either type of hook-up.

b.   Use the tape recorder to rehearse student talks. When a student has prepared a talk, record the delivery. Have the student then listen to his presentation, make changes and improvements, and record the talk again. Continue this process until the talk is satisfactorily delivered.

c.   Conceal the recorder in the classroom. Start it recording be-fore the students arrive. Let it record throughout the lesson. After the lesson, play it back, making a critical analysis of the quality of your voice, grammar, questions, student responses, interest of students, staying on the subject, and class discipline. Then make a written list of items you plan to apply in overcoming the weak spots.

d.   Record stories role played in or out of class by students. Use sound effects in the dramatization such as a closing door, crying baby (by a student), galloping horse (use two pieces of wood on the floor), fire (crumple cellophane in the mike), a cow mooing, or a dog barking. Play back the dramatization to the class and evaluate the message of the presentation.

e.   As a special project, a small group of students might inter-view a bishop or stake president, recording the interview to be played later to the entire class as part of a lesson. It is best if interview ques-tions are written by the students and approved by the teacher before the interview takes place.

f.   Tape recordings are often more desirable than disc recordings for study background music. A tape can be played throughout an entire study period without the interruption of changing the record. Selective study music can also be recorded by the teacher on a tape, since many record albums present a mixture of dramatic emotional music along with meditative music.

g.   The tape recorder is effective when used for recorded narrations of filmstrip and opaque strip presentations.

h.   Classes can tape special short dramatizations and exchange their presentations with other classes. Students might present a short spiritual program in their own class on tape.

i.   Many pre-recorded tapes on gospel subjects are available in meetinghouse libraries. There is a large library of tape recordings available at Brigham Young University, Provo, Utah, of talks by General Authorities of the Church.

56.   Television-Video Tape Recordings

While instructional television is motivating, it is not the type of entertainment we usually see on an evening program. Its major function is to entertain with purpose and thus teach, rather than simply entertain.

There are more than three million students receiving instruction by television in public schools in the United States. Yet much is to be done to solve problems of cost, restrictions of scheduling, and types of programs produced. At the present time the annual and semiannual televised conference sessions are virtually the only Church television programs that fit scheduling by only a limited number of gospel classes.

In public schools where television is used as a major teaching source, the teacher conducts important activities to reinforce understanding and clarify principles being taught. With many classes, content is discussed by the teacher and students before and after the television program. In some classes where the teaching staff is limited, almost total courses are offered on television. More frequently television is used to supplement a course offering specialized instruction. Some colleges are using two-way audio systems where students can ask questions of the "studio-teacher."

Because of the high cost of production, television is proving most effective where a large number of schools become affiliated with an educational television network and coordinate the instructional programs so that they become part of a teacher's regular lesson planning. On some school systems a student sits in a carrel. Before him is space to write, a dial to signal his program for study, a code directory, and a television. He selects from the directory what he would like to study, dials the appropriate code number, and is immediately presented with the program on the screen. The program is cabled from a central system. This is an expensive but effective method of individualized instruction.

The video tape recorder (VTR) is much like an audio tape recorder, although it transmits a picture on a monitor (television screen) as well as sound. A complete VTR set consists of the *recorder* on which a video tape is run on reels (much like an audio tape recorder) the monitor, and a small television camera. Class activities can be filmed and played back immediately on the monitor. The VTR has the advantage over the audio tape of providing a live picture as well as sound. Most VTRs can record regular television programs. These programs can be played back for viewing simply by re-running the video tape cassette or reel.

The VTR has numerous uses in instruction that go well beyond what can be done with a magnetic tape recorder. Teachers or students can carry out such projects as role playing demonstration, reporting, micro-teaching, and interviewing and get immediate playback for study and evaluation. The VTR is an excellent tool for developing teaching and public speaking skills when properly used. It has much potential use in the Church. The cost of a VTR set is from about eight hundred dollars to several thousand. The price is continually being lowered, however, as VTRs are being improved and simplified for general public use.

Chapter 23
NOTES AND REFERENCES

[1]Doyle L. Green, "The Journeys and Ministry of Jesus the Christ," *Improvement Era,* January 1963.

[2]James W. Brown, Richard B. Lewis, and Fred F. Harcleroad, *A-V Instruction Materials and Methods* (New York: McGraw-Hill Book Company, Inc., 1959), p. 139.

[3]Used with permission of Irwin Goodman.

Bibliography

And Ye Shall Teach Them. Provo, Utah: Department of Seminaries and Institutes of The Church of Jesus Christ of Latter-day Saints, 1968.

Avestein, Jean. *How to Draw People and Animals.* New York: Sterling Publishing Co., 1958.

Baker, C. W. *Seeing Is Believing.* Cincinnati, Ohio: Standard Publishing Company, 1960.

Bellack, Arno A., et al. *The Language of the Classroom.* New York: Teachers College Press, 1966.

Bennion, Adam S. *Principles of Teaching.* Salt Lake City: General Boards of the Auxiliary Organizations of The Church of Jesus Christ of Latter-day Saints, 1958.

Bennion, Lowell L. *Six Fundamentals of Good Teaching and Leadership.* Salt Lake City: General Boards of The Mutual Improvement Associations of The Church of Jesus Christ of Latter-day Saints, 1961.

Berger, Peter L., and Thomas Luckmann. *The Social Construction of Reality.* New York: Anchor Books, 1967.

Bloom, Benjamin S., ed. *Taxonomy of Educational Objectives.* New York: Longmans, Green, 1956.

Book of Mormon

Brown, James W., Richard B. Lewis, and Fred F. Horcleroad. *AV Instruction, Media and Methods.* New York: McGraw-Hill Book Company, 1969.

Bruner, Jerome S. *Toward a Theory of Instruction.* New York: W. E. Norton and Company, 1968.

Carnegie, Dale. *The Quick and Easy Way to Effective Speaking.* New York: Association Press, 1962.

Carnegie, Dale. *How to Win Friends and Influence People.* New York: Simon and Schuster, 1951.

Cracker, Lionel and Louis M. Eech. *Oral Reading.* 70 Fifth Avenue, New York: Prentice Hall, Inc.

Dewey, John. *Democracy and Education.* New York: The Free Press, 1966.

Dewey, John. *Experience and Education.* New York: Collier Books, 1938.

Dewey, John. *Logic the Theory of Inquiry.* New York: Holt, Rinehart and Winston, Inc., 1964.

Doctrine and Covenants

Driggs, Howard R. *The Master's Art.* Salt Lake City: Deseret Sunday School Union of The Church of Jesus Christ of Latter-day Saints, 1946.

Dunn, Paul H. *You Too Can Teach.* Salt Lake City: Bookcraft Publishing Co., 1962.

Encyclopedia Brittanica. Chicago: William Benton, Publisher, 1960.

Ensign, The. Salt Lake City: The Church of Jesus Christ of Latter-day Saints. (Monthly Periodical.)

Famous Artists School, Cartooning Course, Westport, Conn.

Finck, Henry. *Success in Music.*

Fromm, Erich. *The Art of Loving.* New York: Bantam Books by Harper and Row, 1963.

Gage, N. L. (ed.). *Handbook of Research on Teaching.* Chicago: Rand McNally & Company, 1963.

Gardiner, Erma Y. *Three Steps to Good Teaching.* Salt Lake City: General Board of Primary Association of The Church of Jesus Christ of Latter-day Saints, 1960.

Gardner, John W. *Self Renewal.* New York: Harper and Row, 1965.

Glasser, William. *Reality Therapy.* New York: Harper and Row, 1965.

Glasser, William. *Schools without Failure.* New York: Harper and Row, 1965.

Great Lives, Great Deeds. New York: The Reader's Digest Association, 1964.

Herbert, John. *A System for Analyzing Lessons;* New York: Teachers College Press, 1967.

Highet, Gilbert. *The Art of Teaching.* New York: Vintage Books, 1950.

Hill, Ida Stewart and William Fawcett Hill. *Learning and Teaching through Discussion.* Chicago: Center for the Study of Liberal Education for Adults, 1958.

Hobbs, Charles R. "An Experimental Study of Selected Group Guidance Techniques in the Seminary Classroom." Unpublished Master's thesis, Brigham Young University, Provo, Utah, 1958.

Hobbs, Charles R. "An Investigation of Selected Educational Conditions within the Latter-day Saint Community." New York: Teachers College, Columbia University, 1970. (Unpublished Dissertation.)

Hobbs, Charles R. "Balance in Teaching, BYU *Studies,* vol. 12, no. 2.

Hudgins, Bryce B. *Problem Solving in the Classroom.* New York: The Macmillan Company, 1966.

Hymns. Salt Lake City: The Church of Jesus Christ of Latter-day Saints, 1958.

Improvement Era. Salt Lake City: Mutual Improvement Association of The Church of Jesus Christ of Latter-day Saints. (Monthly Periodical.)

Instructor. Salt Lake City: Deseret Sunday School Union of The Church of Jesus Christ of Latter-day Saints. (Monthly Periodical.)

Jackson, Philip W. *Life in Classrooms.* New York: Holt, Rinehart and Winston, 1968.

James, William. *Talks to Teachers.* New York: W. W. Norton and Company, 1958.

Johnson, Clair. *Worship in Song.* Salt Lake City: Deseret Book Company, 1962.

Kemp, Jerrold E. *Planning and Producing Audiovisual Materials.* Scranton, Pennsylvania: Chandler Publishing Company, 1968.

Kibler, Robert J. Larry L. Barker, and David T. Miles. *Behavioral Objectives and Instruction.* Boston: Allyn and Bacon, 1970.

Klausmeier, Herbert J. *Principles and Practices of Secondary School Teaching.* New York: Harper and Brothers, 1953.

Klausmeier, Herbert J. *Teaching in the Secondary School.* New York: Harper and Row, 1958.

Kohler, W. *The Mentality of Apes.* New York: Harcourt, Brace and World, 1927.

Lange, Phil C. (ed). *Programed Instruction, The Sixty-Sixth Yearbook of the National Society for the Study of Education.* Part II. Chicago: The University of Chicago Press, 1967.

Lee, Blain Nelson and M. David Merrill. *Writing Complete Affective Objectives.* Los Angeles: Wadsworth Publishing Co., 1972.

Ligon, Ernest M. *A Greater Generation.* New York: The Macmillan Company, 1950.

Ligon, Ernest M. *The Psychology of Christian Personality.* New York: The Macmillan Company, 1957.

McFarland, Kenneth. *Eloquence in Public Speaking.* Englewood Cliffs, New Jersey: Prentice-Hall, Inc., 1961.

McKay, David O. *Gospel Ideals.* Salt Lake City: Improvement Era, 1953.

Mager, Robert F. *Preparing Instructional Objectives.* Palo Alto, California: Fearon Publishers, Inc., 1962.

Malone, Dumas. (ed.). V. 5. *Dictionary of American Biography.* New York: Charles Scribner, 1964.

Middlemiss, Clare. Comp. *Man May Know for Himself: Teachings of President David O. McKay.* Salt Lake City: Deseret Book Company, 1967.

Minor, Ed and Harvey R. Frye. *Techniques for Producing Visual Instructional Media.* New York: McGraw-Hill Book Company, 1970.

New Testament, Bible.

Nightingale, Earl. "The Strangest Secret." (Recording) Success Institutes, Inc.

Northrop, F. S. C. *The Logic of the Sciences and the Humanities.* New York: The World Publishing Company, 1966.

Nutt, Robert H. *How to Remember Names and Faces.* New York: Simon and Schuster, 1951.

Old Testament, Bible.

Pearl of Great Price.

Peters, R. S. "Education as Initiation." *Philosophical Analysis and Education.* Edited by Reginald D. Archambault. London: Routledge & Kegan Paul, 1965.

Peterson, Houston. *Great Teachers.* New York: Vintage Books, 1946.

Polanyi, Michael. *The Tacit Dimension.* New York: Anchor Books, 1967.

Pullias, Earl V. and James D. Young. *A Teacher Is Many Things.* Bloomington: Indiana University Press, 1968.

Reader's Digest. Pleasantville, New York: The Reder's Digest Association. (Monthly periodical.)

Redl, Fritz, and William W. Wattenberg. *Mental Hygiene in Teaching.* New York: Harcourt, Brace and Company, 1959.

Reiser, A. Hamer. *A Reader for the Teacher.* Salt Lake City: Deseret Book Company, 1960.

Rogers, Carl R. *On Becoming a Person.* Boston: Houghton Mifflin Company, 1961.

Sanders, Norris M. *Classroom Questions: What Kinds?* New York: Harper and Row, 1966.

Sawyer, Ruth. *The Way of the Storyteller.* New York: The Viking Press, 1969.

Schain, Robert L. "Discipline How to Establish and Maintain It." Brooklyn, New York: Teachers' Practical Press, Inc.

Scheffler, Israel. *The Language of Education.* Springfield, Illinois: Charles C. Thomas, Publisher, 1960.

Schoenfeld, Clarence A. *Effective Feature Writing.* New York: Harper and Brothers, 1960.

Smith, Joseph Fielding. *Doctrines of Salvation.* V. I. Salt Lake City: Bookcraft, 1954.

Smith, Mary Howard. *Using Television in the Classroom.* New York: McGraw-Hill Book Company, Inc., 1961.

Stoops, Emery, and John Dunworth. *Classroom Discipline.* Montclair, New Jersey: The Economics Press, Inc., 1958.

Teacher Development Inservice Administrator-Instructor Materials. Series 3. Salt Lake City: The Church of Jesus Christ of Latter-day Saints, 1972.

Teacher Development Program, Basic Course, Course Directors Materials. Salt Lake City: The Church of Jesus Christ of Latter-day Saints, 1971.

Teacher Training. Salt Lake City: The Deseret Sunday School Union Board, 1955. (Prepared by the Teacher Training Comittee.)

They See What You Mean. Johnson City, New York: Ozalia Audio-Visual Department, Division of General Anailine and Film Corporation, 1959.

Thut, I. N., and J. Raymond Gerberich. *Foundations of Method for Secondary Schools.* New York: McGraw-Hill Book Company, Inc., 1949.

Tolstoi, Leo. *The Works of Leo Tolstoi.* New York: Blacks Reader Service Company, 1928.

Waethen, Walter B. *Human Variability and Learning.* 1201 Sixteenth Street, N. W., Washington 6, D.C.: Association for Supervision and Curriculum Development, 1961.

Woodruff, Asahel D. *Teaching the Gospel.* Salt Lake City: The Deseret Sunday School Union Board, 1961.

Index